Learning by Doing

A Handbook for Professional Learning Communities at Work™

Richard DuFour

Rebecca DuFour

Robert Eaker

Thomas Many

Solution Tree

Copyright © 2006 by Solution Tree
(formerly National Educational Service)
304 West Kirkwood Avenue
Bloomington, IN 47404
(800) 733-6786 (toll free) / (812) 336-7700
FAX: (812) 336-7790
email: info@solution-tree.com
www.solution-tree.com

Cover Design by Grannan Graphic Design, Ltd.

Printed in the United States of America

ISBN 978-1-932127-93-5

What the Experts Are Saying

"Continuous and sustainable school improvement requires three ingredients: a shared language, an empowered leadership group, and time. *Learning by Doing* provides a compelling framework for continuous and sustainable school improvement. The book offers a clear process for bringing these essential ingredients together. It should be required reading for all professional educators dedicated to the mission of 'Learning for All.'"

—Lawrence W. Lezotte,
Founder of Effective Schools Products

"For the last decade, the authors and their colleagues have been developing a body of work that can and is transforming schools across the country. Like other greats who influence a generation, their books form a logical chain, each section adding to the integrity of the whole. This latest handbook is the next vital link because it takes on the practical challenge of orchestrating change from within. 'Indispensable' is an overused word for books that are simply useful; but this book is, in fact, indispensable for leaders who want to make the right changes, and make them endure. When our country gets serious about good schools for all our children, these books will be the curriculum."

—Jonathon Saphier, Founder and Chairman Emeritus of Teachers 21,
Founder and President of Research for Better Teaching

"Rick DuFour and his colleagues continue to push us to new levels of understanding of how professional learning communities work. They then invite us to join them in developing unique frameworks that can be used in our own schools to create cultures of time, feeling, focus, and persistence aimed at ensuring that every child will succeed. Critical to their approach is aggregating what we know and using this knowledge together, thus compounding its effect. Easily one of the most important new books on school improvement."

—Thomas J. Sergiovanni, Lillian Radford Professor of Education,
Trinity University, San Antonio, Texas

"In *Learning by Doing*, Rick DuFour, Becky DuFour, Bob Eaker, and Tom Many provide a practical approach to understanding the essential elements of PLCs—clarity of purpose, precision in use of concepts and language, learning through doing as part of teachers' daily work, interdependent action through teamwork, and a results orientation that focuses on the learning of every student. Readers will find *Learning by Doing* to be filled with the authors' wisdom and insights informed by years of experience in leading and assisting others in forming PLCs."

—Dennis Sparks, Executive Director,
National Staff Development Council

"There are no more excuses to avoid professional learning communities. With a mountain of evidence, compelling case studies, and a wealth of experience, *Learning by Doing* will transform PLCs from the ambiguous concept practiced in many schools into a practical reality. For the discouraged educator and administrator, the authors provide respect for the time constraints and daily challenges of the busy practitioner, and leaven the lessons with gentle humor. For the complacent and cynical opponent of change, the authors offer a stirring challenge that the alternative to effective professional communities is not the comfort of the good old days, but a fundamental failure to meet our ethical and professional obligations to students and to one another. For those who think that because they have relabeled a dysfunctional faculty meeting a 'professional learning community' they are finished, then they must think again. The self-assessments and reflective exercises in this book will challenge the most experienced PLC leader, while offering hope to those who are starting this process of discovery and collaboration. Many books deserve a glance, perhaps half of them are worthy of a thorough reading, but only a few—and this book is surely in this category—should be devoured. Grab a pen and a colleague and get ready for a challenging and rewarding journey into the heart of professional learning communities."

—Douglas B. Reeves, Founder,
The Leadership and Learning Center

"As professional learning communities become more and more popular, we need more than ever a definitive guide to the whys, whats, and hows of PLCs. This handbook is it: comprehensive, clear, practical, and above all demanding for moving forward with deep PLCs. Anyone committed to PLCs must base their work on this powerful standard."

—Michael Fullan, Special Adviser in Education to the Premier
and the Minister of Education, Ontario, Canada

"'Professional learning community'—three ambitious words that don't often characterize our work in schools. Educators are commonly not professional, and schools are frequently neither hospitable to learning nor communities. With this detailed roadmap, no school leader—teacher, principal, or superintendent—will ever again have to say, 'I'm all for building a PLC . . . but how do you do it?' I wish I had this little volume, which is overflowing with concrete ideas, before me during my own turbulent years as a school principal. It would have enabled us to break out of our inertia and create the PLC we all desperately wanted and deserved."

—Roland S. Barth,
Educator and Consultant

"This may be the best, most practical book yet written on how to implement professional learning communities. It reaches an important threshold—a greater confidence and clarity about the power and potential of PLCs. On every important issue, this book contains excellent tested advice from people who have had immense success implementing learning communities in real schools where they achieved exceptional results. It is that rare book about which one can say: If you read it, and put its principles into action, you can expect results."

—Mike Schmoker,
Educator and Consultant

"This handbook serves as a useful tool for educators and administrators in need of a resource that helps them develop their school-level professional learning community model from conceptualization to implementation. It promotes a dialogue among school teams that engages them in strategic collaboration and problem solving . . . and synthesizes the research and best practices in the authors' previous publications by providing action steps readers can build upon to establish their PLC. Readers will find the concepts proposed in this handbook to be nothing less than insightful as they endeavor to achieve sustained and substantive school improvement. *Learning by Doing* provides a wealth of information and viable steps for schools and districts to achieve optimal levels of achievement through the creation of professional learning communities."

—Barbara Eason-Watkins, Chief Education Officer, Chicago Public Schools

"I have struggled with school improvement for over 40 years. My background in effective schools research gave me a clear picture of what schools were trying to create, but very few met with success. The work of Becky, Rick, and Bob has given me the vehicle needed to successfully implement school improvement initiatives. Professional learning communities provide a structure to support data gathering, goal-setting, implementation strategies, and monitoring and adjusting activities. My Planning for School and Student Success process (*Harbors of Hope,* 2005) is being used in hundreds of schools throughout North America. The process' success is determined by the ability of a school staff to become a PLC. My knowledge of PLC concepts has made a significant difference in my ability to support schools and districts in ensuring success for all students.

—Wayne Hulley, Author and Educator

What Practitioners Are Saying

"Professional Learning Communities at Work™ has been a breath of fresh air for schools everywhere. The work of Richard DuFour, Rebecca DuFour, and Robert Eaker has helped me focus my school leadership on the most important and critical issue in schools: student learning. As schools struggle to raise student achievement and increase their organizational effectiveness, the strategies imbedded in the PLC philosophy provide the answer. I have had the opportunity to use this powerful tool in two schools, and in both cases the result was a tremendous gain in student achievement. I believe if leaders at all levels embraced and understood PLCs, we would see schools improve at a rate never seen before."

—Anthony Muhammad, Principal,
Southfield High School, Southfield, Michigan

"The work of the DuFours and Bob Eaker provides schools with the practical strategies that both challenge and empower administrators and teachers to collaborate on creating a school culture that increases student learning."

—Alan Addley, Principal,
Granby Memorial High School, Granby, Connecticut

"Bradley Elementary School serves as a shining example of what is possible when a faculty implements professional learning community concepts. The fact that we did it from the ground up has helped to show other teachers in our district what is possible. Professional learning communities is now the primary focus in our district for professional development."

—Geri Parscale, Principal,
Bradley Elementary School, Fort Leavenworth, Kansas

"I have had the honor and privilege to work for a year with Rick, Becky, and Bob to learn the importance and impact of PLCs. The evidence is clear and convincing: PLC concepts are the future for improving schools and school districts. Through properly developed PLCs, school leadership teams and guiding coalitions can make significant improvement in student achievement and leadership development."

—William Hall, Director,
Educational Leadership and Professional Development,
Viera, Florida

"Building a PLC has transformed our school from a place where adults came to work to a place where students come to learn. Ours was a school with no shortage of teachers working hard; there was also no shortage of teachers who wanted students to learn. What we were lacking, however, was alignment. Our school improvement effort pre-PLC looked like 25 arrows shot from bows by many marksmen: aiming at targets in many directions, but not hitting much of anything predictably. Professional learning communities provided us with the blueprints for alignment. We are now capitalizing on a collective effort to move toward shared mission, vision, values, and goals. We have moved away from a 'hammer and hope' approach to one of results—*planned and on purpose.*"

—Kenneth C. Williams, Principal,
E.J. Swint Elementary School, Jonesboro, Georgia

Dedication

We have been avid, ongoing students of the research regarding professional learning communities and the leadership necessary to bring PLC concepts to life. Our deepest learning, however, has come from our own work in schools that have embodied those PLC concepts and from our association with colleagues who have initiated and sustained the PLC process in their own schools and districts. These men and women come from varied backgrounds throughout North America and from schools and districts that represent a broad spectrum of sizes and circumstances. More importantly, these colleagues share certain characteristics. First, they are passionate about the potential for PLCs to have an impact on the lives of the students they serve. Second, they have learned by doing: They have developed their expertise by leading through the rough and tumble of PLC initiatives. Third, they are willing to and skillful at sharing their insights with other practitioners. Our own understanding of PLC concepts has been enriched by their efforts and deepened by their insights. We are proud to call them colleagues and friends, and we dedicate *Learning by Doing* to them, our PLC associates.

—Richard DuFour, Rebecca DuFour, and Robert Eaker

To Rick, my friend and mentor, and to Becky and Bob. Thank you for inviting me to be a part of creating and sustaining professional learning communities. And to my father, Dr. Wesley A. Many, I thank you for sharing Willie's story. I am a living legacy to the lessons so beautifully illustrated by that simple tale.

—Thomas Many

Acknowledgements

Our work and our thinking have been shaped and influenced by some of the greatest contemporary educational thinkers in North America. We have benefited immensely from the wisdom of Larry Lezotte, Michael Fullan, Doug Reeves, Rick Stiggins, Roland Barth, Mike Schmoker, Jonathon Saphier, Dennis Sparks, Bob Marzano, and Tom Sergiovanni. Like so many educators, we are indebted to them, and we acknowledge the enormous contribution each has made to our practice, our ideas, and our writing.

We also acknowledge the tremendous support we have received for this project from the Solution Tree family. Rhonda Rieseberg and Suzanne Kraszewski are skillful editors who polished our prose and designed layouts for the book that greatly enhanced its readability. We are grateful for the enthusiasm and energy they devoted to this endeavor.

Finally, each of us owes a tremendous debt of gratitude to Jeff Jones, the president of Solution Tree. Jeff is more than a publisher. He is one of the most ethical, service-oriented business leaders we know. He has been an ardent advocate for spreading the PLC concept across North America, and his passion and his skill have given our ideas a platform we could not have achieved on our own. Finally, he is a friend in every sense of the word. Every author should have the opportunity to work with a publisher like Jeff Jones. More importantly, everyone should know the joy of having someone like him for a friend.

Table of Contents

About the Authors

Richard DuFour, Ed.D., was a public school educator for 34 years, serving as a teacher, principal, and superintendent. He was principal of Adlai E. Stevenson High School in Lincolnshire, Illinois, from 1983 to 1991 and superintendent of the district from 1991 to 2002. During his tenure, Stevenson became what the United States Department of Education (USDE) has described as "the most recognized and celebrated school in America." It is one of only three schools in the nation to win the USDE Blue Ribbon Award on four occasions, and one of the first comprehensive schools the USDE designated as a New America High School, a model of successful school reform. Stevenson has been repeatedly cited in the popular press as one of America's best schools and referenced in professional literature as an exemplar of best practices in education.

Rick is the author of 8 books and more than 50 professional articles. He wrote a quarterly column for the *Journal of Staff Development* for almost a decade. He was the lead consultant and author for the Association for Supervision and Curriculum Development's seven-part video series on the principalship and is the author of two other videos: *How to Develop a Professional Learning Community: Passion and Persistence* (2002) and *Through New Eyes: Examining the Culture of Your School* (2003).

He has received his state's highest award as both a principal and superintendent. He was named one of the top 100 school administrators in North America by *Executive Educator* magazine, was presented the Distinguished Scholar Practitioner Award from the University of Illinois, and was the 2004 recipient of the National Staff Development Council's Distinguished Service Award. He consults with school districts, state departments of education, and professional organizations throughout North America on strategies for improving schools.

Rebecca DuFour, M.Ed., has served as a teacher, school administrator, and central office coordinator. As a former elementary principal, she helped her school earn state and national recognition as a model professional learning community. She was the lead consultant and is the featured principal in the 2003 *Video Journal of Education* program *Elementary Principals as Leaders of Learning* and one of the featured principals in the 2001 production *Leadership in the Age of Standards and High Stakes.*

Becky is the co-author of *Getting Started: Reculturing Schools to Become Professional Learning Communities* (2002) and *Whatever It Takes: How Professional Learning Communities Respond When Kids Don't Learn* (2004). She is a co-editor of *On Common Ground: The Power of Professional Learning Communities* (2005), a collection of essays by leading educational authors and consultants. She is also featured in the three-part video series *Let's Talk About PLC* (2004).

Becky has written for numerous professional journals, reviewed books for the *Journal of Staff Development,* and authored a quarterly column for *Leadership Compass,* published by the National Association of Elementary School Principals. Becky has worked for and consults with professional organizations, school districts, universities, and state departments of education throughout North America.

Robert Eaker, Ed.D., is the former dean of the College of Education and interim executive vice president and provost of Middle Tennessee State University. He is a former fellow with the National Center for Effective Schools Research and Development. He has written widely on the issues of effective teaching, effective schools, helping teachers use research findings, and high expectations for student achievement. He was recognized by *Phi Delta Kappan* as one of the nation's leaders in helping educators translate research into practice.

He is co-author of *Classroom Supervision and Instructional Improvement* (Kendall/Hunt, 1976), *Creating the New American School: A Principal's Guide to School Improvement* (1992), *Professional Learning Communities at Work™: Best Practices for Enhancing Student Achievement* (1998), *Getting Started: Reculturing Schools to Become Professional Learning Communities* (2002), and *Whatever It Takes: How Professional Learning Communities Respond When Kids Don't Learn* (2004). Bob is co-editor of *On Common Ground: The Power of Professional*

Learning Communities (2005), a collection of essays from leading educational authors and consultants. He is also featured in the three-part video series *Let's Talk About PLC* (2004).

Bob has spoken at numerous national meetings held by the National Association of Secondary School Principals, the Association for Supervision and Curriculum Development, and the National Center for Effective Schools Research and Development. He regularly consults with school districts throughout the nation on school improvement issues.

Thomas Many, Ed.D., a superintendent for 16 years, has spent the past 10 years at Kildeer Countryside Community Consolidated School District 96 in Buffalo Grove, Illinois. The students from his district feed into Adlai Stevenson High School where Rick DuFour was superintendent for 11 years. Tom has been a classroom teacher, learning center director, curriculum supervisor, principal, and assistant superintendent.

Tom is a practitioner of professional learning communities and has been involved in initiatives at the state and local level to bring about continuous improvement in schools. Under his direction, District 96 has been recognized as one of the highest achieving and lowest spending districts in Illinois.

Tom has presented at a wide variety of educational conferences and has published several articles that have received national attention. His combination of theoretical expertise and practical hands-on experience make him a compelling and sought-after presenter. He delivers exciting workshops on PLCs throughout the United States and Canada.

Chapter 1

A Guide to Action for Professional Learning Communities at Work™

Wᵉ learn best by doing. We have known this to be true for quite some time. More than 2,500 years ago Confucius observed, "I hear and I forget. I see and I remember. I do and I understand." Most educators acknowledge that our deepest insights and understandings come from action, followed by reflection and the search for improvement. After all, most educators have spent 4 or 5 years *preparing* to enter the profession—taking courses on content and pedagogy, observing students and teachers in classrooms, completing student teaching under the tutelage of a veteran teacher, and so on. Yet almost without exception, they admit that they learned more in their first semester of *teaching* than they did in the 4 or 5 years they spent *preparing* to enter the profession. This is not an indictment of higher education; it is merely evidence of the power of learning that is embedded in the work.

Our profession also attests to the importance and power of learning by doing when it comes to educating our students. We want students to be *actively engaged* in *hands-on authentic exercises* that promote *experiential learning*. How odd then that a profession that pays such homage to the importance of learning by doing is so reluctant to apply that principle when it comes to developing its collective capacity to meet the needs of students. Why do institutions created for and devoted to learning not call upon the professionals within them to become more proficient in improving the effectiveness of schools by actually doing the work of school improvement? Why have we been so reluctant to learn by doing?

A Brief Review

Since 1998 we have published numerous resources with two goals in mind: first, to persuade educators that the most promising strategy for helping all students learn at high levels is to develop a staff's capacity to function

The question confronting most schools and districts is not, "What do we need to know in order to improve?" but rather, "Will we turn what we already know into action?"

as a professional learning community (PLC) and second, to offer specific strategies and structures to help educators create PLCs in their own schools.

In *Professional Learning Communities at Work™: Best Practices for Enhancing Student Achievement* (1998), we provide the conceptual framework for PLCs and the research to support the concepts. We also offer descriptions of how PLC concepts impact the various stakeholders in schools—teachers, principals, students, and parents—and how they impact important school programs such as the curriculum, professional development, and assessment. *Getting Started: Reculturing Your School to Become a Professional Learning Community* (2003) provides specific strategies for beginning the PLC process, describes the cultural shifts that take place, and addresses the most common questions that arise as schools begin their PLC journeys.

In *Whatever It Takes: How Professional Learning Communities Respond When Kids Don't Learn* (2004), we explore how schools at all levels have created systematic interventions that ensure their students receive additional time and support for learning in a timely and directive way. In *On Common Ground: The Power of Professional Learning Communities* (2005), we were privileged to serve as editors and contributors to a collection of writing from North America's leading educational thinkers who share their insights and suggestions for helping make PLC concepts the norm in all schools.

Learning by Doing: A Handbook for Professional Learning Communities at Work™ is the logical next step in our effort to help educators confront the challenges of implementing significant changes in their schools and districts as they work to become PLCs. We rely heavily on current research from a number of different fields, but we also draw upon the insights we have acquired in our work with schools and districts throughout North America.

What Are Professional Learning Communities?

It has been interesting to observe the growing popularity of the term *professional learning community*. In fact, the term has become so commonplace and has been used so ambiguously to describe virtually any loose coupling of individuals who share a common interest in education that it is in danger of losing all meaning. This lack of precision is an obstacle to implementing PLC concepts because, as Mike Schmoker observes, "clarity precedes competence" (2004, p. 85). Thus, we begin this handbook with an attempt to clarify our meaning of the term. To those familiar with our past work, this step may seem redundant, but we are convinced that redundancy can be a powerful tool in effective communication, and we prefer redundancy to ambiguity.

A Focus on Learning

The very essence of a *learning* community is a focus on and a commitment to the learning of each student. When a school or district functions as a PLC, educators within the organization embrace high levels of learning for all students as both the reason the organization exists and the fundamental responsibility of those who work within it. In order to achieve this purpose, the members of a PLC create and are guided by a clear and compelling vision of what the organization must become in order to help all students learn. They make collective commitments clarifying what each member will do to create such an organization, and they use results-oriented goals to mark their progress. Members work together to clarify exactly what each student must learn, monitor each student's learning on a timely basis, provide systematic interventions that ensure students receive additional time and support for learning when they struggle, and extend and enrich learning when students have already mastered the intended outcomes.

A corollary assumption is that if the organization is to become more effective in helping all students learn, the adults in the organization must also be continually learning. Therefore, structures are created to ensure staff members engage in job-embedded learning as part of their routine work practices.

There is no ambiguity or hedging regarding this commitment to learning. Whereas many schools operate as if their primary purpose is to ensure that children are taught, PLCs are dedicated to the idea that their organization exists to ensure that all students learn essential knowledge, skills, and dispositions. All the other characteristics of a PLC flow directly from this epic shift in assumptions about the purpose of the school.

*The very essence of a **learning** community is a focus on and a commitment to the learning of each student.*

A Collaborative Culture With a Focus on Learning for All

A PLC is composed of collaborative teams whose members work *interdependently* to achieve *common goals* linked to the purpose of learning for all. The team is the engine that drives the PLC effort and the fundamental building block of the organization. It is difficult to overstate the importance of collaborative teams in the improvement process. It is equally important, however, to emphasize that collaboration does not lead to improved results unless people are focused on the right issues. Collaboration is a means to an end, not the end itself. In many schools, staff members are willing to collaborate on a variety of topics as long as the focus of the conversation stops at their classroom door. In a PLC, *collaboration* represents a systematic process in which teachers work together interdependently in order to *impact* their classroom practice in ways that will lead to better results for their students, for their team, and for their school.

*A PLC is composed of collaborative teams whose members work **interdependently** to achieve **common goals** linked to the purpose of learning for all.*

Collective Inquiry Into Best Practice and Current Reality

The teams in a PLC engage in collective inquiry into both best practices in teaching and best practices in learning. They also inquire about their current reality—including their present practices and the levels of achievement of their students. They attempt to arrive at consensus on vital questions by building shared knowledge rather than pooling opinions. They have an acute sense of curiosity and openness to new possibilities.

Collective inquiry enables team members to develop new skills and capabilities that in turn lead to new experiences and awareness. Gradually, this heightened awareness transforms into fundamental shifts in attitudes, beliefs, and habits which, over time, transform the culture of the school.

Working together to build shared knowledge on the best way to achieve goals and meet the needs of clients is exactly what *professionals* in any field are expected to do, whether it is curing the patient, winning the lawsuit, or helping all students learn. Members of a *professional* learning community are expected to work and learn together.

Action Orientation: Learning by Doing

Members of PLCs are action oriented: They move quickly to turn aspirations into action and visions into reality.

Members of PLCs are action oriented: They move quickly to turn aspirations into action and visions into reality. They understand that the most powerful learning always occurs in a context of taking action, and they value engagement and experience as the most effective teachers. In fact, the very reason that teachers work together in teams and engage in collective inquiry is to serve as catalysts for action.

Members of PLCs recognize that learning by doing develops a deeper and more profound knowledge and greater commitment than learning by reading, listening, planning, or thinking. Traditional schools have developed a variety of strategies to resist taking meaningful action, preferring the comfort of the familiar. Professional learning communities recognize that until members of the organization "do" differently, there is no reason to anticipate different results. They avoid paralysis by analysis and overcome inertia with action.

A Commitment to Continuous Improvement

Inherent to a PLC are a persistent disquiet with the status quo and a constant search for a better way to achieve goals and accomplish the purpose of the organization. Systematic processes engage each member of the organization in an ongoing cycle of:

- Gathering evidence of current levels of student learning

- Developing strategies and ideas to build on strengths and address weaknesses in that learning

■ Implementing those strategies and ideas

■ Analyzing the impact of the changes to discover what was effective and what was not

■ Applying new knowledge in the next cycle of continuous improvement

The goal is not simply to learn a new strategy, but instead to create conditions for perpetual learning—an environment in which innovation and experimentation are viewed not as tasks to be accomplished or projects to be completed but as ways of conducting day-to-day business, *forever*. Furthermore, participation in this process is not reserved for those designated as leaders; rather, it is a responsibility of every member of the organization.

Results Orientation

Finally, members of a PLC realize that all of their efforts in these areas—a focus on learning, collaborative teams, collective inquiry, action orientation, and continuous improvement—must be assessed on the basis of results rather than intentions. Unless initiatives are subjected to ongoing assessment on the basis of tangible results, they represent random groping in the dark rather than purposeful improvement. As Peter Senge and colleagues conclude, "The rationale for any strategy for building a learning organization revolves around the premise that such organizations will produce dramatically improved results" (1994, p. 44).

This focus on results leads each team to develop and pursue measurable improvement goals that are aligned to school and district goals for learning. It also drives teams to create a series of common formative assessments that are administered to students multiple times throughout the year to gather ongoing evidence of student learning. Team members review the results from these assessments in an effort to identify and address program concerns (areas of learning where many students are experiencing difficulty). They also examine the results to discover strengths and weaknesses in their individual teaching in order to learn from one another. Most importantly, the assessments are used to identify students who need additional time and support for learning. Frequent common formative assessments represent one of the most powerful tools in the PLC arsenal.

Why Don't We Apply What We Know?

As we have shared our work in support of PLCs with educators in every state in the U.S. and every province of Canada, we have become accustomed to hearing the same response: "This just makes sense." It just makes sense that a school committed to helping all students learn at high levels would focus on *learning* rather than teaching, would ensure students had access to the same curriculum, would assess each student's learning on a timely basis using consistent standards

Inherent to a PLC are a persistent disquiet with the status quo and a constant search for a better way to achieve goals and accomplish the purpose of the organization.

Members of a PLC realize that all of their efforts must be assessed on the basis of results rather than intentions.

"Why does knowledge of what needs to be done so frequently fail to result in action or behavior that is consistent with that knowledge?" (Pfeffer & Sutton, 2000, p. 4)

for proficiency, and would create systematic interventions that provide students with additional time and support for learning. It just makes sense that we accomplish more working collaboratively than we do working in isolation. It just makes sense that we would assess our effectiveness in helping all students learn on the basis of results—tangible evidence that they have actually learned. It just makes sense! In fact, we have found little overt opposition to the characteristics of a PLC.

So why don't schools *do* what they already *know* makes sense. In *The Knowing-Doing Gap*, Jeffrey Pfeffer and Robert Sutton (2000) explore what they regard as one of the great mysteries of organizational management: the disconnect between knowledge and action. They ask, "Why does knowledge of what needs to be done so frequently fail to result in action or behavior that is consistent with that knowledge?" (p. 4).

This handbook is our most specific and direct attempt to help educators close the knowing-doing gap by transforming their schools into PLCs. More specifically, it is designed to accomplish the following four objectives:

1. To help educators develop a common vocabulary and a consistent understanding of key PLC concepts

2. To present a compelling argument that the implementation of PLC concepts will benefit students and educators alike

3. To help educators assess the current reality in their own schools and districts

4. To convince educators to take purposeful steps to develop their capacity to function as a PLC

Helping Educators Develop a Common Vocabulary and a Consistent Understanding of Key PLC Concepts

Michael Fullan observes that "terms travel easily . . . but the meaning of the underlying concepts does not" (2005a, p. 67). Terms such as *professional learning community, collaborative teams, goals, formative assessments,* and scores of others have indeed traveled widely in educational circles. They are prevalent in the lexicon of contemporary "educationese." If pressed for a specific definition, however, many educators would be stumped. It is difficult enough to bring these concepts to life in a school or district when there *is* a shared understanding of their meaning. It is impossible when there is no common understanding and the terms mean very different things to different people within the same organization.

Developmental psychologists Robert Kegan and Lisa Laskow Lahey (2001) contend that the transformation of both individuals and organizations requires new language. They write, "The places where we work and live are, among other things, places where certain forms of speech are promoted and encouraged, and places where other ways of talking are discouraged or made impossible" (p. 7). As educators make the cultural shift from traditional schools and districts to PLCs, a new language emerges. Therefore, we have included a glossary of key terms used in implementing PLC concepts to assist in building shared knowledge of both critical vocabulary and the concepts underlying the terms. This glossary begins on page 213. We hope it will add to the precision and clarity of the emerging language that accompanies the creation of PLCs.

Presenting a Compelling Argument That the Implementation of PLC Concepts Will Benefit Students and Educators Alike

Jim Collins (2001) begins his best-selling book *Good to Great* with a provocative observation: "Good is the enemy of great." "Good" organizational performance can cause complacency and inertia instead of inspiring the pursuit of continuous improvement essential to sustained greatness. Despite the persistent attacks on public schools throughout North America by politicians insisting on greater accountability, business leaders demanding better trained workers, and members of the media lamenting the failure of public education, most parents believe their children go to "good" schools. While they may be concerned about the quality of education throughout the country, almost 70% of parents consistently give the schools their oldest child attends a grade of A or B (Rose & Gallup, 2005). So what would cause educators to explore more powerful models for learning if the general perception in the community they serve indicates they are already doing a good job? One strategy, increasingly popular in contemporary North America, is to apply sanctions and punishment for schools that fail to demonstrate improvement. Currently this strategy impacts only a small percentage of schools, and its effectiveness remains very much in question.

Another strategy for motivating a faculty to initiate new practices and procedures is to present a persuasive case that there is a better, more effective, more gratifying way to approach the work. We are convinced that the PLC model makes that compelling case for any educator willing to give it meaningful consideration. The model offers a tangible, realistic, compelling vision of what schools might become. We hope to bring the PLC concept to life in ways that resonate with educators because, after all, "It just makes sense."

Helping Educators Assess the Current Reality in Their Own Schools and Districts

More than 2 decades ago, Naisbitt and Aburdene (1985) offered the common sense conclusion that people find it a lot easier to get from point A to point B if they know where point B is and how to recognize it once they arrive. For many educators, however, school improvement initiatives have been plagued by uncertainty and confusion regarding both points A and B. They have not taken

Educators will find it easier to move forward to where they want to go if they first agree on where they are.

the time to clarify either the current status of their school or what they hope it will become. As a result, efforts to reform their schools have too often been characterized by random stops and starts, rather than by purposeful progression on a path of improvement. A key step in any effective improvement process is an honest assessment of the current reality—a diligent effort to determine the truth (Collins, 2001). Educators will find it easier to move forward to where they want to go if they first agree on where they are.

Even when teachers and administrators make a good faith effort to assess their schools, they face significant obstacles. All schools have cultures: the assumptions, beliefs, expectations, and habits that constitute the norm for a school and guide the work of the educators within it. Perhaps it is more accurate to say that educators *do not* have school cultures, but rather that the school cultures have *them*. Teachers and administrators are typically so immersed in their traditional ways of doing things that they find it difficult to step outside of those traditions to examine conventional practices from a fresh, critical perspective. Therefore, this handbook is designed not only to offer specific examples of PLC practices (to help paint a picture of point B), but also to help educators make a frank and honest assessment of current conditions in their schools (to clarify point A).

Convincing Educators to Take Purposeful Steps to Develop Their Capacity to Function as a PLC

Our greatest hope in developing this handbook is that it will help educators take immediate and specific steps to close the knowing-doing gap in North American education by implementing PLC concepts in their own schools and districts. Once again, it will take action on the part of educators to accomplish this objective. The research on what it takes to improve schools has been very consistent over a number of years. Most educators already know what they should do to help students achieve at higher levels, and if they don't have the necessary knowledge, it is easily accessible to them in a variety of forms. The question confronting most schools and districts is not, "What do we need to know in order to improve?" but rather, "Will we turn what we already know into action?"

Taking Action

Perhaps the greatest insight we have gained in our work with school districts across the continent is that schools that take the plunge and actually begin *doing* the work of a PLC develop their capacity to help all students learn at high levels far more effectively than schools that spend years *preparing* to become PLCs through reading or even training. Educators must develop their collective capacity to function as PLCs, but as Michael Fullan (2005a) notes, "Capacity building is not just workshops and professional development for all. It is the daily habit of *working together*, and you can't learn this from a workshop or course. You need to learn by doing it and having mechanisms for getting better at it on purpose" (p. 69).

In the past we have provided study guides for our books because we discovered that many faculties use our resources in their book study groups. We call the study guide that accompanies this book an "Action Guide" (available at www.solution-tree.com); we cannot stress enough that this resource is not designed for study, but rather for *action*—to help educators take the essential action steps for building their capacity to create and sustain PLCs.

The Format

Each chapter of this handbook includes six parts:

- Part One: The Case Study

- Part Two: Here's How

- Part Three: Here's Why

- Part Four: Assessing Your Place on the PLC Journey

- Part Five: Tips for Moving Forward

- Part Six: Questions to Guide the Work of Your Professional Learning Community

Part One: The Case Study

Each chapter opens with a case study describing some of the issues and challenges that have arisen in a school or district that is attempting to implement PLC concepts. The names of schools and people described in the case studies are fictional, but the situations presented are neither fictional nor hypothetical. They represent the very real issues educators must grapple with and resolve if they are to bring PLC concepts to life in their schools and districts. Readers may be tempted to skip the case studies section of each chapter in order to move quickly to solutions. We urge you to resist that temptation. A critical step in assessing alternative solutions to any problem is to come to an understanding and appreciation of the problem itself. We hope you will take the time to consider each case study carefully, reflect upon the issues it presents, and generate possible strategies for addressing those issues. This reflective process will only be strengthened if readers engage in it collectively with their colleagues prior to considering the rest of the chapter.

Part Two: Here's How

In our work with schools, we have found that "how" questions come in at least two varieties: one type represents a sincere and genuine solicitation of guidance

*Schools that take the plunge and actually begin **doing** the work of a PLC develop their capacity to help all students learn at high levels far more effectively than schools that spend years **preparing** to become PLCs through reading or even training.*

from inquirers who are willing to act, and the other typically comes in waves as a series of "yeah, but . . ." questions. For example, after listening to an explanation of PLC concepts and procedures, a teacher or administrator responds with:

- "Yeah, but . . . how are we supposed to find time to collaborate?"

- "Yeah, but . . . how can we give students extra time and support for learning when our schedule will not allow it?"

- "Yeah, but . . . how can this work in a school this big (or small, or poor, or urban, or rural, or suburban, or low achieving and therefore too despondent, or high achieving and therefore too complacent)?"

- "Yeah, but . . . how can we make this happen with our ineffective principal, unsupportive central office, or adversarial teacher union?"

These questions are less of a search for answers on how to implement PLC concepts successfully and more of a search for a reason to avoid implementation. As Peter Block (2003) says, "Asking 'How?' is a favorite defense against taking action" (p. 11). Block goes on to say, "We act like we are confused, like we don't understand. The reality is that we *do* understand—we get it, but we don't like it" (p. 47–48). Our own work with schools has confirmed that a group that is determined not to act can always find a justification for inaction. Questions about "how" can have a positive impact only if those asking are willing to act on the answers.

Therefore, the "Here's How" sections in this book are written for those who seek ideas, insights, and information regarding how PLC concepts come alive in the real world of schools. Part Two of each chapter describes how educators bring a particular PLC element to life in their school. It will present exemplars for schools to use as a model as they work through the challenges of moving from concepts to action.

There is no precise recipe for school improvement. . . . Even the most promising strategies must be customized for the specific context of each district and each school.

We fully recognize that there is no precise recipe for school improvement (blending two parts collaboration with one part formative assessment does not work). We also understand that even the most promising strategies must be customized for the specific context of each district and each school. The most effective improvement models are those that have been adapted by staff to fit the situation in their schools and communities (Hall & Hord, 1987; Hord, Rutherford, Huling-Austin, & Hall, 1987; Marzano, 2005). Therefore, the "Here's How" sections do not presume to present "The Answer" to problems posed in the case study, because it is the dialogue about and the struggle with those problems at the school and district level that results in the deepest learning and greatest commitment for teachers and administrators. Our hope is that this book can serve as a tool educators can use to initiate the dialogue and to engage in the struggle.

Part Three: Here's Why

Informing others about how something can be done does not ensure they will be persuaded to do it. In fact, we are convinced that one of the most common mistakes school administrators make in the implementation of improvement initiatives is to focus exclusively on "how" while being inattentive to "why." Leaders at all levels must be prepared to anticipate and respond to the inevitable questions and concerns that arise when educators are called upon to engage in new practices. We have included Part Three in each chapter to offer useful tools—research, reasoning, and rationale—to help clarify why the initiative should be undertaken.

Part Three draws upon, but is not limited to, the research base on education. We examine findings from studies in organizational development, change processes, leadership, effective communication, and psychology because the challenges facing contemporary leaders demand that they look outside the narrow scope of their professional field for answers.

Part Four: Assessing Your Place on the PLC Journey

This section calls upon readers to assess the current reality in their own schools as it relates to a particular element of PLC practices. Readers will do hands-on work as they use the charts in this section to assess their policies and practices. They are then asked to present evidence and arguments in support of their assessments.

Part Five: Tips for Moving Forward

Each chapter includes specific suggestions and strategies to assist with the implementation of particular PLC concepts. The primary purpose of this handbook is to encourage people to act, to "learn by doing." Random actions, however, do nothing to enhance the capacity of a staff to function as a PLC. The challenge facing leaders is to identify purposeful and focused actions that contribute to the goal of improved learning for students and staff alike. Part Five offers insight regarding which actions to take and which to avoid. It identifies tactics that offer the greatest leverage for advancing PLC concepts and presents research-based and practitioner-proven tips for pursuing those tactics effectively.

Part Six: Questions to Guide the Work of Your Professional Learning Community

Members of PLCs engage in *collective* inquiry: They learn how to learn together. But it is only when they focus this collective inquiry on the right questions that they develop their capacity to improve student and adult learning.

It has been said that the leader of the past knew how to tell. The leader of the future, however, will have to know how to ask. Those who lead the PLC process should not be expected to have all the answers and tell others what they must do. Leaders should instead be prepared to ask the right questions, facilitate the dialogue, and help build shared knowledge. Part Six will offer some of the "right" questions educators should consider as they work to drive PLC concepts deeper into the culture of their schools and districts.

A Journey Worth Taking

We do not argue that the PLC journey is an easy one, but we know with certainty that it is a journey worth taking.

Despite the popularity of the term *professional learning community*, the *practices* of a PLC continue to represent "the road less traveled" in public education. Many teachers and administrators prefer the familiarity of their current path, even when it becomes apparent that it will not take them to their desired destination. We recognize it is difficult to pursue an uncharted path, particularly when it is certain to include inevitable bumps and potholes along the way. We do not argue that the PLC journey is an easy one, but we know with certainty that it is a journey worth taking. We have seen the evidence of improved learning and heard the testimonials of teachers and principals who have been renewed by establishing common ground, clear purpose, effective monitoring, and collaborative processes that lead to better results. They describe a heightened sense of professionalism and a resurgence of energy and enthusiasm generated by committed people working together to accomplish what could not be done alone. As Robert Evans (1996) writes:

> Anyone part of such a process, or anyone who has seen first-rate teachers engage in reflective practice together, knows its power and excitement. Opportunities to collaborate and to build knowledge can enhance job satisfaction and performance. At their best, they help schools create a self-reflective, self-renewing capacity as learning organizations. (p. 232)

The following chapters will not eliminate the bumps and potholes of the PLC journey, but they will offer some guidance as to how educators can maneuver their way around and through the rough spots on the road. It has been said that the journey of a thousand miles begins with a single step. We urge readers to take that step. Let us begin together.

Chapter 2

A Clear and Compelling Purpose

Principal Cynthia Dion left the Professional Learning Communities Institute with the zeal and fervor of a recent convert. She was convinced that the PLC concept was the best strategy for improving student achievement in her school, and she was eager to introduce the concept to her faculty at the Siegfried and Roy Middle School (nickname: The Tigers).

On the opening day of school she assembled the entire staff to share both her enthusiasm for PLCs and her plans for bringing the concept to the school. She emphasized that she was committed to transforming the school into a PLC and that the first step in the process was to develop a new mission statement that captured the new focus of the school. She presented the following draft to the staff and invited their reaction:

> It is our mission to ensure all our students acquire the knowledge and skills essential to achieving their full potential and becoming productive citizens.

The moment Principal Dion presented the statement a teacher challenged it, arguing that any mission statement should acknowledge that the extent of student learning was dependent upon their ability and effort. Another teacher disagreed with the reference to "ensuring" all students would learn because it placed too much accountability on teachers and not enough on students. A counselor felt the proposed mission statement placed too much emphasis on academics and not enough on the emotional well-being of students. Soon it became difficult to engage the entire staff in the dialogue as pockets of conversation began to break out throughout the room. Principal Dion decided to adjourn the meeting to give staff members more time to reflect on her mission

The very essence of a professional learning community is a focus on and a commitment to the learning of each student.

statement and promised to return to the topic at the after-school faculty meeting scheduled for the next month.

In the intervening weeks fierce lobbying took place among teachers as they argued for and against different variations of a mission statement. When the staff convened for their next faculty meeting, a group of teachers proposed a compromise, a mission statement they felt would be more acceptable to the staff. It stated:

> *It is our mission to give each student the opportunity to learn according to his or her ability and to create a school that is attentive to the emotional needs of every student.*

Principal Dion expressed concern that the statement did not convey a commitment to helping all students learn; instead, it merely promised to give them the *chance* to learn. The ensuing discussion revealed significant differences of opinion, and the respective parties became more entrenched in the defense of their positions. Finally, as the time to end the meeting approached, an impatient staff member proposed a show of hands to determine support for the two different mission statements. Fifty-five percent of the staff preferred the compromise statement, 25% supported the mission presented by the principal, and 20% were indifferent. Principal Dion acknowledged the decision of the majority and said the compromise statement would become the new mission statement of the school.

Principal Dion remained hopeful that this mission statement would inspire new effort and commitment from the staff. As the year wore on, however, she was disappointed to see the staff had returned to business as usual. She became increasingly disenchanted with the PLC concept. After all, she had engaged the staff in clarifying the mission of the school, just as she had been advised to do at the PLC Institute. There was virtually no evidence, however, that this new mission had impacted either teacher practice or student achievement. She resolved to find another improvement model during the summer.

Reflection

Consider Principal Dion's efforts to develop a clear and compelling purpose for the school with her staff. What advice would you give Principal Dion if you were called upon to mentor her as she was beginning to initiate this process with her staff?

Part Two
Here's How

Despite her good intentions and initial enthusiasm, Principal Dion struggled with two significant factors that adversely impacted her efforts:

1. The process she utilized in attempting to build consensus

2. Her failure to move the dialogue beyond the philosophical debate about the mission of the school

A Failure to Build Consensus

How would a PLC work to build consensus, and what steps would it take to move from dialogue to action? Leaders of a PLC recognize it is a mistake to launch an improvement initiative without the support of a guiding coalition. As John Kotter (1996) of the Harvard Business School concluded in his definitive study of the change process:

> No one individual is ever able to develop the right vision, communicate it to large numbers of people, eliminate all obstacles, generate short-term wins, lead and manage dozens of change projects and anchor new approaches deep in an organization's culture. A strong, guiding coalition is always needed—one with a high level of trust and shared objectives that appeal to both head and heart. Building such a team is always an essential part of the early stages of any effort to restructure a set of strategies. (p. 52)

The challenge Principal Dion faced was not "selling" staff on *her* version of the school's mission, but rather engaging in a process that would help the staff co-create a mission (Senge, Kleiner, Roberts, Ross, & Smith, 1994). A guiding coalition is a powerful tool in that process. It could be composed of existing structures in the school such as a school improvement committee, department chairpeople, or representatives of the teacher's association. Alternatively, she could create a new structure such as a task force convened for the specific purpose of leading an improvement process. In any case, a principal benefits by working through the issues with a small group of key staff members and securing them as allies before engaging the entire faculty. In fact, a comprehensive study of effective school leadership concluded the creation of a guiding coalition or leadership team is a critical first step in the complex task of leading a school (Marzano, Waters, & McNulty, 2005).

In presenting the proposal to the entire staff at one time, Principal Dion used a forum—a large group—that was ill-suited to the dialogue that facilitates consensus. Most people will have questions when significant change is

> The creation of a guiding coalition or leadership team is a critical first step in the complex task of leading a school.

Build consensus one small group at a time.

proposed, and they will want those questions answered before they are willing to give their consent for moving forward. The large-group forum she used in the case study allowed those skeptical of the proposal to dominate the discussion before the idea had been fully considered. A more intimate venue with a small number of staff would have been more effective. Principal Dion might have asked teachers to meet with her in small groups during a preparation period to engage in this dialogue, particularly if she was willing to cancel an after-school faculty meeting to compensate teachers for their lost time. She might have hired enough substitute teachers to free small groups of teachers to meet with her during the school day. Had she done so, she would have found it easier to build consensus one small group at a time rather than in an entire faculty.

The biggest *process* mistake Ms. Dion made was her failure to build shared knowledge among the staff. Although she had apparently learned of concepts and strategies at the PLC Institute that convinced her of the benefits of a PLC, she did nothing to share that learning with her colleagues in the school. When a school functions as a PLC, staff members attempt to answer questions and resolve issues by building shared knowledge. Members of a *learning* community learn together. When all staff members have access to the same information, it increases the likelihood that they will arrive at similar conclusions. Without access to pertinent information, they resort to debating opinions or retreating to a muddied middle ground.

Time spent up front building shared knowledge results in faster, more effective, and most importantly, more committed action later in the improvement process.

Working with her guiding coalition, Ms. Dion might have presented information to help the staff assess the current reality of the school. For example, she could have presented data to help paint a picture of the school's current reality. The data picture worksheet (A Data Picture of Our School, pages 17 and 18) assists in the gathering and presentation of information to help clarify the existing conditions of the school. Anecdotes and stories about students who were not being successful could also help establish what the school experience was like for some students. The coalition could have also presented staff with a synthesis of research on topics such as professional learning communities, improving schools, clear academic goals for every student, and high expectations for student achievement to support the premise that schools are most effective when staff members define their purpose as helping students learn rather than ensuring they are taught. The staff might have heard testimonials from other schools that had adopted PLC concepts or conducted site visits to see a PLC in action. Time spent up front building shared knowledge results in faster, more effective, and most importantly, more committed action later in the improvement process (Patterson, Grenny, McMillan, & Switzler, 2002).

A Data Picture of Our School

Student Achievement Results

Indicator	Year 20___–20___	Year 20___–20___	Year 20___–20___	Facts About Our Data
Based on Our School Assessment Data				
Based on Our District Assessment Data				
Based on Our State Assessment Data				
Based on Our National Assessment Data				

Student Engagement Data

Average Daily Attendance				
Percentage of Students in Extra-Curricular Activities				
Percentage of Students Using School's Tutoring Services				
Percentage of Students Enrolled in Most Rigorous Courses Offered				
Percentage of Students Graduating Without Retention				
Percentage of Students Who Drop Out of School				
Other Areas in Which We Hope to Engage Students, Such as Community Service				

Discipline Data

Number of Referrals/Top Three Reasons for Referrals				
Number of Parent Conferences Regarding Discipline				
Number of In-School Suspensions				

(continued)

A Data Picture of Our School (continued)

Discipline Data (continued)

Indicator	Year 20___–20___	Year 20___–20___	Year 20___–20___	Facts About Our Data
Number of Detentions/Saturday School				
Number of Out-of-School Suspensions				
Expulsions/Other				

Survey Data

Student Satisfaction or Perception Assessment				
Alumni Satisfaction or Perception Assessment				
Parent Satisfaction or Perception Assessment				
Teacher Satisfaction or Perception Assessment				
Administration Satisfaction or Perception Assessment				
Community Satisfaction or Perception Assessment				

Demographic Data

Free and Reduced Lunch				
Percent Mobility				
Percent Special Education				
Percent English as a Second Language				
Ethnicity				
Other				

Learning by Doing © 2006 Solution Tree ■ www.solution-tree.com

Confusing Mission With Action

The biggest mistake made by Principal Dion and her staff was confusing *writing* a mission statement with *living* a mission. No school has ever improved simply because the staff wrote a mission statement. In fact, we have found no correlation between the presence of a written mission statement, or even the wording of a mission statement, and a school's effectiveness as a PLC. The words of a mission statement are not worth the paper they are written on unless people begin to *do* differently.

> The words of a mission statement are not worth the paper they are written on unless people begin to *do* differently.

What could Principal Dion have done to bring the mission to life in her school? First, after engaging staff in building shared knowledge on the specific practices and characteristics of schools where all students were learning at high levels, she might have asked them to describe in vivid detail the school they hoped to create. For almost 30 years, beginning with the Effective Schools research, those who have examined the practices of improving schools have cited the same characteristics again and again:

- A safe and orderly environment

- Clear and focused academic goals for each student

- Frequent monitoring of each student's learning

- Additional opportunities to learn for those who struggle initially

- A collaborative culture

- High expectations for each student

- Strong leadership

- Effective partnerships with parents

For each of these characteristics, she might have asked the staff to describe specific practices that would embed the conditions in their school, such as creating systems to monitor each student's learning of key concepts every 4 weeks, developing an intervention plan to give struggling students extra time and support for learning during the school day, organizing teachers into collaborative teams based on common courses or grade levels, and designing a schedule that provides teachers with time to collaborate.

Once the staff agreed on the school they hoped to create, the principal and her guiding coalition could have then led the staff in a discussion of the specific commitments each member would need to honor in order to become the school they had envisioned. Principal Dion might have modeled a willingness to make commitments by identifying the specific things she was prepared to do to support the effort to transform the school. She could have shared her commitments with the staff and asked for their reactions, revisions, and additions.

Members of the guiding coalition could have then led the staff in a process to clarify their collective commitments.

Principal Dion might also have asked the faculty to identify the indicators that should be monitored to assess the progress they made in creating their agreed-upon school. Benchmarks could have been established for what they hoped to achieve in the first 6 months, the first year, and the first 3 years. Each team of teachers could have been asked to establish specific team goals that, if accomplished, would have contributed to achieving school-wide goals and to moving the school toward the ideal the staff had described.

Of course, all of this dialogue would impact the school only if purposeful steps were taken to demonstrate that creating the school of their hopes, honoring their commitments, and achieving their goals were the collective responsibility of every member of the staff. How is that message best communicated? The most powerful communication is not a function of what is written or said, but rather, once again, what is *done*. As James Autry (2001), author of *Servant Leadership*, wrote, "Those around you in the workplace—colleagues and employees—can determine who you are only by observing what you do . . . the only way you can manifest your character, your personhood, and your spirit in the workplace is through your behavior" (p. 1). Or to paraphrase Ralph Waldo Emerson, what you do stands over you all the while and thunders so loudly that I cannot hear what you say to the contrary.

Consider some of the specific actions the principal and staff might have taken to convey their commitment to improving their school:

1. **Initiating structures and systems to foster qualities and characteristics consistent with the school they are trying to create.** When something is truly a priority in an organization, people do not hope it happens; they develop and implement systematic plans to ensure that it happens. For example, if the staff was committed to creating a collaborative culture, steps could be taken to organize teachers into teams, build time for collaboration into the contractual workday, develop guidelines and parameters to guide the work of teams, and so on. True priorities are not left to chance but are carefully and systematically addressed.

2. **Creating processes to monitor critical conditions and important goals.** In most organizations, what gets monitored gets done. A critical step in moving an organization from rhetoric to reality is to establish the indicators of progress to be monitored, the process for monitoring them, and the means of sharing results with people throughout the organization. For example, if the staff agreed student learning was the priority in their school, procedures to monitor each student's learning on a timely and systematic basis would be imperative.

3. **Reallocating resources to support the proclaimed priorities.** Marshall McLuhan observed, "Money talks because money is a metaphor." The actual legal tender may have little intrinsic value, but how it is expended, particularly in times of scarcity, reveals a great deal about what is valued. Money, however, is not the only significant resource in an organization, and in contemporary public education, time is even scarcer than money. As Phil Schlecty (1990) wrote:

   > The one commodity that teachers and administrators say they do not have enough of, even more than money, is time; time to teach, time to converse, time to think, time to plan, time to talk, time to go to the restroom or have a cup of coffee. Time is indeed precious in schools. (p. 73)

   Decisions about the spending of precious resources are some of the most unequivocal ways organizations communicate what is important. Had Principal Dion created a schedule that provided teachers with time to collaborate and students with time for additional support for learning when they experienced difficulty, she would have sent the message that teacher collaboration and student learning were viewed as priorities in the school.

4. **Posing the right questions.** The questions posed by an organization—and the effort and energy spent in the pursuit of answers—not only communicate priorities but also direct members in a particular direction. In too many schools the prevalent question is, "What is wrong with these kids?"—a question that typically has little impact on improving student achievement. Principal Dion and her staff could have conveyed their commitment to student learning by devoting time to the pursuit of critical questions aligned with that goal, questions such as:

   - What knowledge and skills should every student acquire as a result of this unit of instruction?

   - How will we know when each student has acquired the essential knowledge and skills?

   - How will we respond when some students do not learn?

   - How will we respond when some students have clearly achieved the intended outcomes?

5. **Modeling what is valued.** Example is still the most powerful teacher. In his study of effective leadership, Daniel Goleman (2002) found that a leader's emotions are contagious. If a leader resonates energy and enthusiasm, an organization thrives; if a leader spreads negativity and dissonance, it flounders. If Principal Dion hopes the staff will make a

Example is still the most powerful teacher. . . . If a leader resonates energy and enthusiasm, an organization thrives; if a leader spreads negativity and dissonance, it flounders.

commitment to high levels of learning for all students, she must demonstrate her own commitment by focusing on learning with laser-like intensity and keeping the issue constantly before the faculty. If she hopes to build a culture in which teachers collaborate, she must engage the staff in collaborative decision-making and provide the time and support essential for effective collaboration. As one study concluded, "The single most powerful mechanism for creating a learning environment is that the leadership of the organization be willing to model the approach to learning they want others to embrace" (Thompson, 1995, p. 96).

6. **Celebrating progress.** When an organization makes a concerted effort to call attention to and celebrate progress toward its goals, the commitments it demonstrates in day-to-day work, and evidence of improved results, people within the organization are continually reminded of the priorities and what it takes to achieve them. Furthermore, this provides real-life models by which they can assess their own efforts and commitment. If Principal Dion devoted a part of every staff meeting to a celebration of steps forward on the journey of school improvement, the faculty would soon learn what was noted, appreciated, and valued in their school.

7. **Confronting violations of commitments.** If Principal Dion hopes to convey what is important and valued, she must be prepared to confront those who act in ways that are contrary to the priorities of the school and the commitments of the staff. Leaders who are unwilling to promote and defend improvement initiatives put those initiatives at risk.

Part Three
Here's Why

"To truly reform American education we must abandon the long-standing assumption that the central activity is teaching and reorient all policy making and activities around a new benchmark: student learning." (Fiske, 1992, p. 253)

Given the many demands on teachers and principals, why should they take the time to consider and build shared knowledge regarding the questions posed in this chapter? What evidence is there that reflection upon and dialogue about these issues will be beneficial?

Engaging members of an organization in reflective dialogue about the fundamental purpose of the organization, as Principal Dion attempted to do, can be a powerful strategy for improvement. In fact, the first question any organization must consider if it hopes to improve results is the question of purpose (Drucker, 1992). Why does our organization exist? What are we here to do together? What exactly do we hope to accomplish? What is the business of our business? (Bardwick, 1996; Champy, 1995; Senge, Kleiner, Roberts, Ross, & Smith, 1994)

Research has repeatedly found a correlation between clarity of purpose and effective schools (Lezotte, 1991). As one study concluded, "There is no point in thinking about changes in structure until the school achieves reasonable consensus about its intellectual mission for children" (Newmann & Wehlage, 1996, p. 295). Lickona and Davidson (2005) found that:

> Great schools "row as one"; they are quite clearly in the same boat, pulling in the same direction in unison. The best schools we visited were tightly aligned communities marked by a palpable sense of common purpose and shared identity among staff—a clear sense of "we." By contrast, struggling schools feel fractured; there is a sense that people work in the same school but not toward the same goals. (p. 65)

Educators who believe that merely clarifying or reaffirming their mission will somehow improve results are certain to be disappointed. In fact, in many schools, developing a mission statement has served as a substitute, rather than a catalyst, for meaningful action. Merely drafting a new mission statement does not automatically change how people act, and therefore writing a mission statement does nothing to close the knowing-doing gap (Pfeffer & Sutton, 2000).

Engaging staff members in a dialogue to reaffirm their mission can be an important step in the improvement process, but transforming schools also requires that educators become clear about the vision, values (that is, collective commitments), and goals that drive the daily workings of the school.

Imagine that the foundation of a PLC rests upon the four pillars of mission, vision, values, and goals (see the chart on page 24). Each of these pillars asks a different question of the educators within the school. When teachers and administrators have worked together to consider those questions and reach consensus regarding their collective positions on each question, they have built a solid foundation for a PLC. Much work remains to be done, for these are just a few of the steps in the thousands of steps that must be taken in the never-ending process of continuous improvement. But addressing these questions improves the likelihood that all subsequent work will have the benefit of firm underpinnings. If staff members have not considered the questions, have done so only superficially, or are unable to establish common ground regarding their positions on the questions, any and all future efforts to improve the school will stand on shaky ground.

Mission

The mission pillar asks the question, "Why?" More specifically, it asks, "Why do we exist?" The intent of this question is to help reach agreement regarding the fundamental purpose of the school. This clarity of purpose can help establish priorities and becomes an important factor in guiding decisions.

"Why do we exist?"

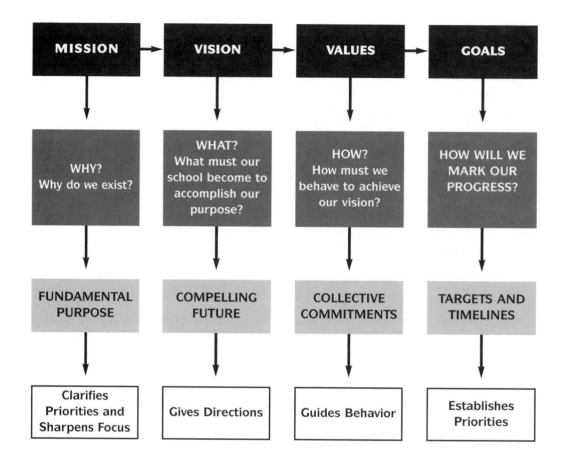

Vision

"What must we become in order to accomplish our fundamental purpose?"

The vision pillar asks "What?": "What must we become in order to accomplish our fundamental purpose?" In pursuing this question, a staff is attempting to create a compelling, attractive, realistic future that describes what they hope their school will become. Vision provides a sense of direction and a basis for assessing both the current reality of the school and potential strategies, programs, and procedures to improve upon that reality. Researchers within and outside of education have routinely cited the importance of developing shared vision (Autry, 2001; Blanchard, 1996; Eastwood & Louis, 1992; Kotter, 1996; Kouzes & Posner, 1996; Newmann & Wehlage, 1996; Schlecty, 1997; Senge, 1990; Tichy, 1997). The conclusion of Burt Nanus (1992) is typical: "There is no more powerful engine driving an organization toward excellence and long-range success than an attractive, worthwhile and achievable vision of the future, widely shared" (p. 3). The very first standard for school administrators drafted by the Interstate School Leaders Licensure Consortium (1996) calls upon educational leaders to "promote the success of all students by facilitating the development, articulation, implementation and stewardship of a vision of learning that is shared and supported by the school community" (p. 10).

Values

In their study of high-performing organizations, Collins and Porras (1997) found that although creating a vision can be a helpful step in the improvement process, it is never sufficient. Teachers and administrators must also tackle the collective commitments they must make and honor in order to achieve the shared vision for their school or district. The third pillar of the foundation, the values pillar, is an attempt to clarify these collective commitments. It does not ask, "Why do we exist?" or, "What do we hope to become?" Rather, it asks, "How must we behave to create the school that will achieve our purpose?" The focus shifts from philosophical musings regarding mission or the shared hopes for the school of the future to commitments to act in certain ways—starting today. Clarity on this topic guides the individual work of each member of the staff and outlines how each person can contribute to the improvement initiative. When members of an organization understand the purpose of their organization, know where it is headed, and then pledge to act in certain ways to move it in the right direction, they don't need prescriptive rules and regulations to guide their daily work. Policy manuals and directives are replaced by commitments and covenants. As a result, members of the organization enjoy greater autonomy and creativity than their more rigidly supervised counterparts.

"How must we behave to create the school that will achieve our purpose?"

Leaders benefit from clearly defined commitments as well. When leaders in traditional hierarchical structures address an employee's inappropriate behavior and demand change, their rationale tends to be, "Because the rules say we have to do it," or, "Because I am the boss, and I said so." If, however, the members of the organization have specified collective commitments, leaders operate with the full weight of the moral authority of the group behind them. Inappropriate behavior is presented as a violation of collective commitments and the leader moves from the role of "boss" to the promoter and protector of what the members have declared as important or sacred.

Finally, achieving agreement about what we are prepared to start doing, and the *implementation* of that agreement, is one of the most effective strategies for closing the knowing-doing gap. Those who "do" develop deeper knowledge, greater self-efficacy, and a stronger sense of ownership in results than those who talk about what should be done.

Shared values (or, as we prefer, collective commitments) have been described as the "vital social glue that infuses an organization with passion and purpose" (Bolman & Deal, 2000, p. 185). Creating a community of shared values has been described as one of the most crucial jobs of a leader (Lezotte, 1997; Tichy, 1997). For over 2 decades both organizational and educational researchers have cited the importance of attention to this crucial element of organizational effectiveness (Champy, 1995; Collins & Porras, 1997; Fullan, 2001; Heskett & Schlesinger,

1996; Kanter, 1995; Kouzes & Posner, 1996; Marks, Doanne, & Secada, 1996; Mandl & Sethi, 1996; Newmann & Wehlage, 1996; Peters & Waterman, 1982; Senge, Kleiner, Roberts, Ross, & Smith, 1994; Sergiovanni, 2005; Steele, 1996). We believe that attention to clarifying collective commitments is one of the most important and, regrettably, least-utilized strategies in building a PLC.

Goals

"How will we know if all of this is making a difference?"

The final pillar of the foundation asks members to clarify the specific goals they hope to achieve as a result of their improvement initiative. The goals pillar identifies the targets and timelines that enable a staff to answer the question, "How will we know if all of this is making a difference?"

Goals provide staff members with a sense of their short-term priorities and the steps to take to achieve the benchmarks. Effective goals foster both the results orientation of a PLC and individual and collective accountability for achieving the results. They help close the gap between the current reality and where the staff hopes to take the school (the shared vision).

Furthermore, goals are absolutely essential to the collaborative team process. We define a team as a group of people working together *interdependently* to achieve a *common goal* for which members are held *mutually accountable.* In the absence of a common goal, there can be no true team. Effective goals generate joint effort and help collaborative teams clarify how their work can contribute to school-wide or district-wide improvement initiatives.

Perhaps most importantly, measurable, results-oriented goals are essential to sustaining the momentum of any improvement initiative. We are often asked how a school can support and nourish the effort to build a PLC over time. Experts on the process of organizational change offer very consistent advice regarding that question (see the feature box on page 27).

When schools create short-term goals and routinely celebrate as those goals are achieved, they foster a sense of confidence and self-efficacy among the staff. Confidence is merely "the expectation of success" (Kanter, 2005), and when people expect to be successful they are more likely to put forth the effort to ensure it. Thus, goals play a key role in motivating people to honor their commitments so the school moves closer to fulfilling its fundamental purpose of learning for all students. We will have more to say about goals in chapter 6, but, once again, educational researchers and organizational theorists consider measurable goals as a key element in improvement (Champy, 1995; Consortium on Productivity in Schools, 1995; Drucker, 1992; Katzenbach & Smith, 1993; Klein, Medrich, & Perez-Ferreiro, 1996; Kotter, 1996; Marzano, 2003; Nanus, 1992; Newmann, King, & Youngs, 2000; Schlecty, 1997; Schmoker, 1999; Senge, Kleiner, Roberts, Ross, & Smith, 1994; Symonds, 2004; Tichy, 1997).

What the Experts Say . . .
How Can a School Support and Nourish the Effort to Build a PLC Over Time?

"Complex change strategies risk losing momentum if there are no short-term goals to meet and celebrate. Most people won't go on the long march unless they see compelling evidence . . . that the journey is producing expected results. Without short-term wins, too many people will give up. But creating short-term wins is different from hoping for short-term wins."

—John Kotter (1996, p. 11)

"Milestones that are identified, achieved, and celebrated represent an essential condition for building a learning organization."

—John Thompson (1995, p. 96)

"The most effective change processes are incremental—they break down big problems into small, doable steps and get a person to say 'yes' numerous times, not just once. They plan for small wins that form the basis for a consistent pattern of winning that appeals to people's desire to belong to a successful venture. A series of small wins provides a foundation of stable building blocks for change."

—James Kouzes and Barry Posner (1987, p. 219)

"Specific goals should be designed to allow teams to achieve small wins as they pursue their common purpose. Small wins are invaluable to building members' commitment and overcoming the obstacles that get in the way of achieving a meaningful, long-term purpose."

—J. Katzenbach and D. Smith (1993, p. 54)

"When people see tangible results, however incremental at first, and see how the results flow from the overall concept, they will line up with enthusiasm. People want to be a part of a winning team. They want to contribute to producing visible, tangible results. When they feel the magic of momentum, when they begin to see tangible results—that's when they get on board."

—Jim Collins (2001, p. 175)

"[Leaders build momentum] by encouraging participants to savor the joys of successive small accomplishments that signal milestones along the way toward achieving more ambitious goals."

—Dov Eden (1990, pp. 186–87)

Leaders must realize that the most important element in communicating is congruency between their actions and their words. It is not essential that leaders are eloquent or clever; it is imperative, however, that they demonstrate consistency between what they say and what they do.

The Importance of Effective Communication

Marcus Buckingham (2005) contends that the one thing leaders of any organization must know to be effective is the importance of clarity: communicating clearly and consistently the purpose of the organization, the primary clients it serves, the future it is creating, the indicators of progress it will track, and the specific actions members can take immediately to achieve its long-term purpose and short-term goals. Michael Fullan (2001) agrees effective leaders provide clarity for those in the organization and lists the ability to create coherence as one of the five core components of leadership. Effective communication is indeed an "essential prerequisite" of great leadership (Tichy, 1997).

Powerful communication is simple and succinct, driven by a few key ideas, and is repeated at every opportunity (Collins, 2001; Pfeffer & Sutton, 2000; Tichy, 1997). Leaders must realize, however, that the most important element in communicating is congruency between their actions and their words. It is not essential that leaders are eloquent or clever; it is imperative, however, that they demonstrate consistency between what they say and what they do (Collins & Porras, 1997; Drucker, 1992; Kouzes & Posner, 1987; Maxwell, 1995; Ulrich, 1996). When leaders' actions are inconsistent with what they contend are their priorities, they overwhelm all other forms of communication (Kotter, 1996).

One of the most effective ways leaders communicate priorities is by what they pay attention to (Kouzes & Posner, 1999; Peters & Austin, 1985). In subsequent chapters, we will provide specific examples of leaders communicating what is valued by creating systems and structures to promote priorities, by monitoring what is essential, by re-allocating time, by asking the right questions, and by the way in which they respond to conflict. In this chapter, we present a powerful tool for communication that is often overlooked and underutilized: celebration.

Celebration

Celebration is a particularly powerful tool for communicating what is valued and for building community (Deal & Key, 1998; Kouzes & Posner, 1999). When celebrations continually remind people of the purpose and priorities of their organizations, members are more likely to embrace the purpose and work toward agreed-upon priorities. Regular public recognition of specific collaborative efforts, accomplished tasks, achieved goals, team learning, continuous improvement, and support for student learning remind staff of the collective commitment to create a PLC. The word *recognize* comes from the Latin "to know again." Recognition provides opportunities to say, "Let us all be reminded, let us all know again, what is important, what we value, and what we are committed to do. Now let's all pay tribute to someone in the organization who is living that commitment."

Celebrations allow for expressions of both appreciation and admiration. Appreciation lets others know we have received something we value, something we are happy to have. Admiration conveys the message that we have been inspired or instructed by observing the work and commitments of others. When admiration and appreciation are repeatedly expressed, organizations create a culture of ongoing regard that sustains effort because such language is "like pumping oxygen into the system" (Kegan & Lahey, 2001, p. 102).

Celebrations also provide an opportunity to use one of the oldest ways in the world to convey the values and ideals of a community: telling stories. As Kouzes and Posner (1999) write: "The intention of stories is not just to entertain. . . . They are also intended to teach. Good stories move us. They touch us, they teach us, and they cause us to remember" (p. 25). Good stories appeal to both the head and the heart and are more compelling and convincing than data alone. Stories are a leader's most powerful weapon in the arsenal for communicating priorities (Gardner, 1990), and the ability of an individual to weave vibrant stories that lead others to a shared understanding of a better future is the "ultimate hallmark of world-class champion leaders" (Tichy, 1997, p. 173). Good stories personify purpose and priorities. They put a human face on success by providing examples and role models that can clarify for others what is noted, appreciated, and valued.

Most schools and districts, however, will face a significant challenge as they attempt to integrate meaningful celebration into their cultures. The excessively egalitarian culture of schools (Lortie, 1975) makes it difficult to publicly recognize either individuals or teams. In most schools and districts, generic praise ("You are the best darn faculty in the state!") or private praise ("I want to send you a personal note of commendation") are acceptable—public recognition is not. Generic and private praise are ineffective in communicating priorities because neither conveys to the members at large what specific actions and commitments are valued, and therefore neither is effective in shaping behavior or beliefs. As Peter Drucker (1992) advises, "Changing behavior requires changing recognition and rewards. For over a quarter of a century we have known that people in organizations tend to act in response to being recognized and rewarded" (p. 195). Tom Peters (1987) put it this way: "Well-constructed recognition settings provide the single most important opportunity to parade and reinforce the specific kinds of new behaviors one hopes others will emulate" (p. 307).

An excellent predictor of the future behavior of any organization is to examine the people and events it elects to honor (Buckingham, 2005). This is true of schools in particular. In his study of school culture, sociologist Robert Evans (1996) concluded, "The single best low-cost, high-leverage way to improve performance, morale, and the climate for change is to dramatically increase the levels of meaningful recognition for—and among—educators" (p. 254).

We offer the following suggestions to those who face the challenge of incorporating celebration into the culture of their school or district:

1. **Explicitly state the purpose of celebration.** The rationale for public celebration should be carefully explained at the outset of every celebration. Staff members should be continually reminded that celebration represents:

    ■ An important strategy for reinforcing the shared purpose, vision, collective commitments, and goals of the school or district

    ■ The most powerful tool for sustaining the improvement initiative

2. **Make celebration everyone's responsibility.** Recognizing extraordinary commitment should be the responsibility of everyone in the organization, and each individual should be called upon to contribute to the effort. If the formal leader is the sole arbiter of who will be recognized, the rest of the staff can merely sit back and critique the choices. Every staff member should have the opportunity to publicly report when they appreciate and admire the work of a colleague.

3. **Establish a clear link between the recognition and the behavior or commitment you are attempting to encourage and reinforce.** Recognition must be specifically linked to the purpose, vision, collective commitments, and goals of the organization if it is to play a role in shaping culture. As we wrote in 1998, "Recognition will have little impact if a staff believes the recognition is presented randomly, that each person deserves to be recognized regardless of his or her contribution to the improvement effort, or that rewards are given for factors unrelated to the goal of creating a learning community" (DuFour & Eaker, 1998, p. 145). It is imperative, therefore, that clear parameters are established for recognition and rewards. The answer to the question, "What behavior or commitment are we attempting to encourage with this recognition?" should be readily apparent. Recognition should always be accompanied with a story relating the efforts of the individual back to the core foundation of the school or district. It should not only express appreciation to and admiration for the individual, but it should also provide others with an example they can emulate.

4. **Create opportunities to have many winners.** Celebration will not have a significant effect on the culture of a school if most people in the organization feel they have no opportunity to be recognized. In fact, celebration can be disruptive and detrimental if there is a perception that

---

**Four Keys for Incorporating Celebration
Into the Culture of Your School or District**

1. Explicitly state the purpose of celebration.

2. Make celebration everyone's responsibility.

3. Establish a clear link between the recognition and the behavior or commitment you are attempting to encourage and reinforce.

4. Create opportunities for many winners.

---

recognition and reward are reserved for an exclusive few (Dilworth, 1995; Peters & Austin, 1985). Establishing artificial limits on appreciation—such as, "We honor no more than five individuals per meeting," or, "Only those with five or more years of experience are eligible"—lessens the impact celebration can have on a school or district. Developing a PLC requires creating systems specifically designed not only to provide celebrations, *but also to ensure that there are many winners.*

Frequent public acknowledgements for a job well done and a wide distribution of small symbolic gestures of appreciation and admiration are far more powerful tools for communicating priorities than infrequent "grand prizes" that create a few winners and many losers. An effective celebration program will convince every member of the staff that he or she can be a winner and that his or her efforts can be noted and appreciated.

Adlai Stevenson High School in Lincolnshire, Illinois, is often cited as a school that has used celebration to communicate purpose and priorities and to shape culture (Deal & Peterson, 1999; DuFour & Eaker, 1998; Kanold, 2006; Schmoker, 1999). Stevenson does not offer a "Teacher of the Year" program, but it has distributed thousands of "Super Pat" awards (small tokens of appreciation that represent a "pat on the back" for a job well done) to hundreds of teachers in the past decade. In fact, in the past 20 years Stevenson has *never* had a faculty meeting without celebrating the effort and commitment of individuals and teams. Stevenson also surveys its seniors each year to ask, "Which member of the staff has had the most profound impact on your life and why?" The heartfelt responses of the students are then published in an internal "Kudos Memorandum" and distributed to the entire staff each quarter. Staff members have read thousands of testimonials citing specific examples of how they and their colleagues are making a difference in the lives of students. Stevenson employees receive ongoing reminders of the priorities of their school and the commitments that are being honored in order to achieve those priorities, and every member of the staff feels like he or she has the opportunity to be recognized and celebrated as a winner.

Study after study of what workers want in their jobs offer the same conclusion: they want to feel appreciated (Kouzes & Posner, 1999). Yet Kegan and Lahey (2001) concluded that "nearly every organization or work team we've spent time with astonishingly undercommunicates the genuinely positive, appreciative, and admiring experiences of its members" (p. 92).

One of the most frequent concerns raised by educators who are wary of making celebration a part of their school or district is that if celebration is frequent, it will lose its impact to motivate. Yet research has drawn the opposite conclusion; it reaffirms that frequent celebration communicates priorities, connects people to the organization and to each other, and sustains improvement initiatives (Kegan & Lahey, 2001; Kouzes & Posner, 1999; Peters, 1987).

Can celebration be overdone? Absolutely. The criterion for assessing the appropriateness of recognition for a team or individual should be the sincerity with which the recognition is given. A commendation should represent genuine and heartfelt appreciation and admiration. If that sincerity is lacking, celebration can be counterproductive.

Part Four
Assessing Your Place on the PLC Journey

The PLC Continuum

In each chapter of this handbook, you will be asked to reflect upon the current conditions in your school or district and assess the alignment of those conditions with the principles and practices of a PLC. The assessment will present a four-point continuum:

1. **Pre-Initiation Stage.** The school has not yet begun to address this principle or practice of a PLC.

2. **Initiation Stage.** An effort has been made to address this principle or practice, but the effort has not yet begun to impact a critical mass of staff members.

3. **Developing Stage.** A critical mass of staff has begun to engage in the practice. Members are being asked to modify their thinking as well as their traditional practices. Structural changes are being made to support the transition.

4. **Sustaining Stage.** The principle or practice is deeply embedded in the culture of the school. It is a driving force in the daily work of staff. It is deeply internalized and staff would resist attempts to abandon the principle or practice.

District leaders may lead the entire administration through the survey or ask randomly selected representatives from each school to complete it. Principals would typically invite the entire staff to participate. Both district- and school-based groups will benefit from the perceptions of others (community members, parents, students, and support staff) as they engage in the process.

We recommend that all those participating in this endeavor work quietly and independently to make individual assessments before making comparisons. We also recommend that staff members be encouraged to be as objective and honest as possible in making their assessments. Each participant should be prepared to cite evidence and anecdotes to support his or her conclusions on each characteristic. Remember that if you are to move your school or district toward greatness, you must have "the discipline to confront the facts of your current reality whatever they might be" (Collins, 2001, p. 13).

> Discrepancies in assessment provide a rich opportunity for learning. . . . Delve into one another's thinking to see if you can clarify discrepancies and establish common ground.

Once they complete their individual assessments, participants should share their conclusions and engage in dialogue to clarify, as accurately as possible, the current status of their school or district. Discrepancies in assessment provide a rich opportunity for learning. Often groups have a tendency to gloss over disagreements. One person contends the school is in the pre-initiation stage while another thinks it is developing, and to avoid discussion, they might merely compromise and settle for the initiation stage. Avoid this temptation. Delve into one another's thinking to see if you can clarify discrepancies and establish common ground.

Where Do We Go From Here?

You will complete this phase of the process by turning to the "Where Do We Go From Here?" planning worksheet that follows the continuum (page 36). Each worksheet presents a principle or practice of a PLC and calls upon participants to develop a specific plan for moving forward. *Beware of plans that call for study, training, discussions, or anything less than specific action to advance your school.* The plan should specify what needs to be done, by whom, a timeline for completion, and how both its implementation and impact will be monitored.

Consider each indicator of a professional learning community described in the left column of the Where Do We Go From Here? Worksheet on page 36, and then answer the questions listed at the top of the remaining four columns.

The Professional Learning Community Continuum

Element of a PLC	Pre-Initiation Stage	Initiation Stage	Developing Stage	Sustaining Stage
Mission: **Is it evident that learning for all is our core purpose?**	No effort has been made to engage faculty in identifying what they want students to learn or how they will respond if students do not learn. School personnel view the mission of the school as teaching rather than learning.	An attempt has been made, typically by the central office, to identify learning outcomes for all grade levels or courses, but this attempt has not impacted the practice of most teachers. Responding to students who are not learning is left to the discretion of individual teachers.	Teachers are clear regarding the learning outcomes their students are to achieve. They have developed strategies to assess student mastery of these outcomes, they monitor the results, and they attempt to respond to students who are not learning.	Learning outcomes are clearly articulated to all stakeholders in the school, and each student's attainment of the outcomes is carefully monitored. The school has developed systems to provide more time and support for students experiencing initial difficulty in achieving the outcomes. The practices, programs, and policies of the school are continually assessed on the basis of their impact on learning. Staff members work together to enhance their effectiveness in helping students achieve learning outcomes.
Shared Vision: **Do we know what we are trying to create?**	No effort has been made to engage faculty in describing preferred conditions for their school.	A vision statement has been developed for the school, but most staff are unaware of or are unaffected by it.	Staff members have worked together to describe the school they are trying to create. They have endorsed this general description and feel a sense of ownership in it. School improvement planning and staff development initiatives are tied to the shared vision.	Staff members routinely articulate the major principles of the shared vision and use those principles to guide their day-to-day efforts and decisions. They honestly assess the current reality in their school and continually seek effective strategies for reducing the discrepancies between the conditions described in the vision statement and their current reality.

Element of a PLC	Pre-Initiation Stage	Initiation Stage	Developing Stage	Sustaining Stage
Shared Values: How must we behave to advance our vision?	Staff members have not yet articulated the attitudes, behaviors, or commitments they are prepared to demonstrate in order to advance the mission of learning for all and the vision of what the school might become. If they discuss school improvement, they focus on what other groups must do.	Staff members have articulated statements of beliefs or philosophy for their school; however, these value statements have not yet impacted their day-to-day work or the operation of the school.	Staff members have made a conscious effort to articulate and promote the attitudes, behaviors, and commitments that will advance their vision of the school. Examples of the core values at work are shared in stories and celebrations. People are confronted when they behave in ways that are inconsistent with the core values.	The values of the school are embedded in the school culture. These shared values are evident to new staff and to those outside of the school. They influence policies, procedures, and daily practices of the school as well as day-to-day decisions of individual staff members.
Goals: What are our priorities?	No effort has been made to engage the staff in setting and defining school improvement goals related to student learning. If goals exist, they have been developed by the administration.	Staff members have participated in a process to establish goals, but the goals are typically stated as projects to be accomplished or are written so broadly that they are impossible to measure. The goals do not yet influence instructional decisions in a meaningful way.	Staff members have worked together to establish long- and short-term improvement goals for their school. The goals are clearly communicated. Assessment tools and strategies have been developed and implemented to measure progress toward the goals.	All staff pursue measurable performance goals as part of their routine responsibilities. Goals are clearly linked to the school's shared vision. Goal attainment is celebrated and staff members demonstrate willingness to identify and pursue challenging stretch goals.
Communication: How do we communicate what is important?	There is no clear, consistent message regarding the priorities of the school or district. Initiatives are changing constantly and different people in the organization seem to have different pet projects.	A small group of leaders in the school or district is declaring the importance of a program or initiative. Their efforts have yet to impact practice to any significant degree.	The school or district is beginning to align practices with stated priorities. New structures have been created to support the initiative, resources have been re-allocated, and systems for monitoring the priorities have been put into place. Evidence of progress is noted and publicly celebrated.	The priorities of the school or district are demonstrated in the everyday practices and procedures of the school and the assumptions, beliefs, and behaviors of the staff. The priorities are evident to students, parents, new staff members, and even visitors to the school or district. Stories of extraordinary commitment to the priorities are part of the lore that binds people together.

Where Do We Go From Here? Worksheet

Effective Communication

Describe one or more aspects of a professional learning community that you would like to see in place in your school.	What steps or activities must be initiated to create this condition in your school?	Who will be responsible for initiating or sustaining these steps or activities?	What is a realistic timeline for each step or phase of the activity?	What will you use to assess the effectiveness of your initiative?
The school communicates its focus on learning consistently and persistently. It develops specific plans to improve levels of learning.				
The school monitors learning on a timely basis. Staff members model a personal commitment to learning. The driving questions of the school focus on learning.				
Resources are allocated to promote learning.				
Evidence of learning is celebrated. There is a systematic response to students who are not learning.				
Staff members who are inattentive to student learning are confronted.				

Learning by Doing © 2006 Solution Tree ■ www.solution-tree.com

Part Five
Tips for Moving Forward:
Building the Foundation of a PLC

1 **Move quickly to action.** Remember that you will not progress on the PLC continuum or close the knowing-doing gap until people in the school or district begin to "do" differently. We have seen educators devote years to studying, debating, rewording, and revising different elements of the foundation, thereby giving the illusion of meaningful action. In most instances a staff should be able to consider and resolve all of the questions of the foundation in a matter of weeks. They may need to return to the foundation in the future to make changes as the vision becomes clear, the need for additional commitments arises, or new goals emerge. Perfection is not the objective: action is. Once again, the school or district that actually does the work of a PLC will develop its capacity to help all students learn far more effectively than the school or district that spends years preparing to be a PLC.

2 **Build shared knowledge when asking people to make a decision.** Asking uninformed people to make decisions is bound to result in uninformed decisions. Members of a PLC resolve issues and answer important questions by asking, "What information do we need to examine together to make a good decision?" and then building shared knowledge regarding that information. Learning together is, by definition, the very essence of a *learning* community. Furthermore, giving people access to the same information increases the likelihood that they will arrive at the same conclusions. All staff should have direct access to user-friendly information on the current reality in their school or district as well as access to best practices and best thinking regarding the issue under consideration.

3 **Use the foundation to assist in day-to-day decisions.** Addressing the foundation of a PLC will impact the school only if it becomes a tool for making decisions. Posting mission statements in the building or inserting a vision statement or goals into a strategic plan does nothing to improve a school. When proposals are considered, the first questions that should be asked are:

- Is this consistent with our purpose?

- Will it help us become the school we envision?

- Are we prepared to commit to do this?

- Will it enable us to achieve our goals?

An honest assessment of these questions can help shorten debate and lead the group to the right conclusion.

 Use the foundation to identify existing practices that should be eliminated. Once your foundation has been established, use it to identify and eliminate any practices that are inconsistent with its principles. As Jim Collins (2001) wrote:

> Most of us have an ever-expanding "to do" list, trying to build momentum by doing, doing, doing—and doing more. And it rarely works. Those who build good to great companies, however, made as much use of "stop doing" lists as "to do" lists. They had the discipline to stop doing all the extraneous junk. (p. 139)

Translate the vision of your school into a teachable point of view. Effective leaders create a "teachable point of view": a succinct explanation of the organization's purpose and direction that can be illustrated through stories that engage others emotionally and intellectually (Tichy, 1997). They have a knack for making the complex simple in ways that give direction to those in the organization (Collins, 2001). They use simple language, simple concepts, and the power of common sense (Pfeffer & Sutton, 2000). Develop a brief teachable point of view that captures the vision of your school in a message that is simple, direct, and jargon free.

Write value statements as behaviors rather than beliefs. "We believe in the potential and worth of each of our students" is a morally impeccable statement; however, it offers little insight into what a staff is prepared to do to help each child realize that potential. Another difficulty with belief statements is their failure to assign specific, personal responsibility. A staff may agree with the statement, "We believe in a safe and orderly environment," but feel it is the job of the administration to create such an environment. Simple, direct statements of what we commit to do are preferable to the most eloquent statements of our beliefs. For example, "We will monitor each student's learning on a timely basis and provide additional time and support for learning until the student becomes proficient" helps to clarify expectations far more effectively than assertions about the potential of every child.

Focus on yourself rather than others. In our work with schools, we have found that educators rarely have difficulty in articulating steps that could be taken to improve their schools, but they call upon others to do it: Parents need to be more supportive, students need to be more responsible, the district needs to reduce class size, the state needs to provide more funding, and so on. This external focus on what others must do fails to improve the situation and fosters a culture of dependency (Sparks,

2005). Furthermore, we cannot make commitments on the behalf of others. We can only make them for ourselves. Members of a PLC have an internal focus that acknowledges that there is much that lies within their sphere of influence that could be done to improve their school. They create a culture of self-efficacy and optimism by concentrating on what is within their collective power to do (Goleman, 2002, p. 87).

 Recognize that the process is nonlinear. Although we present the four pillars sequentially, the process of clarifying purpose, vision, collective commitments, and goals is nonlinear, nonhierarchical, and nonsequential. Working on the foundation is cyclical and interactive. Writing purpose and vision statements can help shape commitments and goals, but as those commitments are honored and goals are achieved, purpose and vision become more real, clearer, and more focused.

 That is what you do that matters, not what you call it. When concepts take on a label, they accumulate baggage. People get the impression that a proposal represents the latest fad, or they settle for a superficial understanding rather than really engaging in an assessment of the underlying ideas. There are schools and districts throughout North America that call themselves professional learning communities yet demonstrate none of the characteristics of a PLC. There are schools that could serve as model PLCs that are unfamiliar with the term. We are not advocating that faculties be asked to vote to become a PLC or take a PLC pledge. In fact, it may be more helpful to never use the term. What is important is that we first engage staff members in building shared knowledge of certain key assumptions and critical practices and then call upon them to act in accordance with that knowledge.

(continued)

Part Six
Questions to Guide the Work of Your Professional Learning Community

For Clarifying the Mission of Your School or District, Ask:

1. What is our fundamental purpose?

2. Why was this school built? What have we been brought here to do together?

3. Does the concept of public education for all children mean that all students shall learn or merely that they will be required to attend school?

4. What happens in our school or district when a student experiences difficulty in learning?

For Clarifying the Vision for Your School or District, Ask:

1. Can you describe the school we are trying to create?

2. What would our school look like if it were a great place for students? What would it look like if it were a great place for teachers?

3. It is 5 years from now and we have achieved our vision as a school. In what ways are we different? Describe what is going on in terms of practices, procedures, relationships, results, and climate.

4. Imagine we have been given 60 seconds on the nightly news to clarify the vision of our school or district to the community. What do we want to say?

For Clarifying the Collective Commitments (Values) of Your School or District, Ask:

1. What are the specific commitments we must honor to achieve our purpose and vision?

_____

_____

2. What are the specific behaviors we can exhibit to make a personal contribution to the success of our school?

_____

_____

3. What commitments are we prepared to make to each other?

_____

_____

4. What commitments or assurances are we prepared to make to every student in our school?

_____

_____

5. What are the "must dos" and the taboos for this staff?

_____

_____

6. What agreements are shared among all of us?

_____

_____

For Clarifying the Goals of Your School or District, Ask:

1. How will we know if we are making progress toward achieving our vision?

_____

_____

2. How will we know if we are more effective 3 years from now than we are today?

_____

_____

3. If we achieve our shared vision, what will student achievement look like in our school?

_____

_____

4. What are the most essential conditions and factors we must monitor on an ongoing basis?

_____

_____

For Clarifying How Effective You Are at Communicating Priorities, Ask:

1. What are the most important factors that drive the day-to-day decisions in our school or district?

_____

_____

2. What are the priorities in our school or district?

_____

_____

3. What systems have been put in place to monitor progress in our priority areas?

_____

_____

4. What gets paid the closest attention in this school or district?

_____

_____

Final Thoughts

The consideration of these questions can help a staff lay the foundation for a professional learning community, but important work remains to be done. A staff that embraces the premise that the very purpose of the school is to help all students learn will face the very challenging questions of, "Learn what?" and, "How will we know if each student has learned?" We turn our attention to these critical questions in the next chapter.

Chapter 3

Creating a Focus on Learning

Professional learning communities create an intensive focus on learning by clarifying exactly what students are to learn and by monitoring each student's learning on a timely basis.

Part One
The Case Study: What Do We Want Our Students to Learn, and How Will We Know When They Have Learned It?

Principal Dan Matthews had worked successfully with a task force of committed teachers to build support for professional learning community (PLC) concepts among the staff of Genghis Khan High School (nickname: The Fighting Horde). They drafted and approved a new vision statement, endorsed their collective commitments, and established school improvement goals. Principal Matthews then asked department chairs to help teachers work together in their collaborative teams to clarify the most essential learning for students by asking, "What knowledge, skills, and dispositions should each student acquire as a result of this course and each unit of instruction within this course?"

After a few weeks, the department chairs proposed modifications to Principal Matthews' request. The math chair reported that teachers felt the state standards had already clarified what students were to learn, and they saw no point in addressing a question that had already been answered. The English chair informed Principal Matthews that several teachers from her department had worked very hard on the committee that wrote the district's language arts curriculum, and they felt their work was being dismissed as irrelevant or ineffective. The head of the social studies department complained that the teachers in her department were unable to agree on the most essential learning for students because so many were personally invested in particular units that they refused to abandon. After considerable discussion, the principal accepted the recommendations of the department chairs:

1. Every teacher would be provided with a copy of the state standards and district curriculum guide for their area.

2. Teachers would be asked to adhere to the state and district guideline.

3. Teacher teams would no longer be required to clarify the essential learning of their courses.

The task force proposal to engage teachers in creating common assessments for their courses also met with resistance on the part of some teachers. Art teachers argued that there was no way to assess the most essential outcomes of their courses on paper and pencil tests; therefore, they believed they should be exempt from common assessments. Science teachers pointed out that their textbooks included test questions at the end of each chapter, and they could simply use these chapter tests as their common assessments. The English department noted that there were not enough copies of the required novels for all students to read the same novel simultaneously. They argued that since students were reading different novels at different times, common assessments were impossible. The social studies department insisted teachers lacked both the time and expertise to develop quality assessments. They took the position that if common assessments were to be created, they should be developed by the district office. The math department chair contended that he spent 2 years trying to get his teachers to embrace the only test that really mattered: the state test. He finally persuaded them to sit down as a department to analyze the results, assess strengths and weaknesses in student learning, and adjust their curriculum and instruction based on the results. To now ask them to create common, teacher-made assessments would send mixed messages and divert their attention from the state test.

After reviewing these concerns, Principal Matthews and the task force agreed to withdraw the proposal to require teams of teachers to develop common assessments.

Reflection

Consider Principal Matthews' efforts and the efforts of the task force to engage teachers in clarifying the essential outcomes of their courses and developing common assessments. If you were called upon to consult with the school, what advice would you offer?

Part Two
Here's How

The principal and task force confronted a common dilemma in this case study: There were certain important tasks in which they hoped to engage the staff in order to further their agreed-upon commitment to learning for all students; however, they wanted the staff to be a part of the process and to feel empowered as the school moved forward.

- Should they insist that the faculty develop common outcomes and common assessments for their courses, or should they abandon processes vital to a PLC because of the objections raised by the staff?

- Is the school better served by a culture of control that demands adherence to certain practices or a culture of freedom that encourages individual autonomy?

In their study of high-performing organizations, Collins and Porras (1997) discovered ineffective organizations succumbed to the "Tyranny of Or—the rational view that cannot easily accept paradox, that cannot live with two seemingly contradictory forces at the same time. We must be A or B, but not both" (p. 44). High-performing organizations, however, rejected this false dichotomy and embraced the "Genius of And" by demonstrating the ability to embrace both extremes at the same time. Collins and Porras clarified that the "Genius of And" "is not just a question of 'balance' because balance implies going to the mid-point—fifty-fifty. A visionary company does not seek the gray of balance, but seeks to be distinctly both 'A' and 'B' at the same time" (p. 45).

If Principal Matthews and his task force were to apply these findings to their situation, they would "create a culture of discipline with an ethic of entrepreneurship" (Collins, 2001, p. 124) and embrace the concept of "directed empowerment" (Waterman, 1987). In other words, they would create a school culture that was simultaneously loose and tight.

Schools and districts need not choose between demanding adherence to certain core principles and practices or empowering the staff. Certain critical issues must be addressed and certain important tasks must be accomplished in a PLC. The school or district is tight in those areas, demanding faithfulness to specific principles and practices. At the same time, however, individuals and teams can benefit from considerable autonomy and freedom in terms of how things get done on a day-to-day basis because the school or district is loose about much of the implementation. Members of the school have the benefit of clear parameters that provide direction and coherence to the improvement process; however, they are also given the freedom and tools to make their own contribution to that

Create a school culture that is simultaneously loose *and* tight.

process. This autonomy allows the school community to benefit from the insights and expertise of those who are called upon to do the actual work.

Principal Matthews has every right to expect faculty members to unite around and act in accordance with the common purpose, clear priorities, and systematic procedures of a PLC if the school is to become more effective in helping all students learn. At the same time, teachers have every right to enjoy considerable freedom and autonomy as they build their capacity to function as a PLC.

Exploring the Critical Questions of a Professional Learning Community

One expectation the school must establish is that every teacher will be called upon to work collaboratively with colleagues in clarifying the questions:

- What is it we want our students to learn?

- How will we know when each student has learned it?

The pursuit of these questions cannot be assigned to others. The constant collective inquiry into these questions is a professional responsibility of every faculty member. Nor can the responsibility be left to each teacher to address on his or her own in a school or district committed to providing all students with equal access to a common, challenging curriculum. The questions of "Learn what?" and "How will we know?" are two of the most significant questions a PLC will consider, the very basis of the collective inquiry that drives the work of collaborative teams. Therefore, members of a PLC can neither ship the questions off to someone else to answer nor disregard their colleagues while exploring the questions.

Clarifying What Students Must Learn

*The constant collective inquiry into "What is it we want our students to learn?" and "How will we know when each student has learned it?" is a professional responsibility of **every** faculty member.*

The personal responsibility of each member of the faculty to work with colleagues in the exploration of the "learn what?" question does not mean teacher teams have license to disregard the curriculum and assessment frameworks that have been developed in their state, province, or district. Principal Matthews should provide the staff with the pertinent resources to help them address the questions and should specifically stipulate that:

1. The essential learning they establish must be aligned with state or provincial standards and district curriculum guides.

2. The identified essential learning must ensure students are well prepared to demonstrate proficiency on state, provincial, district, and national assessments.

3. The assessments created by the team must provide timely information on each student's proficiency so students who are struggling can be

provided with additional time and support for learning. The assessment must also be sufficiently precise to ensure the team can ascertain the specific skills with which a particular student needs help.

Some of the resources Principal Matthews should make available to the teacher teams include:

- State or provincial standards

- Recommended standards from professional organizations (for example, from the National Council of Teachers of Math)

- District curriculum guides

- Prerequisite skills for students entering the next course or grade level

- Assessment frameworks (how students will be assessed on state, provincial, national, and district assessments)

- Data on student performance on past assessments

- Examples of student work and the specific criteria to be used in judging the quality of student work

- Recommendations and standards for workplace skills

- Released test items from state and national assessments

- Recommendations on standards and curriculum design from authors such as Reeves, Jacobs, Marzano, Wiggins, and McTighe

This process should be specifically designed to eliminate content from the curriculum. It is impossible for American teachers to adequately address all the state and national standards they have been urged to teach (Consortium on Productivity in Schools, 1995; Kendall & Marzano, 2000). Ultimately, the problem of too much content and too little time forces teachers to either rush through content or to exercise judgment regarding which standards are the most significant and essential. In a PLC this issue would not be left up to each teacher to resolve individually, nor would it deteriorate into a debate between teachers regarding their opinions on what students must learn. Instead, collaborative teams of teachers would work together to build shared knowledge regarding essential curriculum. They would do what people do in learning communities: They would learn together.

The insights of Doug Reeves (2002) are particularly helpful in guiding this work. He offers a three-part test for teams to consider as they assess the significance of a particular standard:

1. **Does it have endurance?** Do we really expect our students to retain the knowledge and skills over time as opposed to merely learning it for a test?

Does the standard have endurance?

Does it have leverage?

Does it develop student readiness for the next level of learning?

What current content can we eliminate because it is not essential?

(Reeves, 2002)

2. **Does it have leverage?** Will proficiency in this standard help the student in other areas of the curriculum and other academic disciplines?

3. **Does it develop student readiness for the next level of learning?** Is it essential for success in the next unit, course, or grade level?

The teams would also benefit from the discussion of a fourth question as they determine the most essential learning for their students: "What content do we currently teach that we can eliminate from the curriculum because it is not essential?" Principal Matthews could help foster a new mindset in the school if he asked each team to identify content it was removing from the curriculum each time the team planned a unit of instruction.

When Tom Many works with schools, he uses a simple process called "Keep, Drop, Create" to engage teachers in dialogue regarding essential learning. At least once a quarter, teachers devote a grade level or departmental meeting to analysis of the intended versus the implemented curriculum. Each member of the team brings his or her lesson plan books and a copy of the essential curriculum. Three pieces of butcher paper are posted on the wall of the meeting room and labeled with one of the three categories: Keep, Drop, or Create. Each member of the team is then given sticky notes in three colors—yellow for Keep, pink for Drop, and green for Create—and is asked to reflect honestly on his or her teaching.

Teams begin their analysis using their lesson plan books as the record of what was actually taught (the implemented curriculum) and copies of state or district curriculum guides to review the intended curriculum. Topics identified in the essential curriculum documents and included in each teacher's lesson plan book are recorded on the Keep page. Topics identified as essential but not addressed in a teacher's lesson plan book (either because the topics have not yet been taught or because they have been omitted) are listed on the Create page. Finally, topics included in a teacher's lesson plan book but not reflected in the essential curriculum documents are put on the Drop page.

This process not only assists in discovering curriculum gaps and topics that must be addressed in upcoming units, but it also helps teams to create a "stop doing" list of topics that are not essential. As teachers engage in this activity over time, they become more clear, more consistent, and more confident in their response to the question, "What must our students know and be able to do as a result of this unit we are about to teach?"

How Will We Know if Our Students Are Learning?

Principal Matthews must also resist any effort to exempt teachers from working together to create the frequent common assessments that enable a team to verify the proficiency of each student in each skill. Frequent monitoring of each student's learning is an essential element of effective teaching, and no teacher should be absolved from that task or allowed to assign responsibility for it to state test makers, central office coordinators, or textbook publishers.

Teachers should be guided by clear expectations and parameters as they develop their common, formative assessments. Such guidelines might call upon teams to:

- Create a specific minimum number of common assessments to be used in their course or grade level during the semester.

- Demonstrate how each item on the assessment is aligned to an essential outcome of the course or grade level.

- Specify the proficiency standard for each skill.

- Clarify the conditions for administering the test consistently.

- Ensure that demonstration of proficiency on the team assessment will be highly correlated to success on high-stakes testing at the district, state, provincial, or national level.

- Assess a few key concepts frequently rather than many concepts infrequently (Reeves, 2004).

Once again, Principal Matthews could support teachers in their efforts to build common assessments by providing them with time to address the task and resources to help them build quality assessments. Such resources might include:

- State or provincial assessment frameworks to make sure staff are familiar with the format and rigor of the state or provincial test

- Released items from state, provincial, and national assessments (for example, see the National Assessment of Educational Progress web site for released items of different disciplines at different grade levels: http://nces.ed.gov/nationsreportcard/)

- Data on student performance on past indicators of achievement

- Examples of rubrics for performance-based assessments

- Recommendations from assessment experts such as Rick Stiggins and Doug Reeves

- Web sites on quality assessments such as the National Center for Research on Evaluation, Standards and Student Testing (CRESST, www.cse.ucla.edu); the Assessment Training Institute (www.assessmentinst.com); and the The Leadership and Learning Center (www.makingstandardswork.com)

- Tests developed by individual members of the team

Frequent monitoring of each student's learning is an essential element of effective teaching; no teacher should be absolved from that task or allowed to assign responsibility for it to state test makers, central office coordinators, or textbook publishers.

Teams should have the autonomy to develop the kind of assessments they believe will result in valid and authentic measures of the learning of their students. They should have autonomy in designating the proficiency targets for each skill; however, they should also be called upon to demonstrate that student success on their assessments is strongly correlated to success on other indicators of achievement the school is monitoring.

Part Three
Here's Why

Organizations are most effective when the people throughout the organization are clear regarding its fundamental purpose. It is not enough that a few key leaders get the big picture. Employees can play a role in the success of their organizations when they know not only how to perform their specific tasks, but also why they do them—when they see how their work contributes to a larger purpose (Covey, 1996; Handy, 1996; Kouzes & Posner, 1987). This clarity of purpose directs their day-to-day actions and decisions. As Jim Collins (2001) noted, "Great organizations simplify a complex world into a single organizing idea, a basic principle or concept that unifies and guides everything" (p. 91).

In chapter 2 we argued that the fundamental purpose—the single organizing idea—that unifies and guides the work of a PLC is ensuring high levels of learning for all students. No school or district can accomplish that purpose unless it can answer the questions:

- Exactly what is each student expected to learn?

- How will students be called upon to demonstrate their learning?

School districts are most effective when these questions are addressed in a systematic way by the professionals most responsible for ensuring learning: classroom teachers.

The premise that every teacher must know what he or she must teach and what students must learn is found in virtually every credible school improvement model. Thirty years ago, Larry Lezotte and his colleagues (1991) identified clear and focused educational goals as an essential correlate of effective schools. In their study of school restructuring, Gary Wehlage, Fred Newmann, and Walter Secada (1996) found that high-quality teaching and learning began when teachers developed a common vision of the academic standards their students were to achieve. Jonathon Saphier (2005) contends that excellent schools use a "crystal clear curriculum" to bring academic focus, coherence, rigor, precision, alignment, and accountability to the daily work of classroom teachers. Doug Reeves (2004) calls upon teachers to identify the most essential curriculum or "power standards" as a first step in improving student achievement. In his summary of 35 years of research, Robert Marzano (2003) concluded the single most powerful impact a school can have on student achievement is providing students with a "guaranteed and viable curriculum" that:

- Gives students access to the same essential learning regardless of who is teaching the class

- Can be taught in the time allotted

All of this research points to the same conclusion: Teachers are most effective in helping all students learn when they are clear regarding exactly what their students must know and be able to do as a result of the course, grade level, or unit of instruction.

This finding presents schools and districts with an important question: "What is the best way to ensure each teacher knows what students must learn?" One approach is to provide each teacher with a copy of the standards that have been established for their subject area or grade level as well as a district curriculum guide for addressing those standards. The assumption behind this practice is that if the right documents are distributed to individual teachers, each will teach the same curriculum as his or her colleagues. This assumption lingers despite decades of evidence that it is erroneous. Almost every veteran educator would agree with the research on the huge discrepancy between the intended curriculum and the implemented curriculum (Marzano, 2003). The former specifies what teachers are called upon to teach; the latter reflects what is actually taught. The idea that all students within the same school have access to the same curriculum has been described as a "gravely misleading myth" (Hirsch, 1996, p. 26), and district curriculum guides have been characterized as "well intended, but fundamentally fictional accounts" of what students are actually learning (Jacobs, 2001, p. 20).

School leaders must do more than deliver curriculum documents to teachers to ensure all students have an opportunity to master the same essential learning. They must engage every teacher in a collaborative process to study, to clarify, and most importantly, to commit to teaching the curriculum. All teachers should be expected to clarify essential learning with their colleagues—even in states or provinces with delineated standards and in districts with highly developed curriculum guides. They should do so because:

1. **Collaborative study of essential learning promotes clarity.** Even if individual teachers take the time to review state and district curriculum standards, it is unlikely they will interpret those standards consistently. Dialogue regarding the meaning of standards and the clarification of what the standards look like in the classroom help promote a more consistent curriculum.

Teachers are most effective in helping all students learn when they are clear regarding exactly what their students must know and be able to do as a result of the course, grade level, or unit of instruction.

2. **Collaborative study of essential learning promotes consistent priorities.** Just because teachers interpret a learning standard consistently does not guarantee that they will assign the same priority to the standard. One teacher may conclude a particular standard is very significant and devote weeks to teaching it while another teacher may choose to spend only a day on the same standard.

3. **Collaborative study of essential learning is crucial to the common pacing required for formative assessments.** If teachers have not agreed on the meaning and significance of what they are being asked to teach, they will not be able to establish common pacing in their courses and grade levels. Common pacing is a prerequisite for common formative assessments, which we believe are some of the most powerful tools for improvement available to a school.

4. **Collaborative study of essential learning can help establish a curriculum that is viable.** One of the most significant barriers to clarity regarding essential learning for students is curriculum overload (Consortium on Productivity, 1995; Reeves, 2004). One analysis concluded it would take up to 23 years to cover adequately all the standards that have been established at the state and national levels (Marzano, 2003). As a result, individual teachers are constantly making decisions regarding what content to omit in their classrooms, making it difficult for subsequent teachers to know what has been taught and what has not (Stevenson & Stigler, 1992). If teachers work together to make these decisions, they can establish a curriculum that can be taught in the allotted time, and they can clarify the scope and sequence of the curriculum with colleagues who teach in the preceding and subsequent courses or grade levels.

5. **Collaborative study of essential learning creates ownership of the curriculum among those who are called upon to teach it.** Attempts to create a guaranteed curriculum for every child throughout a state, province, or district often create a uniform *intended* curriculum but do little to address the *implemented* curriculum. Teachers throughout North America often feel neither ownership of nor accountability for the content they are being asked to teach. They were not meaningfully involved in the process of creating that content, and they often critique the decisions of those who were: state or provincial departments of education, district committees, central office curriculum coordinators, and so on. Others do not debate the merits of the curriculum; they simply ignore it. A guaranteed curriculum exists in theory but not in fact.

Certainly teacher ownership of and commitment to the curriculum their students will be asked to master plays an important role in the quality of student

Collaborative Study of Essential Learning . . .

- Promotes clarity

- Promotes consistent priorities

- Is crucial to the common pacing required for formative assessments

- Can help establish a curriculum that is viable

- Creates ownership of the curriculum among those who are asked to teach it

learning. Successful implementation of any course of study requires people who care about intended outcomes and have a determination to achieve them. One strategy to promote stronger ownership would simply allow each teacher to determine what he or she will teach; however, that strategy eliminates any hope students will have an equal opportunity to learn the same essential content.

So should districts opt for the uniformity that accompanies a curriculum prescribed by a state, province, or district, or should they promote individual teacher autonomy in an effort to generate greater enthusiasm and ownership? The attentive reader will recognize that the wisest course is to reject this "Tyranny of Or" and seek the "Genius of And" by creating processes that promote both equity and allegiance.

Ownership and commitment are directly linked to the extent to which people are engaged in the decision-making process (Axelrod, 2002), and as a result, there is a direct correlation between participation and improved results (Wheatley, 1999). An attempt to bring about significant change in a school without first engaging those who will be called upon to do the work for the change—the meaningful dialogue—creates a context for failure. Seymour Sarason (1996), who studied the culture of schools for over a quarter of a century, described the typical change process:

> "Someone" decides that something will be changed and "others" are then *required* appropriately to implement that change. If others have had no say in the decision, if there was no forum or allotted time for others to express their ideas or feelings, if others come to feel they are not respected, if they feel their professionalism has been demeaned, the stage is set for the change to fail. *The problem of change is the problem of power, and the problem of power is how to wield it in ways that allow others to identify with, to gain a sense of ownership of the process and the goals of the change.* (p. 335)

So what is the best way to engage staff in an improvement process? The greatest ownership and strongest levels of commitment flow to the smallest part of the organization because that is where people's *engagement* levels are highest. Teachers are *de facto* members of their state or provincial systems of education, but they feel greater allegiance to their local district than they do to the state or province. Most teachers, however, feel greater loyalty to their individual schools than they do to their districts. They probably feel even greater allegiance to their departments than they do their schools. If their departments have been organized into teams, they probably feel greater loyalty to their teammates than to the department as a whole. It is at the team level that teachers have the greatest opportunity for engagement, dialogue, and decision-making. When teachers have collaboratively studied the question of "What must our students learn," when they have created common formative assessments as a team to monitor student learning on a timely basis, and when they have promised each other to teach essential content and prepare students for the assessments, they have exponentially increased the likelihood that the agreed-upon curriculum will actually be taught.

We are not advocating that a team of teachers should be free to disregard state, provincial, or district guidelines and pursue their own interests. We are instead contending that one of the most powerful ways to bring the guidelines to life is to create processes to ensure every teacher becomes a true student of them.

When school leaders establish clear expectations and parameters like those we list in part two of this chapter, they create a process that promotes consistency *and* engages teachers in ways that encourage ownership and commitment. Those guidelines also demand accountability because a team must be able to demonstrate that the decisions it has made have led to more students achieving at higher levels as measured by multiple indicators. Furthermore, the team format itself promotes accountability. Teachers recognize that failure to address agreed-upon content will have an adverse impact on their students when they take common assessments and will prevent the team from achieving its goals. Few teachers will be cavalier about letting down their students and their teammates, particularly when evidence of their failure to honor commitments is readily available with each common assessment.

For too long administrators have settled for the illusion of uniformity across the entire district: They dictated curriculum to schools while teachers provided students in the same course or grade level with vastly different experiences. Effective leaders will view engagement in the question of "What do we want our students to know and be able to do?" as a professional obligation incumbent upon every teacher, and they will create the processes and parameters to promote far greater consistency in the *implemented* curriculum.

The Power of Common Assessments

One of the most powerful, high-leverage strategies for improving student learning available to schools is the creation of frequent, common, high-quality formative assessments by teachers who are working collaboratively to help a group of students develop agreed-upon knowledge and skills (Fullan, 2005a; Hargreaves & Fink, 2006; Reeves, 2004; Schmoker, 2003; Stiggins, 2005). Such assessments serve a distinctly different purpose than the state and provincial tests that have become the norm in North America, and we draw from the work of Rick Stiggins (2002, 2005) to clarify the differences.

State and provincial tests are summative assessments: attempts to determine if students have met intended standards by a specified deadline. They are assessments *of* learning, typically measuring many things infrequently. They can provide helpful information regarding the strengths and weaknesses of curricula and programs in a district, school, or department, and they often serve as a means of promoting institutional accountability. The infrequency of these end-of-process measurements, however, limits their effectiveness in providing the timely feedback that guides teacher practice and student learning.

Formative assessments are assessments *for* learning that measure a few things frequently. These timely in-process measurements can inform teachers individually and collectively regarding the effectiveness of their practice. Furthermore, these teacher-made assessments identify which students have learned each skill and which have not, so that those who are experiencing difficulty can be provided with additional time and support for learning. When done well, they advance and motivate, rather than merely check on student learning. The clearly defined goals and descriptive feedback to students provide them with specific insights regarding how to improve, and the growth they experience helps build their confidence as learners (Stiggins, 2002). These timely team assessments, when combined with classroom teachers' skillful ongoing assessment of student proficiency in precise skills on a daily basis, create a powerful synergy for learning.

Doug Reeves (2000) uses an analogy to draw a sharp distinction between summative and formative assessments, comparing the former to an autopsy and the latter to a physical examination. A summative test, like an autopsy, can provide useful information that explains why the patient has failed, but the information comes too late, at least from the patient's perspective. A formative assessment, like a physical examination, can provide both the physician and the patient with timely information regarding the patient's well-being and can help in prescribing antidotes to help an ailing person or to assist a healthy patient in becoming even stronger.

Common, team-developed formative assessments are such a powerful tool in school improvement that, once again, no team of teachers should be allowed to

> Summative assessments are assessments *of* learning that measure many things infrequently.
>
> Formative assessments are assessments *for* learning that measure a few things frequently.

opt out of creating them. Schools can use a variety of assessments: those developed by individual teachers, a state or provincial test, district tests, national tests, tests that accompany textbooks, and so on. But school leaders should never allow the presence of these other assessments to be an excuse for ignoring the need for common, team-made formative assessments for the following reasons:

1. **Common assessments are more efficient than assessments created by individual teachers.** If all students are expected to demonstrate the same knowledge and skills regardless of the teacher to which they are assigned, it only makes sense that teachers would work together to assess student learning. For example, four third-grade teachers will assess their students on four reading skills during a unit. It would be more efficient for each teacher to develop activities or questions for one skill and present them to teammates for review for inclusion on the common assessment than for each teacher to work separately, duplicating the effort of his or her colleagues. It is ineffective and inefficient for teachers to operate as independent subcontractors who are stationed in proximity to others, yet work in isolation. Those who are called upon to complete the same task benefit by pooling their efforts.

2. **Common assessments are more equitable for students.** When schools utilize common assessments they are more likely to:

    -   Ensure that students have access to the same essential curriculum

    -   Use common pacing

    -   Assess the quality of student work according to the same standards

    It is ironic that schools and districts often pride themselves in the fair and consistent application of rules and policies while at the same time ignoring the tremendous inequities in the opportunities students are given to learn and the criteria by which their learning is assessed. Schools will continue to have difficulty helping all students achieve high standards if the teachers within them cannot develop the capacity to define a standard with specificity and assess it with consistency.

3. **Common assessments represent the most effective strategy for determining whether the guaranteed curriculum is being taught and, more importantly, learned.** Doug Reeves (2004) refers to common, teacher-made formative assessments as the "best practice in assessment" (p. 71) and the "gold standard in educational accountability" (p. 114) because they promote consistency in expectations and provide timely, accurate, and specific feedback to both students and teachers. Perhaps most importantly, teachers' active engagement in the development of the assessment leads them to accept greater accountability for the results.

4. **Common assessments inform the practice of individual teachers.** Tests constructed by an individual teacher generate plenty of data (mean, mode, median, percentage of failing students, and so on), but they do little to inform the teacher's practice by identifying strengths and weaknesses in his or her teaching. Common assessments provide teachers with a basis of comparison as they learn, skill by skill, how the performance of their students is similar to and different from the other students who took the assessment. With this information, a teacher can seek assistance from teammates on areas of concern and can share strategies and ideas on skills in which his or her students excelled.

5. **Common assessments build a team's capacity to improve its program.** When collaborative teams of teachers have the opportunity to examine indicators of the achievement of all students in their course or grade level and track those indicators over time, they are able to identify and address problem areas in their program. Their collective analysis can lead to new curriculum, pacing, materials, and instructional strategies designed to strengthen the academic program they offer.

6. **Common assessments facilitate a systematic, collective response to students who are experiencing difficulty.** Common assessments help identify a group of students who need additional time and support to ensure their learning. Because the students are identified at the same time and because they need help with the same specific skills that have been addressed on the common assessment, the team and school are in a position to create a timely, systematic program of intervention. We will address this topic in detail in the next chapter.

Common Assessments . . .

- Are more efficient than assessments created by individual teachers.
- Are more equitable for students.
- Represent the most effective strategy for determining whether the guaranteed curriculum is being taught and, more importantly, learned.
- Inform the practice of individual teachers.
- Build a team's capacity to improve its program.
- Facilitate a systematic, collective response to students who are experiencing difficulty.

Of course the most effective teachers are constantly assessing student learning. Multiple times each day they will check for student understanding, use precise assessments, and engage students in reviewing their own comprehension and progress. This ongoing, daily assessment is crucial to good teaching and can serve as a powerful motivator for students, and we endorse it whole-heartedly. We are certainly not suggesting that common formative assessments take the place of this continuous monitoring. There will be times, however, that assessments become more formal, and we think there are compelling reasons that at least some of those formal assessments be developed by the team rather than by the individual teacher.

One of the most important factors in student learning is the quality of the teaching they receive (Haycock, 1998; Marzano, 2003; Wright, Horn, & Sanders, 1997). And the "most immediate and direct influence on teaching expertise is the workplace of the school itself" (Saphier, 2005, p. 220). As Jonathan Saphier (2005) goes on to say:

> The reason Professional Learning Communities increase student learning is that they produce more good teaching by more teachers more of the time. Put simply, PLC improves teaching, which improves student results, especially for the least advantaged of students. (p. 23)

Teachers in a PLC work together collaboratively in constant, deep collective inquiry into the questions, "What is it our students must learn?" and "How will we know when they have learned it?" The dialogue generated from these questions results in the academic focus, collective commitments, and productive professional relationships that enhance learning for teachers and students alike. School leaders cannot waffle on this issue. Working with colleagues on these questions is an ongoing professional responsibility from which no teacher should be exempt.

Part Four
Assessing Your Place on the PLC Journey

The PLC Continuum

Working individually and quietly, review the continuum of a school's progress on the PLC journey (on pages 60 and 61). Which point on the continuum gives the most accurate description of the current reality of your school or district? Be prepared to support your assessment with evidence and anecdotes.

After working individually, share your assessment with colleagues. Where do you have agreement? Where do you find discrepancies in the assessments? Listen to the rationales of others in support of their varying assessments. Are you able to reach agreement?

Where Do We Go From Here?

The challenge confronting a school that has engaged in the collective consideration of a topic is answering the questions, "So what?" and, "What, if anything, are we prepared to do differently?" Now consider each indicator of a professional learning community described in the left column of the Where Do We Go From Here? Worksheets on pages 62–64, and then answer the questions listed at the top of the remaining four columns.

(continued)

The Professional Learning Community Continuum

Element of a PLC	Pre-Initiation Stage	Initiation Stage	Developing Stage	Sustaining Stage
Clarity Regarding What Students Must Know and Be Able to Do	There has been little effort to establish a common curriculum for students. Teachers are free to determine what they will teach and how long they will teach it.	District leaders have established curriculum guides that attempt to align the district curriculum with state standards. Representative teachers may have assisted in developing the curriculum guides. The materials have been distributed to each school, but there is no process to determine whether the designated curriculum is actually being taught.	Teachers have worked with colleagues to review state standards and district curriculum guides. They have attempted to clarify the meaning of the standards, establish pacing guides, and identify strategies for teaching the content effectively.	Teachers have worked in collaborative teams to build shared knowledge regarding state standards, district curriculum guides, trends in student achievement, and expectations of the next course or grade level. As a result of this collective inquiry, teachers have established the essential learning for each unit of instruction and are committed to instruct their students in the essential learning according to the team's agreed-upon pacing guide. They know the criteria they will use in judging the quality of student work, and they practice applying those criteria until they can do so consistently. They demonstrate a high level of commitment to the essential curriculum, to their students, and to their teammates.

Learning by Doing © 2006 Solution Tree ■ www.solution-tree.com

Element of a PLC	Pre-Initiation Stage	Initiation Stage	Developing Stage	Sustaining Stage
Assessing Whether Students Have Learned the Essential Curriculum	Each teacher creates the assessments he or she will use to monitor student learning. Assessments may vary widely in format and rigor from one teacher to another. The assessments are used primarily to assign grades rather than to inform teacher and student practice. State or provincial tests are administered in the school, but teachers pay little attention to the results.	District officials analyze the results of state and provincial tests and report the results to each school. Principals are expected to work with staff to improve upon the results. The district may also administer district-level assessments in core curricular areas. These assessments have been created by key central office personnel, by representative teachers serving on district committees, or by testing companies who have sold their services to the district. Classroom teachers typically feel little commitment to the assessments and pay little attention to the results.	Teachers have worked together to analyze results from state and district tests and to develop improvement strategies to apply in their classrooms. They have discussed how to assess student learning on a consistent and equitable basis. Parameters are established for assessments, and individual teachers are asked to honor those parameters as they create tests for their students. Teachers of the same course or grade level may create a common final exam to help identify strengths and weaknesses in their program.	Every teacher has worked with colleagues to develop a series of common, formative assessments that are aligned with state or provincial standards and district curriculum guides. The teams have established the specific proficiency standards each student must achieve on each skill. The team administers common assessments multiple times throughout the school year and analyzes the results together. Team members then use the results to inform and improve their individual and collective practice, to identify students who need additional time and support for learning, and to help students monitor their own progress toward agreed-upon standards.

Where Do We Go From Here? Worksheet
Clearly Defined Outcomes

Describe one or more aspects of a professional learning community that you would like to see in place in your school.	What steps or activities must be initiated to create this condition in your school?	Who will be responsible for initiating or sustaining these steps or activities?	What is a realistic timeline for each step or phase of the activity?	What will you use to assess the effectiveness of your initiative?
Teachers in the school have worked together to clarify and focus on the essential outcomes for each course, each grade level, and each unit of instruction. These common essential outcomes reflect the teachers' efforts to build shared knowledge regarding best practice.				

Where Do We Go From Here? Worksheet
Monitoring Each Student's Learning

Describe one or more aspects of a professional learning community that you would like to see in place in your school.	What steps or activities must be initiated to create this condition in your school?	Who will be responsible for initiating or sustaining these steps or activities?	What is a realistic timeline for each step or phase of the activity?	What will you use to assess the effectiveness of your initiative?
Teachers in the school have worked together to clarify the criteria they use in judging the quality of student work and they apply the criteria consistently.				
Teachers in the school have worked together to monitor student learning through frequent, team-developed common formative assessments that are aligned to state and local standards.				

Where Do We Go From Here? Worksheet
How Individuals and Teams Use Assessment Information
to Improve Their Professional Practice

Describe one or more aspects of a professional learning community that you would like to see in place in your school.	What steps or activities must be initiated to create this condition in your school?	Who will be responsible for initiating or sustaining these steps or activities?	What is a realistic timeline for each step or phase of the activity?	What will you use to assess the effectiveness of your initiative?
Each teacher and team receives relevant feedback. Information is provided regarding the extent to which students meet agreed upon standards of mastery on a valid test in comparison to all the students in the school attempting to meet the same standard. The teams utilize formative tests throughout the year to: ■ Identify students who need additional time and support. ■ Help individual teachers identify areas of strength and weakness in their instruction. ■ Help the team measure progress towards its goals and identify areas in need of attention.				

Part Five
Tips for Moving Forward:
Clarifying and Monitoring Essential Learning

1 **Less is more.** Remember that the main problem with curriculum in North America is not that we do not do enough, but rather that we attempt to do too much. As Doug Reeves (2005) writes, "While academic standards vary widely in their specificity and clarity, they almost all have one thing in common: there are too many of them" (p. 48). We recommend that teams start by identifying the 8 to 10 most essential outcomes students will be expected to achieve in their course or subject area for that semester. There is nothing sacred about that total; it is merely meant to serve as a guideline for team dialogue.

2 **Focus on proficiency, rather than coverage, in key skills.** Teachers throughout North America are confronted with a multitude of standards, and they fear that any one of them may be addressed on state and provincial tests. Therefore, they focus on covering the content rather than ensuring students become proficient in the most essential skills. But not all standards are of equal importance. Some are vital to a student's success and others are simply nice to know. By focusing on essential skills, teachers prepare students for 80% to 90% of the content that will be addressed on state and provincial tests and provide them with the reading, writing, and reasoning skills to address any question that could appear (Reeves, 2002).

A common core curriculum can allow for some variation within courses and grade levels. A frequent, but often unstated, objection to common curriculum is that teachers may be forced to forgo their favorite unit, the one they most enjoy and are most passionate about. But a common core curriculum does not mean a uniform curriculum. A team could develop a curriculum and pacing guide that members feel will enable them to address all of the essential skills in 15 weeks of an 18-week semester. This provides each member of the team with 3 weeks to teach his or her favorite thing. The team's common assessment will cover the common curriculum, while individual teachers can create their own assessments for content unique to their students.

3 **Recognize that common assessments might create teacher anxiety.** Common assessments are likely to create anxiety among teachers who recognize that the results from these assessments could be used to expose weaknesses in their instruction. The inner voice of teachers may very well say, "But what if I am the weakest teacher on my team? My teammates will lose respect for me. The principal may use the results in my evaluation. If the results become public parents may demand that their children be removed from my class. I don't want to participate in a process that can be used to humiliate or punish me. I would rather work in blissful ignorance than to be made aware of the fact that I may be ineffective."

These very real and understandable human emotions should be acknowledged, but should not be allowed to derail the effort to create common curriculum and common assessments. There are certain things leaders can do in an attempt to address these initial concerns. For example, teachers could be assured that their individual results from the assessments will not be distributed to their teammates. Each teacher could see how his or her students performed on each skill compared to the total group of students who took the test, but not compared to other individual teachers on the team. Principals could promise teachers that the results will not leave the building, appear in board of education reports, or show up in district newsletters. They could assure staff that student performance on common assessments will not be used as a factor in teacher evaluation. The process to assess student learning should be distinct from the process to evaluate teachers. Certainly a teacher's failure to contribute to the team process or unwillingness to change practices to improve results when students are not being successful are topics that can be addressed in the teacher's evaluation; however, scores from common assessments should not be.

 Use technology as a tool to support the process. Teachers should not be expected to become either statisticians or data entry clerks in order to analyze the data generated from common assessments. A variety of software programs provide teachers with user-friendly analysis to help them identify the strengths and weaknesses of their students' learning at a glance.

 Districts can play a role. Districts make a mistake when they create common assessments as a substitute for teacher-developed assessments at the team level. Districts should create their own assessments to monitor student learning throughout the entire district, but these assessments should supplement rather than replace team-level assessments. Districts can also create test item banks as a resource for teachers, but teams should be expected to engage in the process of developing their own tools to answer the question, "How do we know our students are learning?"

 Create shared understanding of the term "common assessment." Once again, we have discovered that people who use the same terms do not necessarily assign the same meaning to those terms. For example, a team of teachers that agrees to use the quiz provided at the end of each chapter of the textbook could claim they are using common assessments, but they would not experience the benefits outlined in this chapter. Common assessments "are developed collaboratively in grade-level and departmental teams and incorporate each team's 'collective wisdom' (professional knowledge and experience) in determining the selection, design, and administration of those assessments" (Ainsworth & Viegut, 2006).

Countryside Kildeer School District 96 in suburban Chicago worked with staff to create a shared understanding of the term. Teachers there recognized that their common assessments were to be:

- Connected to the guaranteed and viable curriculum

- Given on a regular and frequent basis to all students enrolled in the same course or grade level

- Administered at about the same time

- Created by a collaborative team of teachers

- Analyzed by that collaborative team of teachers

- Considered highly formative (to identify weaknesses in student learning in order to provide students with additional opportunities to learn)

- Used to help students see their progress toward a well-defined standard

7 **Use assessments as a means rather than an end.** In too many schools in North America, the pursuit of higher test scores has become a preoccupation of the staff. Test scores should be an indicator of our effectiveness in helping all students learn rather than the primary focus of the institution. They should be viewed as a means rather than an end. Doug Reeves (2004) does a wonderful job of providing schools with fail-safe strategies to improve test scores: increase the dropout rate, assign higher percentages of students to special education, warehouse low-performing students in one school, create magnet programs to attract enough high-performing students to a low-performing school to raise its average, eliminate electives to devote more time to areas of the curriculum that are tested, and so on. Sadly, these strategies are routinely being used in schools that are attempting to increase scores without improving learning.

Educators will not be driven to extraordinary effort and relentless commitment to achieve the goal of increasing student performance on the state test by five points. Most entered the profession because they felt they could make a significant difference in the lives of their students, and school leaders are more effective in marshalling and motivating faculty efforts when they appeal to that moral purpose.

Test scores will take care of themselves when schools and the people within them are passionately committed to helping each student develop the knowledge, skills, and dispositions essential to his or her success.

Part Six
Questions to Guide the Work of Your Professional Learning Community

To Clarify Essential Learning, Ask:

1. What is it we want all students to know and be able to do as a result of this course, grade level, or unit of instruction?

   _____

   _____

2. How can we be sure each student has access to the same knowledge and skills regardless of who is teaching the course?

   _____

   _____

3. What knowledge and which skills in our curriculum pass the three-part test: endurance, leverage, and necessity for success at the next level?

   _____

   _____

4. What material can we eliminate from our curriculum?

   _____

   _____

5. Is our curriculum preparing students for success on high-stakes tests?

   _____

   _____

6. Is our curriculum preparing students for success at the next level?

   _____

   _____

7. How should we pace the curriculum to ensure that all students have the opportunity to master the essential learning?

   _____

   _____

To Monitor Student Learning, Ask:

1. How will we monitor the learning of each student, on each essential skill, on a timely basis?

_____

_____

2. What are the criteria we will use in judging the quality of student work?

_____

_____

3. What evidence do we have that we apply the criteria consistently?

_____

_____

4. What evidence do we have that we use the results of common assessments to identify students who require additional time and support for learning?

_____

_____

5. What evidence do we have that we are using the results from common assessments to identify strengths and weaknesses in our individual teaching?

_____

_____

6. What evidence do we have that we are using the results of common assessments as part of a continuous improvement process that is helping our team get better results?

_____

_____

7. Does student performance on our team assessments correlate with their achievement on other assessments at the district, state, provincial, or national level?

   - Does student performance on our assessments correlate with the grades they are earning in my course or grade level?

   - Do our assessment practices encourage or discourage learning on the part of our students?

_____

_____

Final Thoughts

When teachers work together to establish clarity regarding the knowledge, skills, and dispositions all students are to acquire as a result of each course, grade level, and unit of instruction, schools take a significant step forward on their PLC journey. When those same teachers establish frequent common formative assessments that provide timely feedback on each student's proficiency, their schools advance even further, because these assessments help identify students who are experiencing difficulty in their learning. If, however, the school does nothing to assist those students, little has been accomplished. The next chapter explores the critical question, "What happens in your school when kids don't learn?"

Chapter 4

How Will We Respond When Some Students Don't Learn?

<table>
<tr>
<td>

Part One
The Case Study: Systematic Interventions
Versus an Educational Lottery

</td>
</tr>
</table>

Marty Mathers, principal of the Puff Daddy Middle School (nickname: the Rappers), knew that his eighth-grade algebra teachers were his most challenging team on the faculty. The team was comprised of four people with very strong personalities who had difficulty finding common ground.

Peter Pilate was the most problematic teacher on the team from Principal Mather's perspective. The failure rate in his classes was three times higher than the other members of the team, and parents routinely demanded that their students be assigned to a different teacher. Ironically, many of the students who failed Mr. Pilate's class demonstrated proficiency on the state math test. Principal Mathers had raised these issues with Peter, but found Peter to be unreceptive to the possibility of changing any of his practices. Peter insisted that the primary reason students failed was because they did not complete their daily homework assignments in a timely manner. He refused to accept late work, and he explained that the accumulation of zeros on missed assignments led to the high failure rate. He felt strongly that the school had to teach students to be responsible, and he made it clear that he expected the principal to support him in his effort to teach responsibility for getting work done on time.

Alan Sandler was known by the students as the "cool" teacher. He had excellent rapport with his students and a great sense of humor that made his classroom an entertaining environment. Most of his students earned As and Bs in

Professional learning communities create a systematic process of interventions to ensure students receive additional time and support for learning when they experience difficulty. The intervention process is timely and students are directed rather than invited to utilize the system of time and support.

his course; however, each spring, almost half of them would fail to meet the proficiency standard on the state exam.

Principal Mathers was aware of yet another trend in Charlotte Darwin's math classes. He knew they could start out with a large number of students in her algebra sections each year because by early October she would recommend that many of them be transferred to the pre-algebra program. She felt it was unfair to keep students in a program where they lacked the skills for success. The students who remained in her algebra class usually scored slightly above the state average on their proficiency examination.

Henrietta Higgins was a true joy to have on the faculty. She was relentless in holding students accountable but perfectly willing to sacrifice her personal time to help students be successful. She monitored their achievement constantly, and if a student began to fall behind, she required the student to meet with her before or after school for intensive tutoring. Her students always met or exceeded the proficiency standard on the state assessment.

Principal Mathers was increasingly uncomfortable knowing that students' experiences in the eighth grade math program varied so greatly depending on which teacher they had, but he was uncertain of how to address the situation. Two parent phone calls in late September convinced him he could no longer ignore the disparities in the program.

The first phone call came from a parent who objected to Charlotte Darwin's recommendation to move her student to pre-algebra. The parent was familiar with the math program at the high school and recognized that if her son did not complete algebra in the eighth grade, he would never have access to the honors math program there. She was certain her son could be successful if he was given some extra time and support to master content in which he was experiencing some initial difficulty. She had asked Ms. Darwin to tutor her son after school, and Ms. Darwin had flatly refused to do so. The parent was aware that Ms. Higgins routinely tutored students after school, and she demanded that Principal Mathers either direct Ms. Darwin to provide the same service for her son or transfer her son to Ms. Higgins' class.

Principal Mathers knew he could not demand that Ms. Darwin extend her contractual day to tutor students after school. He also realized that she was a single parent who constantly struggled to find quality day care for her pre-school-aged child. He felt the only solution was to transfer the student to Ms. Higgins class.

Before he could make the transfer, he received a second parent complaint, but this time Ms. Higgins was the target. The parent objected to the fact that Ms. Higgins was demanding her son stay after school to get extra help in math.

She needed her son to come home immediately after school because he was responsible for caring for his younger sister until his mother came home from work. She did not want her daughter left unsupervised. Her son could not come in before school either because he walked his sister to school. She argued that none of the other math teachers required students to stay after school, and she felt it was unfair for Ms. Higgins to do so.

Principal Mathers certainly did not want to undermine Ms. Higgins. His initial thought was to pursue the easy solution: transfer the two students into the other teacher's class. He recognized, however, that this strategy offered only a temporary solution and left the real problem unresolved. He was uneasy about a program that was, in his mind, inherently unfair in its treatment of students. It was as if the school was playing an educational lottery with the lives of children—rolling the dice to see which students would receive an excellent opportunity to learn algebra and which would not. He was determined to address this inequity, but he was not sure how.

Reflection

Consider the dilemma presented in this case study; it is a dilemma that is played out in schools throughout North America each day. Assuming that Principal Mathers has no additional resources to hire after-school tutors, how can he best address this problem?

Part Two
Here's How

Principal Mathers and his school are confronting the question, "How will we respond when our students don't learn?" Each individual teacher has been left to resolve this question on his or her own. The result is that students who experience difficulty in learning are subject to very different experiences. The solution requires a *systematic* process of intervention to ensure students receive additional time and support for learning according to a school-wide plan:

- The process should ensure students receive the intervention in a *timely* fashion—at the first indication they are experiencing difficulty.

- The process should *direct* rather than invite students to devote the extra time and take advantage of the additional support until they are experiencing success.

■ Most importantly, students should be guaranteed they will receive this time and support *regardless of who their teacher might be.*

Principal Mathers should present the current reality to the staff and ask them to assess that reality in terms of its effectiveness, efficiency, and most importantly, its equity. An honest evaluation of the facts could only lead to certain conclusions. The current practice is ineffective as demonstrated by both local and state indicators: a high failure rate in some classes and a high percentage of students failing to meet the state proficiency standard. It is inefficient: Some teachers give up personal time, the school staff has to make schedule changes, and students sacrifice time in the summer to repeat failed courses. Finally, it is patently unfair.

Once the staff has confronted the "brutal facts" of their current situation, Principal Mathers could lead them through an analysis of best practices in responding to students who are not learning. The research in this area is clear: In order to help all students learn at high levels, schools must provide students who are experiencing difficulty in learning with additional time and support for learning in a timely, directive, and systematic way.

The next step in this process requires the principal and staff to brainstorm ideas to create an intervention system that is timely, directive, systematic, and within the school day. Then staff members would identify the collective commitments essential to the success of their new intervention system. They would set specific, results-oriented student-achievement goals to help monitor the effectiveness of the system. Finally, they would implement that system, monitor its impact, and make adjustments and improvements based on their results.

In our video program *Through New Eyes: Examining the Culture of Your School* (2003), we ask audiences to view a scene of a student who experiences difficulty in making the transition from middle school to high school and, very importantly, to view the scenario through the eyes of the student. Three different teachers respond to the student in three very different ways, but in each case the burden for addressing the student's problems in the course falls to the respective teacher. In fact, the individual teacher is the only person in the school who even realizes the student is having difficulty for the first 9 weeks of the school year.

After viewing and discussing the scene, teachers acknowledge that the *school* never responded to the student. There was no *collective* response. What happened when the student struggled was left to the idiosyncrasies and beliefs of each of the school's overburdened teachers. We then ask the question, "Is what you saw in the scene a fairly accurate account of what typically happens in school?" Every audience has answered in the affirmative.

In order to help all students learn at high levels, schools must provide students who are experiencing difficulty in learning with additional time and support for learning in a timely, directive, and systematic way.

We then show a second scene with the same student experiencing the same difficulty in school; however, in this school, there is a collective response to the student. He is provided with a study hall to ensure he has extra time during the school day to receive additional support. He also meets daily with a faculty advisor and an upperclassman mentor. His counselor visits with him each week. His grades are monitored every 3 weeks. When he continues to experience difficulty, he is assigned to a tutoring center in place of his study hall and his grades are monitored on a weekly basis. When his struggles persist, he is moved from the tutoring center to a guided study hall where his homework is monitored each day and all materials are provided to ensure he will complete his work. He is required to join a co-curricular activity, and his coach advises him he must be passing all of his classes if he wants to be on the team. His progress is monitored on a weekly basis by a Student Support Team led by his counselor. In short, he is *surrounded* by caring adults, all of whom are attempting to help him be successful in his classes and who consistently express their confidence in his ability to be successful through additional effort.

Audiences invariably acknowledge that the caring environment created through this timely, directive, and systematic intervention plan benefits the student far more than what traditional schools typically offer. *But it is not just the student who benefits from this systematic support.* In the first scene (and in most schools), the only person who knows the student is struggling in algebra is the algebra teacher. The only person responsible for resolving the student's algebra problem is the algebra teacher. In the second scene, an army of adults is there to help the algebra teacher help the student. The teacher is not alone.

The good news is that the second scenario is not merely a dream, but something that is happening in schools throughout North America. In *Whatever It Takes: How Professional Learning Communities Respond When Kids Don't Learn* (2004), we describe four very different schools that have created systematic interventions to ensure their students receive additional time and support for learning. In each case, the schools created their systems with their existing resources. In each case, however, it was imperative that the staff agree to modify the schedule and assume new roles and responsibilities.

We know of schools at all levels that have built systems of time and support within the constraints of union contracts, central office guidelines, and state mandates. Although it is impossible to anticipate all the nuances of all the schedules of all the districts in North America, and then offer specific solutions to scheduling questions, we can offer this generalization: Faculties determined to work together to create a schedule that ensures students will receive extra time and support for learning in a timely, directive, and systematic way will be able to do so. The key question the staff of any school must consider in assessing the

It is not just the student who benefits from this systematic support. An army of adults is there to help the teacher help the student. The teacher is not alone.

appropriateness and effectiveness of their daily schedule is, "Does the schedule provide access to students who need additional time and support during the school day in a way that does not require them to miss new direct instruction?"

Part Three
Here's Why

We have known for more than 30 years that effective schools create a climate of high expectations for student learning; that is, such schools are driven by the assumption that all students are able to achieve the essential learning of their course or grade level (Brophy & Good, 2002; Cotton, 2000; Georgiades, Fuentes, & Snyder, 1983; Lezotte, 1991; Newmann & Wehlage, 1996; Purkey & Smith, 1983). One of the most authentic ways to assess the degree to which a school is characterized by "high expectations" is to examine what happens when some of its students do not learn (Lezotte, 1991).

When schools do not create systems of time and support for students who experience initial difficulty in their learning, teachers are forced to enter into an unstated, implicit contract with their students. We described this subtle message in *Whatever It Takes: How a Professional Learning Community Responds When Kids Don't Learn* (2004):

> Kids, there is a very important concept in this unit we are about to begin, and I really want all of you to learn it. But I can only devote 3 weeks to this concept, and then we have to push on to cover all the other concepts I am supposed to teach you this year. The schedule limits us to 50 minutes a day, and I can't make it 55 minutes. So, during this unit, time to learn will be constant: you all will have 50 minutes a day for 3 weeks. When it comes to giving you individual attention and support, I'll do the best I can. But I can't spend a lot of class time helping a few of you who are having difficulty if the rest of the kids have learned it. That is not fair to those students. So, in effect, you will all have essentially the same amount of support during this unit. (pp. 34–35)

Whenever a school makes time and support for learning constant (that is, fixed), the variable will always be student learning. Some students, probably most students, will learn the intended skill in the given time and with the given support. Some students will not. What happens to those who do not learn is left to the discretion of the individual teachers to whom they are assigned.

Professional learning communities make a conscious and sustained effort to reverse this equation: They advise students that learning is the constant—"All

"In the factory model of schooling, quality was the variable. . . . We held time constant and allowed quality to vary. We must turn that on its head and hold quality constant, and allow time to vary."
(Cole & Schlechty, 1993, p. 10)

of you will learn this essential skill"—and then recognize that if they are to keep that commitment, they must create processes to ensure that students who need additional time and support for learning will receive it.

Schools must come to regard time as a tool rather than a limitation. For too long learning has been a prisoner of time with students and teachers being held captive by clock and calendar (Goldberg & Cross, 2005). Of course schools could lengthen the school day or the school year to create more time, but faculties typically are not in a position to do so unilaterally and are understandably unwilling to do so unless they are compensated accordingly. Faculties can, however, examine the way they are using the existing time available to them to create more opportunities for students to learn.

> Schools must come to regard time as a tool rather than a limitation.

"Opportunity to learn" has been recognized as a powerful variable in student achievement for more than 30 years (Lezotte, 2005; Marzano, 2003). Research on the topic has typically focused on whether or not the intended curriculum was actually implemented in the classroom; that is, were the essential skills actually taught? We are arguing that opportunity to learn must move beyond the question of "Was it taught?" to the far more important question of "Was it learned?" If the answer to that question is no for some students, then the school must be prepared to provide additional opportunities to learn during the regular school day in ways that students perceive as helpful rather than punitive.

In the previous chapter, we made the case for the use of common, formative teacher-developed assessments as a powerful tool for school improvement. These assessments help collaborative teams of teachers answer the question, "How do we know if our students are learning?" It is pointless to raise this question, however, if the school is not prepared to intervene when it discovers that some students are not learning. The lack of a systematic response to ensure that students receive additional opportunities for learning reduces the assessment to yet another summative test administered solely to assign a grade. The response that occurs *after* the test has been given will truly determine whether or not it is being used as a formative assessment. If it is used to ensure students who experience difficulty are given additional time and support as well as additional opportunities to demonstrate their learning, it is formative; if additional support is not forthcoming, it is summative.

Many teachers have come to the conclusion that their job is not just difficult—it is *impossible.* If schools continue to operate according to traditional assumptions and practices, we would concur with that conclusion. Individual teachers working in isolation as they attempt to help all of their students achieve at high levels will eventually be overwhelmed by the tension between covering the content and responding to the diverse needs of their students in a fixed amount of time with virtually no external support.

It is disingenuous for any school to claim its purpose is to help all students learn at high levels and then fail to create a system of interventions to give struggling learners additional time and support for learning.

We cannot make this point emphatically enough: *It is disingenuous for any school to claim its purpose is to help all students learn at high levels and then fail to create a system of interventions to give struggling learners additional time and support for learning.* If time and support remain constant in schools, learning will always be the variable.

Furthermore, we cannot meet the needs of our students unless we assume collective responsibility for their well-being. Sarason (1996) described schools as a "culture of individuals, not a group . . . [with] each concerned about himself or herself" (p. 367), a place in which "each teacher dealt alone with his or her problems" (p. 321), an environment in which teachers "are only interested in what they do and are confronted within their encapsulated classrooms" (p. 329). The idea so frequently heard in schools, "These are *my* kids, *my* room, and *my* materials," must give way to a new paradigm of "These are *our* kids, and we cannot help all of them learn what they must learn without a collective effort." As Saphier (2005) writes, "The success of our students is our joint responsibility, and when they succeed, it is to our joint credit and cumulative accomplishment" (p. 28).

Part Four
Assessing Your Place on the PLC Journey

The PLC Continuum

Working individually and quietly, review the continuum of a school's progress on the PLC journey (on page 79). Which point on the continuum gives the most accurate description of the current reality of your school or district? Be prepared to support your assessment with evidence and anecdotes.

After working individually, share your assessment with colleagues. Where do you have agreement? Where do you find discrepancies in the assessments? Listen to the rationales of others in support of their varying assessments. Are you able to reach agreement?

Where Do We Go From Here?

The challenge confronting a school that has engaged in the collective consideration of a topic is answering the questions, "So what?" and, "What, if anything, are we prepared to do differently?" Now consider each indicator of a professional learning community described in the left column of the Where Do We Go From Here? Worksheet on page 80, and then answer the questions listed at the top of the remaining four columns.

The Professional Learning Community Continuum

Element of a PLC	Pre-Initiation Stage	Initiation Stage	Developing Stage	Sustaining Stage
Systematic Interventions Ensure Students Receive Additional Time and Support for Learning	There is no systematic plan either to monitor student achievement on a timely basis or to respond to students who are not learning with additional time and support. What happens when students experience difficulty in learning will depend entirely upon the teacher to whom they are assigned.	The school has created opportunities for students to receive additional time and support for learning before and after school. Students are invited rather than required to get this support. Many of the students who are most in need of help choose not to pursue it.	The school has begun a program of providing time and support for learning within the school day, but unwillingness to deviate from the traditional schedule is limiting the effectiveness of the program. The staff has retained its traditional 9-week grading periods, and it is difficult to determine which students need additional time and support until the end of the first quarter. Additional support is only offered at a specific time of the day or week (for example, over the lunch period or only on Wednesdays), and the school is experiencing difficulty in serving all the students who need help during the limited time allotted.	The school has a highly coordinated, sequential system in place. The system is proactive: It identifies and makes plans for students to receive extra support even before they enroll. The achievement of each student is monitored on a timely basis. Students who experience difficulty are required, rather than invited, to put in extra time and utilize extra support. The plan is multi-layered. If the current level of support is not sufficient, there are additional levels of increased time and support. Most importantly, all students are guaranteed access to this systematic intervention regardless of the teacher to whom they are assigned.

Where Do We Go From Here? Worksheet

Systematic Intervention

Describe one or more aspects of a professional learning community that you would like to see in place in your school.	What steps or activities must be initiated to create this condition in your school?	Who will be responsible for initiating or sustaining these steps or activities?	What is a realistic timeline for each step or phase of the activity?	What will you use to assess the effectiveness of your initiative?
The school has developed a system of interventions that guarantees each student will receive additional time and support for learning if he or she experiences initial difficulty. The interventions are timely and require, rather than invite, students to devote the extra time and receive the additional support for learning. The intervention plan is multi-dimensional. If one intervention strategy proves unsuccessful, the plan provides for alternative strategies to be used.				

Learning by Doing © 2006 Solution Tree ■ www.solution-tree.com

Part Five
Tips for Moving Forward:
Creating Systematic Interventions to Ensure Students Receive Additional Time and Support for Learning

1 **Beware of appeals to mindless precedent.** Appeals to mindless precedent include the phrases, "But we have always done it this way," "We have never done it that way," and the ever-popular, "The schedule won't let us." These appeals pose a formidable barrier to the creation of a PLC.

We have carefully perused both the Old and New Testaments and can find no evidence that any school schedule was carved into stone tablets and brought down from Mount Sinai. Yet in schools throughout North America, the schedule is regarded as sacred—an unalterable, sacrosanct part of the school not to be tampered with in any way. The reverence afforded the schedule is puzzling. A mere mortal created it, and educators should regard it as a tool to further priorities rather than as an impediment to change.

One way to address mindless precedent is to invite those who resort to it to reflect upon and articulate the assumptions that led them to their position. In effect, they are invited to bring their perhaps unexamined assumptions to the surface for dialogue. Advocates for change can inquire about and probe those assumptions, articulate their own assumptions, and invite others to inquire about them as well. The likelihood of well-intentioned people learning from one another and arriving at similar conclusions increases when individual thinking is in clear view and accessible for examination and dialogue (see chapter 5, page 105, for a helpful guide in the use of advocacy and inquiry from Senge, Kleiner, Roberts, Ross, & Smith, 1994).

An advocate for a schedule that provides additional time and support for student learning might present the following argument:

- We contend that our fundamental purpose and most vital priority is to ensure all students learn at high levels.

- Research, as well as our own experience and intuition, make it clear that it is impossible for all students to learn at high levels if some do not receive additional time and support for learning. Even the most ardent advocates of the premise that all students can learn acknowledge that they will not learn at the same rate and with the same support.

- If the only time we offer this service is before or after school, some of our students cannot or will not utilize the services. It will be difficult for us to require those students to do what is necessary to be successful if our only access to them is beyond the school day.

- Therefore, the priority in designing our schedule should be ensuring we have access to students for intervention during the school day in ways that do not deprive them of new direct instruction in their classroom.

- Help me clarify my thinking. Where do you see errors in my logic? What priorities have you identified that are more significant and should take precedence over interventions for students as we build our schedule?

 The system of intervention should be fluid. The system of intervention should not be designed as a permanent support for individual students. When students are experiencing difficulty, they should be directed to the appropriate level of intervention, but only until they have acquired the intended knowledge and skill. Once they have become proficient in the problem area, they should be weaned from the system until they experience difficulty in the future. There should be an easy flow of students into and out of the various levels of the program of support.

Systems of intervention work most effectively when they are supporting teams rather than individual teachers. We know of a school that convinced the Board of Education to provide additional funding to create a support system for students during the day. Three certified teachers were hired to provide tutoring throughout the school day and each created a sign-up sheet that stipulated designated blocks of time they were available to work with students. The sign-up sheets were posted in the faculty workroom, and teachers signed individual students into a designated block on the schedule to utilize the service. This process often proved problematic because the only time available to tutor a student in reading might occur when the classroom teacher was teaching math. Providing the student with extra time in one area meant a loss of instructional time in another. Furthermore, the teachers had not created common essential learning, pacing guides, or assessments. As a result, tutors were often uncertain regarding the specific skills with which a student required assistance. Therefore, teachers were asked to provide materials when they assigned a student to tutoring to ensure the tutor was focused on the right skills and concepts. As time went on, teachers began to regard the tutoring program as a burden that was creating more work for them rather than a helpful service. At the end of the year the program was abandoned.

This example stands in stark contrast to one of the schools featured in *Whatever It Takes* (2004). This rural school had access to very limited resources, and there were no additional dollars available for funding an intervention program; however, the staff chose to re-allocate discretionary funds in their site-based budget and to shift dollars from their state remediation funds in order to create a system of interventions. Two part-time, "floating" tutors were hired to support that system, but neither was a certified teacher.

The teachers in this school were organized into six grade-level teams of four or five members, and each team had clarified the essential learning, adhered to a common pacing guide, and administered common assessments throughout the year. Furthermore, each team had designated a specific 30-minute block of time during the school day when no new direct instruction would take place so students could be provided either additional time and support or enrichment depending upon their demonstrated proficiency.

Following each assessment, the teams identified the students who had been unable to meet the proficiency standard on a particular skill. The tutors would report to the team at the designated period of the day and would typically release the two teachers who had been most effective in teaching that skill to work with struggling students. Thus, the students who experienced the greatest difficulty in mastering a concept were given small-group instruction and individual tutoring by the strongest teachers in that particular concept. During this same 30-minute tutorial block, the tutors and remaining teachers of the grade level provided a variety of enrichment and extension activities to students who had mastered the skill. Each team created its own activities, such as learning centers, silent sustained reading, teacher read-alouds, junior great books groups, computer-based learning activities, and so on. The one rule observed by each team during this tutorial time was that no new direct instruction would take place.

The floating tutors and teaching teams were assisted by a cadre of volunteers recruited by the school: college students, high school students, employees from area businesses, parents, and grandparents. Volunteers were assigned to a specific grade level during the tutoring period and supported both students in the tutorial program and students in the enrichment activities. Most importantly, the volunteers were assured they would able to work directly with students while they were in the school.

Thus, a school with significantly fewer resources but coordinated collaborative teams was able to be successful in creating a system of interventions for students, while a school with extraordinary resources failed because it could not break free from its traditional structure of 28 classrooms that functioned as 28 independent kingdoms. We have witnessed the same lesson repeated over and over again in our work with schools: A school can dabble in PLC concepts or any other school improvement model of their choice; however, they will never experience significant gains in student achievement if they value individual teacher autonomy more than helping all students learn.

 Ensure common understanding of the term "system of interventions." When Kildeer Countryside School District 96 in suburban Chicago asked each of its schools to create a "system of interventions" to provide students with additional time and support for learning, district leaders discovered schools were interpreting the term in very different ways. Therefore, district leaders worked with representatives of the schools to create the SPEED Intervention Criteria to guide the process. According to the criteria, interventions must be:

- Systematic
- Practical
- Effective
- Essential
- Directive

SPEED Intervention Criteria

Systematic: The intervention plan is school-wide, independent of the individual teacher, and communicated in writing (who, why, how, where, and when) to everyone: staff, parents, and students.

Practical: The intervention plan is affordable with the school's available resources (time, space, staff, and materials). The plan must be sustainable and replicable so that its programs and strategies can be used in other schools.

Effective: The intervention plan must be effective and available and operational early enough in the school year to make a difference for the student. It should have flexible entrance and exit criteria designed to respond to the ever-changing needs of students.

Essential: The intervention plan should focus on agreed upon standards and the essential learning outcomes of the district's curriculum and be targeted to a student's specific learning needs as determined by formative and summative assessments.

Directive: The intervention plan should be directive. It should be mandatory—not invitational—and a part of the student's regular school day. Students should not be able to opt out, and parents and teachers cannot waive the student's participation in the intervention program.

Used with permission from Kildeer Countryside School District 96, Buffalo Grove, Illinois.

An intervention plan should recognize the unique context of the school. Faculties should create their own plans rather than merely adopting the program of another school. In *Whatever It Takes* (2004), we offer specific and detailed explanations and examples of how an intervention plan operates in elementary, middle, and high schools. It is important that faculties realize, however, that eventually they are called upon to create their own systems of intervention within the context of their own schools. Once again, engaging staff in the process of exploring and resolving the question, "What will we do when students do not learn in our school?" creates far more ownership in and commitment to the resulting plan than the adoption of someone else's plan.

5 **Realize that no support system will compensate for bad teaching.** A school characterized by weak and ineffective teaching will not solve its problems by creating a system of timely interventions for students. Eventually, that system will be crushed by the weight of the mass of students it is attempting to support. At the same time the school is creating its system of intervention, it must also take steps to build the capacity of every teacher in the school to become more effective in meeting the needs of students. The battle to help all students learn must be fought on both fronts: support for students and support for the professional staff. To focus on one and exclude the other will never result in victory. Principals and teachers must engage in a process of continuous improvement, constantly examining their practices and expanding their repertoire of skills. But no matter how skillful the professional, at the end of each unit of instruction, it is likely some students will not master the intended learning. At that point the system of interventions comes to the aid of both students and teachers. Schools need both skillful teachers and effective, school-wide interventions.

(continued)

Part Six
Questions to Guide the Work of Your
Professional Learning Community

To Develop Systematic Interventions That Ensure Students Receive Additional Time and Support for Learning on a Timely and Directive Basis, Ask:

1. How do we respond in our school when students don't learn?

   _____

   _____

2. How timely is our response? How quickly can we identify a student who is experiencing difficulty?

   _____

   _____

3. How proactive are we? What steps do we take to identify the students who will need us most before they come to our school?

   _____

   _____

4. How directive is our response? Do we require students to put in extra time and utilize the extra support, or do we merely encourage them to do so?

   _____

   _____

5. How systematic is our response? Is there a plan in place that ensures students will receive additional time and support for learning independent of the classroom teacher?

   _____

   _____

6. Who oversees the system of response? Who makes the determination to move a student from one level of intervention to another?

   _____

   _____

7. How extensive is our response? How much time do we have each day and each week to support student learning through our interventions? Do we have multiple layers in our intervention plan?

   _____

   _____

8. How might we adjust our schedule to give us greater access to students who are not successful within the traditional school schedule?

_____

_____

9. How fluid is our response? Can we easily move students in and out of interventions based on their demonstrated proficiency?

_____

_____

Final Thoughts

A school-wide system of interventions requires a collaborative culture: a school culture in which staff members work together to provide each student with access to the same essential learning and a culture in which the proficiency of each student is assessed in a way that is timely, authentic, and consistent. In many schools and districts, however, educators squander precious time that has been provided for collaboration on topics that have no impact on student achievement. Chapter 5 delves into this problem and offers strategies for creating high-performing collaborative teams.

Chapter 5

Building the Collaborative Culture of a Professional Learning Community

**Part One
The Case Study:
Are We Engaged in Collaboration
or "Coblaboration"?**

Members of a professional learning community recognize they cannot accomplish their fundamental purpose of high levels of learning for all students unless they work together collaboratively. The collaborative team is the fundamental building block of a PLC.

Principal Joe McDonald was puzzled. He knew that building a collaborative culture was the key to improving student achievement. He could cite any number of research studies to support his position. He had worked tirelessly to promote collaboration and had taken a number of steps to support teachers working together. He organized each grade level in the Nemo Middle School (nickname: The Fish) into an interdisciplinary team composed of individual math, science, social studies, and language arts teachers. He created a schedule that gave teams time to meet together each day. He trained staff in collaborative skills, consensus building, and conflict resolution. He emphasized the importance of collaboration at almost every faculty meeting. He felt he had done all the right things, and for 3 years he had waited patiently to reap the reward of higher levels of student learning. But to his dismay and bewilderment, every academic indicator of student achievement monitored by the school had remained essentially the same.

Principal McDonald decided to survey the faculty to see if he could discover why all the collaboration had yielded no gains in student achievement. The satisfaction survey he developed revealed that, with very few exceptions, teachers felt their collaborative time had strengthened the bond between teachers. Specialist teachers—those in art, music, physical education, technical education, and special education—were less enthusiastic and expressed some resentment about being lumped together in one collaborative team. In general, however, teachers seemed to enjoy working together.

Principal McDonald then decided to make a concerted effort to observe personally the workings of the teams. At the first meeting he attended, a seventh-grade team focused on the behavior of a student who had become increasingly disruptive. The team agreed to schedule a parent conference so they could present their concerns to the parent as a group. An eighth-grade team brainstormed strategies for achieving their team goal of reducing disciplinary referrals for tardiness to class. At a meeting of a second seventh-grade team, he observed a lively debate about whether or not members should accept late work from students, and if so, how many points they should deduct for each day the work was late. The fourth team he observed assigned roles and responsibilities to each member to ensure all the tasks associated with an upcoming field trip were addressed.

By the end of the fourth meeting, Principal McDonald experienced a revelation: There had been no gains in student achievement because the topics addressed by the collaborative teams were only remotely related to student learning! Armed with this insight, he convened a meeting of the faculty and shared his conclusion that teams needed to shift the focus of their dialogues to curriculum, assessment, and instruction.

The proposal met with less than wild enthusiasm. Teachers pointed out that each member of their interdisciplinary teams taught different content. How could a seventh-grade science teacher engage in meaningful work on curriculum, assessment, and instruction with a seventh-grade social studies teacher? The team of specialist teachers was even more emphatic that it was impossible for them to have meaningful conversations on those topics because of the different courses they taught. Teachers argued that since they did not share content with the colleagues on their team, it made sense that they would use their team time to focus on the one thing they did have in common: their students.

Other teachers accused Principal McDonald of abandoning the middle school concept and its commitment to the "whole child." One highly emotional teacher charged Principal McDonald with selling out—of disregarding the emotional well-being of the children in the pursuit of higher test scores.

Principal McDonald was genuinely stunned by the reaction of the staff. He had always believed they enjoyed working together in their teams, and he assumed that merely shifting the focus of their collaboration would be a relatively simple matter. It now appeared, however, that although the staff was happy to collaborate regarding some aspects of the school's program, they were either disinterested or adamantly opposed to addressing others. Dispirited, he retreated to his office to ponder next steps.

Reflection

Why did Principal McDonald's efforts to build a collaborative culture in his school go awry? What steps might he take to improve upon the situation?

Part Two
Here's How

The situation in this school reflects one of the most pervasive problems in building PLCs. Most educators have gradually, sometimes grudgingly, come to acknowledge that collaborating with one's colleagues is preferable to working in isolation. Slowly, structures have been put in place to support collaboration. Increasingly staff members are assigned into teams, given time for collaboration during their contractual day, and provided with training to assist them as they begin the challenge of working together. Administrators and teachers alike take pride that the goal has been accomplished: Professionals in the building are collaborating with each other on a regular basis. The anticipated gains in student achievement, however, often fail to materialize.

We cannot stress this next point too emphatically: *The fact that teachers collaborate will do nothing to improve a school. The pertinent question is not, "Are they collaborating?" but rather, "What are they collaborating about?"* Collaboration is not a virtue in itself, and building a collaborative culture is simply a means to an end, not the end itself. The purpose of collaboration—to help more students achieve at higher levels—can only be accomplished if the professionals engaged in collaboration *are focused on the right things.*

What are the "right things" a staff would direct their attention to if high levels of learning were the focus of their collaborative efforts? Once again, we return to the four questions that drive the work of a PLC:

- What is it we want our students to learn?

- How will we know if each student has learned it?

- How will we respond when some students do not learn it?

- How can we extend and enrich the learning for students who have demonstrated proficiency?

The fact that teachers collaborate will do nothing to improve a school. The purpose of collaboration can only be accomplished if the professionals engaged in collaboration *are focused on the right things.*

Principal McDonald must first form an alliance with key members of the staff to help build a deeper understanding of the real purpose of their collaboration and then create supports and parameters to guide staff dialogue to the right topics. Staff must work together to resolve a variety of issues as they create an effective collaborative culture focused on learning.

How Should We Organize Staff Into Teams to Promote a Focus on Learning?

The interdisciplinary team model used in the case study school can be an effective structure for collaboration, but only if certain steps are taken to change the nature of the conversation. If teachers share no common content or objectives, inevitably they will turn their attention to the one thing they do have in common: their students. A seventh-grade team's discussions regarding Johnny's behavior and Mary's attitude can be appropriate and beneficial, but at some point the team should clarify the knowledge, skills, and dispositions Johnny and Mary are to acquire as a result of their seventh-grade experience.

Therefore, each team in the school should be asked to create an overarching curricular goal that members will work together interdependently to achieve. For example, Principal McDonald could make staff aware of the power of nonfiction writing to improve student achievement in mathematics, science, social studies, and reading (Reeves, 2006). He could then ask each grade-level team to develop a goal to increase student achievement by becoming more effective in the instruction of nonfiction writing. The seventh-grade team would confront a series of questions as they worked together to achieve this goal, questions such as:

- How can we integrate nonfiction writing into each of our different subject areas?

- What criteria will we use in assessing the quality of student writing?

- How will we know if we are applying the criteria consistently?

- What are the most effective ways to teach nonfiction writing?

- Is there a member of the team with expertise in this area who can help the rest of us become more effective?

- How will we know if our students are becoming better writers?

- How will we know if the focus on writing is impacting achievement in our respective courses?

- What strategies will we put in place for students who struggle with nonfiction writing?

- How can we enrich the learning experience for students who are already capable writers?

- Are there elements of the seventh-grade curriculum we can eliminate or curtail to provide the time necessary for greater emphasis on nonfiction writing?

Principal McDonald could also foster a greater focus on learning if he created a schedule that allowed teachers to meet in content area teams as well as in grade-level teams. Middle schools make a mistake when they put all their eggs in the interdisciplinary basket. A seventh-grade math teacher can certainly benefit from conversations with colleagues who teach language arts, social studies, or science, but just as certainly that math teacher can also benefit from conversations with other math teachers. The best middle schools create different team structures to support different purposes and will focus on academic achievement as well as the behavior of their students.

The challenge of how to organize teachers into teams is certainly not limited to middle school. It is important for principals to recognize that the task of building a collaborative culture requires more than bringing random adults together in the hope they will discover a topic of conversation. The first and most fundamental task is to bring together those people whose responsibilities create an inherent mutual interest in exploring the four critical questions.

Much work will remain in terms of helping teams develop their capacity to improve student learning, but that outcome is far more difficult to achieve without organizing teams appropriately.

Team Structures

The best team structure is simple: a team of teachers who teach the same course or grade level. These teachers have a natural common interest in exploring the critical questions of learning. In some instances, however, a single person may be the only teacher of a grade level or content area (such as in very small schools or courses outside of the core curriculum). How does the only first-grade teacher or the only art teacher in a school become a member of a meaningful collaborative team?

Vertical teams. Vertical teams link teachers with those who teach content above and/or below their students. For example, the sole first-grade teacher could become a member of the school's primary team. The members of that team would work together to:

- Clarify the essential outcomes for students in kindergarten, first grade, and second grade

- Develop assessments for the students in each grade level

- Analyze the results of each assessment

- Offer suggestions for improving results

The first and most fundamental task of building a collaborative culture is to bring together those people whose responsibilities create an inherent mutual interest in exploring the critical questions of a PLC.

Each teacher would have the benefit of two "critical friends" who could offer suggestions for improvement as the team examined indicators of student achievement. Furthermore, as teachers examine evidence indicating students are having difficulty in a particular skill in the grade level beyond the one they are teaching, they can make adjustments to their own instruction, pacing, and curriculum.

Vertical teams can also cut across schools. A teacher could join a team that brings the district's art teachers together on a regular basis to explore critical questions. An elementary school art teacher could work with the middle school teacher to clarify the prerequisite skills students should have acquired as they enter the middle school art program. The K–12 vertical team format can be a powerful tool for strengthening the program of an entire district.

Electronic teams. Proximity is not a prerequisite for an effective collaborative team. Teachers can use technology to create powerful partnerships with colleagues across the district, the state, or the world. Several web sites have been created for the expressed purpose of bringing teachers together into electronic teams. Apple Computers offers www.iSightEd.com, a site that provides educators and professionals with a forum to find each other, share ideas, and ask questions. Microsoft has partnered with the National Staff Development Council to create electronic teams of teachers. Open Text has created a division called "First Class" (www.firstclass.com) to create electronic partnerships between school districts, schools, and teachers in Canada and the United States. The College Board has created electronic discussion groups for each area of the Advanced Placement program along with sample syllabi, course descriptions, free-response questions, and tips for teaching the AP content. A French teacher in Madison, Wisconsin, can no longer complain he has no opportunity to be a member of a collaborative team when he can meet electronically each week with a teammate in Green Bay. The fact that there is no teammate across the hall does not eliminate the possibility of powerful collaboration.

Logical links. Specialist teachers can become members of grade-level or course-specific teams that are pursuing outcomes linked to their areas of expertise. A physical education teacher can join a sixth-grade team in an effort to help students learn percentages. Each day he could help students learn to calculate the percentage of free throws they made in basketball or their batting averages. A music teacher we know joined the fourth-grade team and wrote a musical based on key historical figures students were required to learn that year. A special education teacher joined a biology team because of the difficulties her students were experiencing in that course. She disaggregated the scores of special education students on each test and became a consultant to the team on supplementary materials, instructional strategies, and alternative

---

Team Structures

- **Vertical teams** link teachers with those who teach content above or below their students.

- **Electronic teams** use technology to create powerful partnerships with colleagues across the district, the state, or the world.

- **Logical links** put teachers together in teams that are pursuing outcomes linked to their areas of expertise.

---

assessments to help special education students achieve the intended outcomes of the course.

In short, teachers should be organized into structures that allow them to engage in meaningful collaboration that is beneficial to them and their students. The fundamental question in organizing teams is this: "Do the people on this team have a shared responsibility for responding to the critical questions in ways that enhance the learning of their students?" The effectiveness of any particular team structure will depend on the extent to which it supports teacher dialogue and action aligned with those questions.

How Can We Find Time for Collaboration?

It is also imperative that teachers be provided with time to meet during their contractual day. We believe it is insincere and disingenuous for any school district or any school principal to stress the importance of collaboration and then fail to provide time for collaboration. One of the ways in which organizations demonstrate their priorities is allocation of resources, and in schools, one of the most precious resources is time.

We also recognize that many districts face real-world constraints in providing time for collaboration. Releasing students from school so that teachers can collaborate may create childcare hardships for some families. Hiring substitute teachers to give teams of teachers time to work together may be cost prohibitive in some districts. Furthermore, teachers and administrators alike are often reluctant to lose precious instructional time so that teachers can meet in teams. Nonetheless, we have worked with school districts throughout North America that have been able to create regularly scheduled weekly time for collaboration within real-world parameters: They bring teachers together during their contractual day while students are on campus, in ways that do not cost money, and that result in little or no loss of instructional time.

Teachers should be organized into structures that allow them to engage in meaningful collaboration that is beneficial to them and their students.

One of the ways in which organizations demonstrate their priorities is allocation of resources, and in schools, the most precious resource is time.

The issue of finding time for collaboration has been addressed effectively—and often—in the professional literature and is readily available for those who are sincerely interested in exploring alternatives. Therefore, the following strategies do not form a comprehensive list; rather, they illustrate some of the steps schools and districts have taken to create the prerequisite time for collaboration.

Common preparation. Build the master schedule to provide daily common preparation periods for teachers of the same course or department. Each team should then designate one day each week to engage in collaborative, rather than individual, planning.

Parallel scheduling. Schedule common preparation time by assigning the specialists (physical education teachers, librarians, music teachers, art teachers, instructional technologists, guidance counselors, foreign language teachers, and so on) to provide lessons to students across an entire grade level at the same time each day. The team should designate 1 day each week for collaborative planning. Some schools build back-to-back specials classes into the master schedule on each team's designated collaborative day, thus creating an extended block of time for the team to meet.

Adjusted start and end time. Gain collaborative time by starting the workday early or extending the workday 1 day each week to gain collaborative team time. In exchange for adding time to the end of 1 workday, teachers get the time back on the other end of that day. For example, on the first day of each school week, the entire staff of Adlai Stevenson High School in Lincolnshire, Illinois, begins their work day at 7:30 AM rather than the normal 7:45 AM start time. From 7:30 to 8:30 AM, the entire faculty engages in collaborative team meetings. Students begin to arrive at 7:40 AM, as usual, but the start of class is delayed from the normal 8:05 until 8:30 AM. Students are supervised by administrative and non-instructional staff in a variety of optional activities, such as breakfast, library and computer research, open gym, study halls, and tutorials. To make up for the 25 minutes of lost instructional time, 5 minutes is trimmed from five of the eight 50-minute class periods. The school day ends at the usual time (3:25 in the afternoon) and buses run on their regular schedules. Stevenson teachers are free to leave at 3:30 rather than 3:45, the traditional conclusion of their work day. By making these minor adjustments to the schedule on the first day of each week, the entire faculty is guaranteed an hour of collaborative planning to start each week, but their work day or work week has not been extended by a single minute.

Shared classes. Combine students across two different grade levels or courses into one class for instruction. While one teacher or team instructs the students, the other team engages in collaborative work. The teams alternate instructing and collaborating to provide equity in learning time for students and teams. Some schools coordinate shared classes so older students adopt younger students and serve as literacy buddies, tutors, and mentors during shared classes.

Group activities, events, and testing. Teams of teachers coordinate activities that require supervision of students rather than instructional expertise, such as watching a DVD or video, conducting resource lessons, reading aloud, attending assemblies, or testing. Nonteaching staff members supervise students while teachers engage in team collaboration.

Banking time. Over a designated period of days, extend the instructional minutes beyond the required school day. After you have banked the desired number of minutes, end the instructional day early to allow for faculty collaboration and student enrichment. For example, in a middle school the traditional instructional day ends at 3:00 PM, students board buses at 3:20, and the teachers' contractual day ends at 3:30. The faculty may decide to extend the instructional day until 3:10. By teaching an extra 10 minutes for nine days in a row, they "bank" 90 minutes. On the tenth day, instruction stops at 1:30 and the entire faculty has collaborative team time for 2 hours. The students remain on campus and are engaged in clubs, enrichment activities, assemblies, and so on, sponsored by a variety of parent and community partners and co-supervised by the school's nonteaching staff.

In-service and faculty meeting time. Schedule extended time for teams to work together on staff development days and during faculty meeting time. Rather than requiring staff to attend a traditional whole-staff in-service session or sit in a faculty meeting while directives and calendar items are read aloud, shift the focus and use of these days and meetings so members of teams have extended time to learn with and from each other.

Visit the National Staff Development Council's web site for more ideas on finding time to collaborate: www.nsdc.org.

Finding Time for Collaboration

- Provide common preparation time.
- Use parallel scheduling.
- Adjust start and end times.
- Share classes.
- Schedule group activities, events, and testing.
- Bank time.
- Use in-service and faculty meeting time wisely.

How Can We Help Teams Focus on the Issues That Impact Student Learning?

This question gets to the heart of the matter. Once again, merely assigning teachers to groups will not improve a school, and much of what passes for "collaboration" among teachers is more aptly described as "coblaboration," a term coined by David Perkins (2003). Those who hope to improve student achievement by developing the capacity of staff to function as a professional learning community must create and foster the conditions that move educators from mere work groups to high-performing collaborative teams.

What distinguishes a group from a team? We define a team as:

> A group of people working *interdependently* to achieve a *common goal* for which members are held *mutually accountable*.

A collection of teachers does not truly become a team until they must rely upon one another (and need one another) to accomplish a goal that none could achieve individually. We will have more to say about the importance of goals in the next chapter.

Professional learning communities do not merely require *teams*—they call for *collaborative* teams. There are many terms in education that have been used so indiscriminately that they have virtually lost their meaning, and "collaboration" is certainly near the top of that list. We have defined collaboration in a PLC as:

> A *systematic process* in which educators work together interdependently to analyze and *to impact their professional practice* in order to achieve better results for their students, their team, and their school.

It is only when educators hold themselves accountable to the standard described in this definition that they are truly "co-laboring" in ways that benefit students.

A *systematic process* is a combination of related parts, organized into a whole in a methodical, deliberate, and orderly way, toward a particular aim. It is not intended to be invitational or indiscriminate. Those who develop systematic practices do not hope things happen a certain way; they create specific structures to ensure certain steps are taken.

In a PLC the process of collaboration is specifically designed to *impact* educator practice in ways that lead to better results. Over and over again we have seen schools in which staff members are willing to collaborate about any number of things—dress codes, tardy policies, the appropriateness of Halloween parties—provided they can return to their classrooms and continue to do what they have always done. Yet in a PLC, the reason teachers are organized into

A collection of teachers does not truly become a team until they must rely upon one another (and need one another) to accomplish a goal that none could achieve individually.

teams, the reason they are provided with time to work together, the reason they are asked to focus on certain topics and complete specific tasks, is so that when they return to their classrooms they will possess and *utilize* an expanded repertoire of skills, strategies, materials, and ideas in order to impact student achievement in a positive way.

Principals must do more than assign teachers into teams and hope for the best: They must establish clear parameters and priorities that guide the work of the teams toward the goal of improved student learning. The Critical Issues for Team Consideration worksheet (pages 100–101) is a useful tool toward that end. First, it directs the team's attention to issues that impact practice and, thus, student achievement. Second, it calls upon the team to generate products that flow directly from the dialogue and decisions regarding those issues. One of the most effective ways to enhance the productivity of a team is to insist that it *produce*. In this case, it must produce artifacts related to the team's collective inquiry into the critical questions focused on learning.

Principal McDonald might have avoided some of the initial confusion regarding how teams were expected to use their time had he presented them with the Critical Issues for Team Consideration worksheet and then worked with the teams to help them establish a timeline for the completion of team products. Imagine if the principal and staff had created the following timeline to guide the dialogue of teams:

By the end of . . .

- The second week of school we will present our team norms.

- The fourth week of school we will present our team SMART goal.

- The sixth week of school we will present our list of the essential knowledge, skills, and dispositions our students will acquire during this semester.

- The eighth week of school we will present our first common assessment.

- The tenth week of school we will present our analysis of the results from the common assessments, including areas of strength and strategies for addressing areas of concern.

This kind of documentation of clearly established expectations is a tremendous benefit to teams. They lose no time debating the question, "Why are we here?" or focusing on the trivial because they have been guided toward conversations specifically related to teaching and learning. Furthermore, this process of gathering and reviewing team products on a regular basis is one of the most effective strategies for monitoring the progress of teams. It soon becomes evident when a team is struggling, and support can be provided on a timely basis.

Critical Issues for Team Consideration

Team Name:_____

Team Members: _____

Use the following rating scale to indicate the extent to which each statement is true of your team.

1	2	3	4	5	6	7	8	9	10
Not True of Our Team				**Our Team Is Addressing This**				**True of Our Team**	

1. _____ We have identified team norms and protocols to guide us in working together.

2. _____ We have analyzed student achievement data and established SMART goals to improve upon this level of achievement we are working interdependently to attain. (SMART Goals are Strategic, Measurable, Attainable, Results-Oriented, and Timebound. SMART Goals are discussed at length in chapter 6.)

3. _____ Each member of our team is clear on the knowledge, skills, and dispositions (that is, the essential learning) that students will acquire as a result of (1) our course or grade level and (2) each unit within the course or grade level.

4. _____ We have aligned the essential learning with state and district standards and the high-stakes assessments required of our students.

5. _____ We have identified course content and topics that can be eliminated so we can devote more time to the essential curriculum.

6. _____ We have agreed on how to best sequence the content of the course and have established pacing guides to help students achieve the intended essential learning.

7. _____ We have identified the prerequisite knowledge and skills students need in order to master the essential learning of each unit of instruction.

8. _____ We have identified strategies and created instruments to assess whether students have the prerequisite knowledge and skills.

9. _____ We have developed strategies and systems to assist students in acquiring prerequisite knowledge and skills when they are lacking in those areas.

10. _____ We have developed frequent common formative assessments that help us to determine each student's mastery of essential learning.

11. _____ We have established the proficiency standard we want each student to achieve on each skill and concept examined with our common assessments.

12. _____ We use the results of our common assessments to assist each other in building on strengths and addressing weaknesses as part of an ongoing process of continuous improvement designed to help students achieve at higher levels.

13. _____ We use the results of our common assessments to identify students who need additional time and support to master essential learning, and we work within the systems and processes of the school to ensure they receive that support.

14. _____ We have agreed on the criteria we will use in judging the quality of student work related to the essential learning of our course, and we continually practice applying those criteria to ensure we are consistent.

15. _____ We have taught students the criteria we will use in judging the quality of their work and provided them with examples.

16. _____ We have developed or utilized common summative assessments that help us assess the strengths and weaknesses of our program.

17. _____ We have established the proficiency standard we want each student to achieve on each skill and concept examined with our summative assessments.

18. _____ We formally evaluate our adherence to team norms and the effectiveness of our team at least twice each year.

> If teachers are to work collaboratively to clarify the essential learning for their courses and grade levels, write common assessments, and jointly analyze the results, they must overcome the fear that they may be exposed to their colleagues and principals as ineffective.

The Importance of Explicit Team Norms

A reluctance to change their traditional classroom practices is not the only reason educators tend to drift away from substantive conversations about teaching and learning if parameters are not in place to guide their work. Conversations about the trivial are safer. If teachers are to work collaboratively to clarify the essential learning for their courses and grade levels, write common assessments, and jointly analyze the results, they must overcome the fear that they may be exposed to their colleagues and principals as ineffective. After all, you were hired for your professional expertise, but what if the results from a common assessment demonstrate that while students taught by your colleagues are successful, your students are not? We have seen evidence that some teachers would prefer not to know their strengths and weaknesses in relationship to their colleagues because it is not worth the risk of being exposed and vulnerable.

In his review of the dysfunctions of a team, Patrick Lencioni (2003) contends that the first and most important step in building a cohesive and high-performing team is the establishment of vulnerability-based trust. Individuals on effective teams learn to acknowledge mistakes, weaknesses, failures, and the need for help. They also learn to recognize and value the strengths of other members of the team and are willing to learn from one another.

The fear of vulnerability leads to the second dysfunction of a team: avoidance of productive conflict. Dysfunctional teams prefer artificial harmony to insightful inquiry and advocacy. As a result, they avoid topics that require them to work interdependently. Even decisions that would appear to require joint effort fail to generate genuine commitment from individuals on the team. Members settle for the appearance of agreement rather than pushing each other to pledge to honor the agreement through their actions. The avoidance of conflict and lack of commitment lead to yet another dysfunction of a team: avoidance of accountability. Team members are unwilling to confront peers who fail to work toward team goals or to honor team decisions. Finally, since members are unwilling to commit to purpose, priorities, and decisions, and are unwilling to hold each other accountable, they inevitably are inattentive to results. When teams demonstrate the five dysfunctions of a team—the inability to establish trust, engage in honest dialogue regarding disagreements, make commitments to one another, hold each other accountable, and focus on results—the team process begins to unravel (Lencioni, 2003).

Leaders can address these dysfunctions in several ways. First, and very importantly, they can model vulnerability, enthusiasm for meaningful exploration of disagreements, articulation of public commitments, willingness to confront those who fail to honor decisions, and an unrelenting focus on and accountability for results. For example, Principal McDonald could acknowledge that he made a mistake in his initial approach to creating high-performing teams and admit that he needs the help of the faculty in altering the team process so that it benefits students. He could invite open dialogue about specific proposals to refocus teams on matters impacting learning and help build shared knowledge regarding the advantages and disadvantages of each proposal. He could make commitments to the staff regarding what he is prepared to do to support their efforts and address their concerns. He could demonstrate his commitment to the decisions they reach by confronting those who violate them. Finally, he could clarify the indicators they would monitor as a school to maintain their focus on results.

Furthermore, Principal McDonald could help staff members engage in professional dialogue designed to address the dangers of a dysfunctional team. Teams benefit not only from clarity regarding the purpose of their collaboration, but also from clarity regarding what is expected of each member. Once again, simply putting people in groups does not ensure a productive, positive experience for participants. Most educators can remember a time when they worked in a group that was painfully inefficient and excruciatingly ineffective. But teams increase their likelihood of performing at high levels when they clarify their expectations of one another regarding procedures, responsibilities, and relationships.

All groups establish norms—"ground rules or habits that govern the group" (Goleman, 2002, p. 173)—regardless of whether or not they take the time to reflect upon and articulate the norms they prefer for their team. When individuals work through a process to create explicitly stated norms, and then commit to honor those norms, they increase the likelihood they will begin to function as a collaborative team rather than as a loose collection of people working together.

Here again, members of a learning community will begin the challenging task of creating team norms by *building shared knowledge* regarding best practices and alternative strategies for implementing those practices. For example, one study of high-performing teams (Druskat & Wolf, 2001) found that members consistently demonstrated high emotional intelligence as evidenced by the following characteristics:

- **Perspective taking.** Members are willing to consider matters from the other person's point of view.

- **Interpersonal understanding.** Members demonstrate accurate understanding of the spoken and unspoken feelings, interests, and concerns of other group members.

- **Willingness to confront.** Members speak up when an individual violates norms, but the confrontation is done in a caring way aimed at building consensus and shared interpretations of commitments.

- **Caring orientation.** Members communicate positive regard, appreciation, and respect. A close personal relationship is not a prerequisite of an effective team, but mutual respect and validation are critical.

- **Team self-evaluation.** The group is willing and able to evaluate its effectiveness.

- **Seeking feedback.** The group solicits feedback and searches for evidence of its effectiveness from external sources as part of a process of continuous improvement.

- **Positive environment.** The group focuses on staying positive: positive affect, positive behavior, and the pursuit of positive outcomes. Members cultivate positive images of the group's past, present, and future.

- **Proactive problem-solving.** Members actively take the initiative to resolve issues that stand in the way of accomplishing team goals.

- **Organizational awareness.** Members understand their connection to and contribution to the larger organization.

- **Building external relationships.** The team establishes relationships with others who can support their efforts to achieve their goals.

Garmston and Wellman (1999, p. 37) identified seven norms of collaboration for teams. They contend that when team members practice the following norms, they promote the productive dialogue essential to effective teams:

1. Pausing

2. Paraphrasing

3. Probing for specificity

4. Putting ideas on the table

5. Paying attention to self and others

6. Presuming positive intentions

7. Pursuing a balance between advocacy and inquiry

In their Protocols for Effective Advocacy and Protocols for Effective Inquiry (page 105), Senge, Kleiner, Roberts, Ross, & Smith, (1994, p. 253–258) offer detailed suggestions to assist teams in moving from polite acquiescence to meaningful dialogue that helps clarify the thinking of each member of the group.

The National Staff Development Council devoted an entire issue of their publication *Tools for Schools* (1999) to the topic of team norms. The issue includes a rationale for norms, a format for creating norms, sample team norms, and sources for exploring the topic more fully. (See pages 210–212 in the appendix for a copy of NSDC's Developing Norms document.)

Protocols for Effective Advocacy

1. State your assumptions.	*Here is what I think.*
2. Describe your reasoning.	*Here are some reasons why I arrived at this conclusion.*
3. Give concrete examples.	*Let me explain how I saw this work in another school.*
4. Reveal your perspective.	*I acknowledge that I am looking at this from the perspective of a veteran teacher.*
5. Anticipate other perspectives.	*Some teachers are likely to question . . .*
6. Acknowledge areas of uncertainty.	*Here is one issue you could help me think through.*
7. Invite others to question your assumptions and conclusions.	*What is your reaction to what I said? In what ways do you see things differently?*

Protocols for Effective Inquiry

1. Gently probe underlying logic.	*What led you to that conclusion?*
2. Use nonaggressive language.	*Can you help me understand your thinking here?*
3. Draw out their thinking.	*Which aspects of what you have proposed do you feel are most significant or essential?*
4. Check for understanding.	*I'm hearing that your primary goal is . . .*
5. Explain your reason for inquiring.	*I'm asking about your assumption because I feel . . .*

All of this information should be made available to teams who are called upon to create norms. We also recommend that members of a team have an honest and open dialogue about the expectations they bring to the process by asking each member to reflect upon and discuss his or her past experience with teams. Ask each participant to describe a time when he or she was a member of a group, committee, task force, or so on that proved to be a negative experience. Then ask each participant to explain the specific behaviors or conditions that made it so negative. Next, invite each participant to describe a personal experience in which he or she felt the power and synergy of an effective team. Record the answers and turn the group's attention to identifying norms that would avoid the negative and promote the positive aspects of membership on a team *if* all participants pledged to honor those norms.

We offer the following additional tips for creating norms.

1. **Each team should create its own norms.** Asking a committee to create norms that will be honored by all teams is ineffective. Committees cannot make commitments for us: we have to make them for ourselves. Furthermore, norms should reflect the experiences, hopes, and expectations of the members of a specific team.

2. **Norms should be stated as commitments to act or behave in certain ways rather than as beliefs.** The statement, "We will arrive to meetings on time and stay fully engaged throughout the meeting," is more powerful than, "We believe members should be considerate of each other."

3. **Norms should be reviewed at the beginning and end of each meeting for at least 6 months.** Norms only impact the work of a team if they are put into practice over and over again. Teams should not confuse writing norms with living norms.

4. **Teams should formally evaluate their effectiveness at least twice a year.** This assessment should include exploration of the questions:
   - Are we adhering to our norms?
   - Do we need to establish a new norm to address a problem occurring on our team?
   - Are we working interdependently to achieve our team goal?

5. **Teams should focus on a few essential norms rather than creating an extensive laundry list.** Less is more when it comes to norms. People do not need a lot of rules to remember, just a few commitments to honor.

6. **Violations of team norms must be addressed.** Failure to confront clear violations of the commitments members have made to each other will undermine the entire team process.

Team norms are not intended to serve as rules, but rather as commitments: public agreements shared among the members (Kegan & Lahey, 2001). Effective teams do not settle for "sorta agreements"; they identify the very specific commitments members have made to each other.

Finally, explicit norms do not ensure each member will observe the agreement, but they do offer a powerful tool for addressing violations, which can then lead to team learning. When done well, norms can help establish the trust, openness, commitment, and accountability that move teams from the trivial to the substantive.

Leaders can and should take each of the purposeful steps presented in this chapter: creating teams on the basis of a common interest in pursuing the critical questions of learning, providing them with time to collaborate, guiding them to the most powerful questions that impact learning, asking teams to create specific products that should flow from their dialogue, and helping them to create norms that facilitate the trust, openness, and commitment essential to effective teams. Those steps can help create the structure for meaningful team dialogue; however, two more critical steps must be taken to help turn the focus of the team to improved student learning:

1. Collaborative teams must develop and pursue SMART goals.

2. Individual teachers and teams must have access to relevant and timely information.

These steps will be considered in the following chapters.

Part Three
Here's Why

Why is it so important to organize a staff into collaborative teams in which people work together interdependently to achieve common goals rather than continuing the long-standing tradition of teacher isolation? The very reason any organization is established is to bring people together in an organized way to achieve a collective purpose that cannot be accomplished by working alone. As Pfeffer and Sutton (2000) wrote: "Interdependence is what organizations are all about. Productivity, performance, and innovation result from *joint* action, not just individual efforts and behavior" (p. 197). The degree to which people are working together in a coordinated, focused effort is a major determinant of the effectiveness of any organization.

Furthermore, the collaborative team has been cited repeatedly in organizational literature as the most powerful structure for promoting the essential

*"Interdependence is what organizations are all about. Productivity, performance, and innovation result from **joint** action, not just individual efforts and behavior." (Pfeffer & Sutton, 2000, p. 197)*

Collaborative time can be squandered if educators do not use that time to focus on issues most directly related to teaching and learning.

interdependence of an effective enterprise. Experts on effective teams offer very consistent advice regarding collaboration and teams (see "The Power of Teams," on page 109).

As we mentioned earlier in the chapter, simply organizing people into teams does not improve a school. Steps must be taken to ensure that those team members engage in *collaboration* on the issues that most impact student learning. Educational research has repeatedly linked collaboration with school improvement (see "Linking Collaboration With School Improvement," page 110). In fact, the case for teachers working together collaboratively is so compelling that we are not aware of any credible research explicitly opposed to the concept.

We have, however, heard individuals oppose providing educators with time to collaborate. They typically frame their objection by arguing the time a teacher spends collaborating with colleagues is time that could have been spent teaching students, and thus represents unproductive time. Once again, research from both organizational development and education refute that position. Effective organizations and effective schools build time for reflection and dialogue into every process. The goal is not merely to do more of what we have always done (regardless of its effectiveness), but to create a culture of continuous improvement, to discover ways to become better at achieving our purpose, forever (Black, Harrison, Lee, Marsh, & William, 2004; Champy, 1995; Collins & Porras, 1997; Darling-Hammond, 1996; Dolan, 1994; Goldsmith, 1996; Kouzes & Posner, 1987; Schein, 1996).

Common sense advises, however, that collaborative time can be squandered if educators do not use that time to focus on issues most directly related to teaching and learning. Michael Fullan's (2001) caution should be self-evident: "Collaborative cultures, which by definition have close relationships, are indeed powerful, but unless they are focusing on the right things they may end up being powerfully wrong" (p. 67).

Effective leaders will direct the work of teams to the critical questions, because those are the conversations that have the biggest impact on student achievement. Clarifying what students must learn, monitoring the learning of each student, responding to students who need additional time and support for learning, and challenging students who have already mastered the intended outcomes are the most critical tasks in a school. It is imperative, therefore, that educators work together interdependently to become more skillful in these critical areas, and that these questions become the priority within and among collaborative teams. The extensive research base to support the focus on these questions was presented in chapter 3.

It is crucial not to overlook the significance of teams developing explicit norms to guide their work in the process of building the capacity of teachers to

The Power of Teams

"Empowered teams are such a powerful force of integration and productivity that they form the basic building block of any intelligent organization. Given the right context, teams generate passion and engagement. In addition, a team is something to belong to, a support group and political unit with more clout than the individuals in it." —Pinchot & Pinchot (1993, p. 66)

"We are at a point in time where teams are recognized as a critical component of every enterprise—the predominant unit for decision making and getting things done. . . . Working in teams is the norm in a learning organization." —Senge, Kleiner, Roberts, Ross, & Smith (1994, p. 51)

"The leader of the future will master the art of forming teams. Future leaders will master teamwork, working with and through others because no one person can master all the sources of information to make good decisions." —Ulrich (1996, p. 213)

"Teams bring together complementary skills and experience that exceed those of any individual on the team. Teams are more effective in problem solving. Teams provide a social dimension that enhances work. Teams motivate and foster peer pressure and internal accountability. Teams have more fun." —Katzenbach & Smith (1993, p. 19)

"The best way to achieve challenging goals is through teamwork. Where single individuals may despair of accomplishing a monumental task, teams nurture, support, and inspire each other." —Tichy (1997, p. 143)

"People who collaborate learn from each other and create synergy. That is why learning organizations are made up of teams that share a common purpose. Organizations need togetherness to get things done and to encourage the exploration essential to improvement." —Handy (1995, p. 47)

"Learning organizations are fast, focused, flexible, friendly and fun. To promote these characteristics they are far more likely to be organized into teams than in old-fashioned hierarchies." —Kanter (1995, p. 73)

"We have known for nearly a quarter of a century that self-managed teams are far more productive than any other form of organizing. There is a clear correlation between participation and productivity." —Wheatley (1999, p. 152)

"Collaboration is a social imperative. Without it people can't get extraordinary things done in organizations." —Kouzes & Posner (2003, p. 20)

Linking Collaboration With School Improvement

- Gordon Cawelti: "The New Effective Schools" in *Best Practices, Best Thinking and Emerging Issues in School Leadership*

- Linda Darling-Hammond: *The Right to Learn*

- Kenneth Eastwood and Karen Seashore Louis: "Restructuring That Lasts"

- Michael Fullan: *Change Forces*

- Steve Klein, E. Medrich, and V. Perez-Ferreiro: *Fitting the Pieces: Education Reform That Works*

- Robert Marzano: *What Works in Schools*

- Milbrey McLaughlin and Joan Talbert: *Professional Learning Communities and the Work of High School Teaching*

- The National Commission on Teaching and America's Future: *No Dream Denied*

- The National Education Association: "The Keys Initiative"

- Fred Newmann and Gary Wehlage: *Successful School Restructuring*

- Doug Reeves: *The Leader's Guide to Standards*

- Richard Sagor: "Collaborative Action Research for Educational Change" in *Rethinking Educational Change with Heart and Mind.*

- Jonathon Saphier: *John Adams' Promise*

- Mike Schmoker: *Results: The Key to Continuous School Improvement*

- Karen Seashore Louis, Sharon Kruse, and Helen Marks: "School-wide Professional Community" in *Authentic Achievement*

- Southern Regional Education Board: *Things That Matter Most in Improving Student Learning*

- Judith Warren Little: "The Persistence of Privacy: Autonomy and Initiative in Teachers' Professional Relations"

work together collaboratively. Norms can help clarify expectations, promote open dialogue, and serve as a powerful tool for holding members accountable. As one study of high-performing teams concluded:

> When self-management norms are explicit and practiced over time, team effectiveness improves dramatically, as does the experience of team members themselves. Being on the team becomes rewarding in itself—and those positive emotions provide energy and motivation for accomplishing the team's goals. (Goleman, Boyatzis, & McKee, 2002, p. 182)

Another review of the research on high-performing teams concluded that explicit team norms helped to increase the emotional intelligence of the group by cultivating trust, a sense of group identify, and belief in group efficacy (Druskat & Wolf, 2001). Finally, norms can be a powerful tool at that inevitable moment when someone on the team fails to honor a norm. Referring back to the norms can help "the members of a group to 're-member,' to once again take out membership in what the group values and stands for; to 'remember,' to bring the group back into one cooperating whole" (Kegan & Lahey, 2001, p. 194).

Part Four
Assessing Your Place on the PLC Journey

The PLC Continuum

Working individually and quietly, review the continuum of a school's progress on the PLC journey (page 112). Which point on the continuum gives the most accurate description of the current reality of your school or district? Be prepared to support your assessment with evidence and anecdotes.

After working individually, share your assessment with colleagues. Where do you have agreement? Where do you find discrepancies in the assessments? Listen to the rationales of others in support of their varying assessments. Are you able to reach agreement?

Where Do We Go From Here?

The challenge confronting a school that has engaged in the collective consideration of a topic is answering the questions, "So what?" and, "What, if anything, are we prepared to do differently?" Now consider each indicator of a professional learning community described in the left column of the Where Do We Go From Here? Worksheet on page 113, and then answer the questions listed at the top of the remaining four columns.

The Professional Learning Community Continuum

Element of a PLC	Pre-Initiation Stage	Initiation Stage	Developing Stage	Sustaining Stage
Collaborative Teams of Teachers Focus on Issues That Directly Impact Student Learning	There is no systematic plan in place to assign staff members to teams or provide them with time to collaborate. Teachers work in isolation with little awareness of the strategies, methods, or materials used by their colleagues.	Some structures have been put into place for teachers who may be interested in collaborating. Teachers are encouraged but not required to participate. Topics tend to focus on matters other than classroom instruction and student learning.	Time has been provided during the contractual day for teachers to work together in teams on a regular basis (at least once a week). Guidelines have been established in an effort to ensure staff members use collaborative time to address topics that will impact instruction. Teams are attempting to develop positive relationships and implement specific procedures, but they may not be convinced the collaborative team process is beneficial. Leaders of the school are seeking ways to monitor the effectiveness of the teams.	Self-directed teams represent the primary engine of continuous improvement in the school. Team members are skillful in advocacy and inquiry, hold each other accountable for honoring the commitments they have made to one another, consistently focus on the issues that are most significant in improving student achievement, and set specific measurable goals to monitor improvement. The collaborative team process serves as a powerful form of job-embedded staff development, helping both individual members and the team in general become more effective in helping students learn at high levels. Staff members consider their collaborative culture vital to the effectiveness of their school.

Learning by Doing © 2006 Solution Tree ■ www.solution-tree.com

Where Do We Go From Here? Worksheet
A Commitment to a Collaborative Culture

Describe one or more aspects of a professional learning community that you would like to see in place in your school.	What steps or activities must be initiated to create this condition in your school?	Who will be responsible for initiating or sustaining these steps or activities?	What is a realistic timeline for each step or phase of the activity?	What will you use to assess the effectiveness of your initiative?
Teachers work together as members of collaborative teams. The members of each team work interdependently to achieve common goals.				
Each team is provided with time to meet and uses that time to engage in collective inquiry on questions specifically linked to gains in student achievement.				
Each team adopts and observes protocols that clarify how members will fulfill their responsibilities to the team.				
Each team is asked to generate and submit products, which result from their discussion of critical questions.				

Part Five
Tips for Moving Forward: Building a Collaborative Culture Through High-Performing Teams

 Ensure that teams are created on the basis of shared responsibility for pursuing the critical questions of teaching and learning with a particular group of students: for example, by course or by grade level.

 Work with staff to find creative ways to provide more time for team collaboration, including ways of using existing time more effectively.

 Disperse leadership more widely by identifying team leaders for any team with more than three people. Meet with team leaders on a regular basis to identify problematic areas of the process and develop strategies for resolving those problems.

 Ask teams to build shared knowledge—to learn together—as they approach each new task in the collaborative process.

 Provide teams with tools such as supporting research, templates, exemplars, worksheets, and timelines to assist them in each step of the process.

 Monitor the work of each team through ongoing assessment of their products, regular meetings with team leaders, and formal self-evaluations. Respond immediately to a team that is having difficulty.

 Building-level leadership teams should model everything being asked of the collaborative teams, including meeting on a regular basis, staying focused on issues with the greatest impact on student achievement, establishing and honoring norms, and working toward SMART goals.

 Create procedures to ensure teams are able to learn from one another.

 Look for ways to link teams with relevant resources inside and outside of your building (including other teams).

 Make teams the focus of recognition and celebration (see chapter 2). Take every opportunity to acknowledge the efforts and accomplishments of teams.

Part Six
Questions to Guide the Work of Your Professional Learning Community

To Promote a Collaborative Culture in Your School or District, Ask:

1. Have we organized our staff into collaborative teams?

_____

_____

2. Have teams been organized on the basis of common courses and common grade levels whenever possible?

_____

_____

3. If we have used the interdisciplinary team structure, have members of the team identified specific, overarching student-achievement goals, and do they use those goals to guide their work?

_____

_____

4. Have specialist teachers and singleton teachers found meaningful collaborative teams?

_____

_____

5. Have we avoided assigning people to teams whose disparate assignments make it difficult if not impossible to focus on the critical questions of learning?

_____

_____

6. Have we provided time for teachers to meet in their collaborative teams on a regular basis?

_____

_____

7. Do teams focus on the critical questions of learning identified in this book?

_____

_____

8. Are teams asked to submit specific products according to a designated timeline? Do these products reflect their focus on the critical questions?

_____

_____

9. What systems are in place to monitor the work and the effectiveness of the teams on a timely basis?

_____

_____

10. Has every team developed explicit norms that clarify the commitments members have made to one another regarding how they will work together as a team?

_____

_____

11. Do teams honor the norms they have established? What happens when faculty members do not honor their commitments?

_____

_____

12. Have we given teams the knowledge base, time, and support essential for their effectiveness?

_____

_____

Final Thoughts

A collaborative culture does not simply emerge in a school or district: Leaders cultivate collaborative cultures when they develop the capacity of their staffs to work as members of high-performing teams. People throughout the organization, however, must always remember that collaboration is a means to an end—to higher levels of learning—rather than the end itself. Chapter 6 addresses the challenge of creating a results orientation that impacts the work of teams, the school, and the district.

Chapter 6

Creating a Results Orientation in a Professional Learning Community

Members of a professional learning community continually assess their effectiveness on the basis of results: tangible evidence their students are acquiring the knowledge, skills, and dispositions essential to their future success.

Part One
The Case Study: Creating a Results Orientation at the School, Team, and Teacher Level

When Aretha Ross was hired as a new superintendent of the Supreme School District, the Board of Education made it clear that its Strategic Plan for School Improvement was the pride of the district. Every 5 years the board engaged the community and staff in a comprehensive planning process intended to provide a sense of direction for the district and all of its schools and programs. A committee of key stakeholders oversaw the creation of the plan during a 6-month development process. Each member was responsible for reporting back periodically to the group he or she represented to ensure accurate representation and ongoing communication. The committee held a series of community focus groups to solicit feedback from hundreds of parents, analyzed quantitative data, and generated qualitative data through a series of surveys to community, staff, and parents. The district mission statement provided the foundation of the document:

> *It is the mission of our schools to provide a rigorous academic curriculum in a safe, caring, and enjoyable learning environment that enables each and every child to realize his or her potential and become a responsible and productive citizen and lifelong learner fully equipped to meet the challenges of the twenty-first century.*

The plan provided the vision for the district and its schools, as well as core beliefs, strategic goals, key objectives, operational principles, and performance outcomes. With its adoption by the Board of Education, it became the blueprint for school improvement in the district. Each school was then called upon to create an annual school improvement plan (SIP) aligned with the district's strategic plan.

Superintendent Ross was impressed by the effort that went into the strategic planning process and with the heft of the resulting document, but she was curious to see how it was implemented in the schools. In late October she scheduled a meeting with Harry Lee Lewis, principal of the Elvis Presley Elementary School (nickname: The Kings), to discuss the improvement process of that school.

Principal Lewis explained that the SIP adopted by the staff the previous month was linked to the district goal of "Preparing students to succeed as members of a global community and global economy." The Presley School Improvement Committee had analyzed the results from the previous state assessment of third and fifth graders and concluded that word recognition was an area of weakness for students. The committee reasoned that students would not be prepared to succeed as members of a global community if they were not proficient in such an important skill. The committee recommended that the staff adopt a school improvement goal of "Improved student achievement in word recognition as indicated on the state assessment." The faculty agreed to this with little debate. Principal Lewis assured Superintendent Ross that this same process was the standard procedure in all of the district's schools.

Superintendent Ross was troubled somewhat by the explanation of this improvement process. She realized the state assessment was administered only to third- and fifth-grade students at Presley, and she questioned how much impact the school's goal was having on the other grade levels. Furthermore, she questioned whether the SIP process described to her fostered the commitment to continuous improvement she hoped to see in every school.

Superintendent Ross decided to do some informal investigating by visiting the third-grade team at Presley as its members met in their weekly meeting. She asked if they felt teachers in other grade levels were helping address the language arts goal established by Presley's School Improvement Committee. After some awkward silence, the team members admitted they did not remember the goal, and asked if she could remind them of it.

Superintendent Ross did not want to generalize based upon one school, so she made arrangements to visit four other schools that week. In each, she discovered a similar situation. She was convinced that despite the board's affection for the Strategic Plan, it was neither impacting practice in the classroom nor contributing to a culture of continuous improvement. She knew there was little reason to believe students would achieve at higher levels until principals and teachers became much more interested in and responsible for improved results. What she did not know was what steps the district might take to foster a results orientation.

Reflection

How does a school or district create a results orientation among administrators and teachers—the very people who are called upon to improve results?

Part Two
Here's How

We have repeatedly listed a *results orientation* as one of the characteristics of a professional learning community. It is a fact, however, that organizations do not focus on results: the people within them do, or they do not. There is little evidence to suggest that centralized formal strategic planning creates such an orientation. In fact, one comprehensive study of strategic planning over a 30-year period chronicled its failure to impact results (Mintzberg, 1994).

If formal, district-led strategic planning processes do not create a results orientation, will handing the improvement process over to schools be a more effective alternative? The Consortium on Productivity in Schools (1995) answered that question with a resounding No! and concluded:

> Site based management cannot overcome lack of clear goals and goal overloading. . . . Site based management does not substitute for the lack of stable, limited, and well-defined goals for schools. . . . Otherwise the agendas of site based school improvement drift into non-academic and administrative matters. (pp. 46–47)

The challenge for Superintendent Ross, and for any leader who hopes to improve student achievement, is to engage all members of the organization in processes to:

- Clarify priorities.

- Establish indicators of progress to be monitored carefully.

- Embed continuous improvement throughout the organization.

In simpler terms, she must help every employee of the district, but particularly teachers and principals, focus on results. No school or district creates a results orientation by accident. Educators shift their focus from activities to outcomes and from intentions to results only when leaders establish effective processes and well-defined parameters to shift collective attention in the right direction.

No school or district creates a results orientation by accident.

One of the most powerful strategies to create a results orientation throughout a district is for leaders to:

1. Identify a limited number of very focused goals.

2. Use well-designed processes to drive those goals into every classroom in every school.

Limit District Goals

We have asked the following question hundreds of times to teachers throughout North America: "How many of you feel that your efforts to improve your school have been hampered by an insufficient number of district and state improvement initiatives?" The question is always met with howls of laughter. Veteran educators have become inured to the sheer volume of frequent, fragmented, and uncoordinated new projects, programs, and reforms that wash upon them in waves. They suffer from what Doug Reeves (2004) has called the "irrefutable law of initiative fatigue" (p. 59) as each new improvement scheme they are called upon to adopt saps energy, resources, and attention from those that preceded it.

Superintendent Ross is far more likely to provide clear and focused direction to staff throughout the district if she replaces the voluminous strategic planning process with a few very specific goals that flow directly from a clearly articulated, compelling purpose for the district and its schools. For example, the district could convey the message that its fundamental purpose is to help all students learn at high levels by adopting such simple goals as these:

■ All students will successfully complete every course and every grade level and will demonstrate proficiency on local, state, and national assessments.

■ We will eliminate the gaps in student achievement that are connected to race, socioeconomic status, and gender.

Replace the voluminous strategic planning process with a few very specific goals that flow directly from a clearly articulated, compelling purpose for the district and its schools.

These broad overarching goals can then be translated into goals for each school, as shown in the following example.

In order to help achieve district goals, schools must:

1. Increase student achievement and close the achievement gap in literacy and numeracy in every elementary school, using a variety of local, state, and national indicators to document improved learning on the part of our students.

2. Increase student achievement and close the achievement gap in all areas of our middle and secondary schools, using a variety of local, state, and national indicators to document improved learning on the part of our students.

3. Provide more students with access to our most rigorous curriculum in each subject area and grade level.

Speak With One Voice

District goals are most powerful when the entire central office speaks with one voice in communicating the significance of the goals. District offices often have a tendency to send mixed messages, thereby creating a cacophony of competing interests. As Becky wrote, "When all central office administrators are separately chanting, 'Pay attention to my department's directive! My initiatives are the priority!' they sow seeds of confusion, frustration, and cynicism in schools" (2003, p. 16).

Superintendent Ross could avoid this by insisting her central office function as a unified team with each member working interdependently to achieve district goals—goals for which they would be held mutually accountable. The district team could then clarify how each member was to contribute to the goals in a coordinated way and how each department could customize services to support schools in their efforts to achieve district goals. The central office could then serve as a clearinghouse for best practices, resources, and training and as a conduit for sharing the effective practices used throughout the district so that schools could learn from one another.

The central office could communicate the importance of these goals by pursuing them with constancy and shielding schools from competing interests and initiatives (McLaughlin & Talbert, 2001). Leaders do not build coherence within their organizations when they announce new priorities every year. Goals such as the ones listed in the previous section should represent a life's work rather than a short-term project, and therefore the district should commit to these goals year after year until they are achieved. New hot topics will be touted on the professional development circuit, political leaders will come and go, and special interest groups will demand schools pay more attention to their cause. Rather than reacting to each shift in the wind by placing more initiatives on their schools, the central office staff must help buffer them from the constant turbulence so educators can stay the course.

The Schaumburg Elementary School District 54 in suburban Chicago has made a concerted effort to create coherence within the district by focusing on a few key goals and protecting schools from competing initiatives. In leading that effort, Superintendent Ed Rafferty surveys every principal, assistant principal, and central office administrator to solicit advice regarding what the district office could do and, equally as important, what it could *stop* doing in order to help schools concentrate on improved student achievement. The district- and school-level leadership at Schaumburg work in partnership to focus

Rather than reacting to each shift in the wind by placing more initiatives on their schools, the central office staff must help buffer educators from the constant turbulence so they can stay the course.

on "first things first," and they recognize that some things need not be done at all. They use the Central Office Effectiveness Feedback Tool (pages 123–125) to obtain honest feedback on how effective the central office is in supporting each school and to gather suggestions for how they can better assist staff in raising student achievement.

Translate District Initiatives Into School Goals

Limiting district goals and initiatives is a necessary step in creating a results orientation, but it is not sufficient. Steps must also be taken to ensure that district goals guide the work of individual schools and the professionals within each classroom. One of the most effective strategies for bringing district goals to life is to insist that all schools create goals that are specifically linked to district goals.

But before this can be done, schools and districts must be in agreement about what is meant by the word "goal"; it is one of those terms that can mean many different things to different people within an organization. The SMART goal acronym (O'Neill & Conzemius, 2005) provides much-needed clarity to the term. Goals are SMART when they are strategic and specific, measurable, attainable, results-oriented, and timebound.

Superintendent Ross should insist that each principal presents a brief, succinct school improvement plan that establishes improvement targets for one or more of the goals established by the district. The school's plan should stipulate both the past level of performance and the improvement goal for the indicator being monitored.

For example, a school might establish the following SMART goals based on the district's two goals ("All students will successfully complete every course and every grade level and will demonstrate proficiency on local, state, and national assessments," and, "We will eliminate the gaps in student achievement that are connected to race, socioeconomic status, and gender.")

1. Our Reality: Last year, 14% of the grades assigned to our students were failing grades.

   Our Goal: This year, we will reduce the percentage of failing grades to 7% or less.

2. Our Reality: Last year, 76% of our students met the proficiency standard on the state math test.

   Our Goal: This year, we will increase the percentage of students meeting the proficiency standard on the state math test to 80% or higher.

Central Office Effectiveness Feedback Tool

The purpose of this information-gathering tool is to obtain honest feedback on how effective the central office is in supporting each of our schools. We also want your feedback on how we can better assist you in raising student achievement. We ask that every principal and assistant principal complete the tool. We also ask that all central office administrators complete the tool, answering each question as they believe it will be answered by building principals. The information will be compiled to determine district trends and used as a basis for improving or restructuring support and services to our schools.

Please check:

❏ Principal   ❏ Assistant Principal   ❏ Central Office Administrator

Given that:

- a high level of student achievement is an expectation for every school,

- there are no new funds available,

- the central office is fully committed to supporting each school in their improvement efforts,

- there are no sacred or untouchable programs or services, and

- honesty with a problem-solving focus is valued,

please provide us with specific feedback on the following questions.

1. What do you feel are the top three priorities of the district?

_____

_____

2. What can the central office do to better support you in getting your job done? Please provide specific suggestions.

_____

_____

3. What tasks required by the central office would you recommend be simplified or eliminated to give you more time to focus on student achievement? Please be specific.

_____

_____

4. What supports need to be changed, restructured, or created to enhance your school improvement efforts? Please be as specific as possible.

_____

_____

5. As a district, in what areas do we need to be tighter? Please be as specific as possible.

_____

_____

6. As a district, in what areas do we need to be looser? Please be as specific as possible.

_____

_____

7. How do you want the principal and assistant principal meetings to be structured?

_____

_____

8. How do you want other administrative meetings to be structured?

_____

_____

9. Do you feel you have the support of the central office when dealing with difficult personnel issues? Please provide specific examples.

_____

_____

10. Is the central office modeling what the district professes to be important? Please provide specific examples.

_____

_____

11. As a district, are we asking the right questions about how to improve student learning? Please be as specific as possible.

_____

_____

12. As a district, are we effectively monitoring the right and important things? Please provide specific examples.

_____

_____

13. As a district, do we pay sufficient attention to celebrations? Please provide specific examples.

_____

_____

14. Does the central office provide a sense of coherence, speak with one voice, and help you in clarifying the important issues, or does it send mixed messages? Please provide specific examples.

_____

_____

15. Check your top two areas of need and then explain what we can do as a district to provide leadership and support for your needs.

❏ Assessment _____

_____

❏ Bilingual Education _____

_____

❏ Curriculum Development and Clarification _____

_____

❏ Data Analysis and Storage _____

_____

❏ Instructional Practices _____

_____

❏ Professional Development _____

_____

❏ Special Education _____

_____

❏ Staffing _____

_____

❏ Systematic and Timely Interventions for Students Who Need Extra Support _____

_____

❏ Technology _____

_____

❏ _____

_____

❏ _____

_____

16. Is there any additional information you would like to give us on our performance as a central office?

_____

_____

_____

_____

_____

_____

Reprinted with permission from Schaumburg Elementary School District 54, Schaumburg, Illinois.

> ## SMART Goals Are:
>
> **S**trategic and Specific
>
> **M**easurable
>
> **A**ttainable
>
> **R**esults-Oriented
>
> **T**imebound

3. Our Reality: Last year, 10% of the graduating class completed advanced placement courses or the capstone course in a departmental sequence.

    Our Goal: This year, we will increase the percentage of students taking advanced placement or capstone courses in a departmental sequence to 20% or higher.

Notice the link between these goals and the district goals. Each school goal, if attained, would contribute to progress toward the district goals.

Link School Goals to Team Goals

The next critical step in this process is to ensure that each collaborative team translates one or more of the school goals into a SMART goal that drives the work of the team. As we wrote earlier, the very definition of a team is "*a group of people working **interdependently** to achieve a **common goal** for which members are held **mutually accountable**.*" One of the most powerful strategies for building the capacity of staff to work effectively in collaborative teams is to create the conditions that require them to work together to accomplish a specific goal. The SMART Goal Worksheets on pages 127–132 provide examples of how different school goals might be translated into SMART goals for collaborative teams. A blank SMART Goal Worksheet appears on page 133.

Focus on Results, Not Activities

Once again, a school that defines its purpose as "High levels of learning for all students" will insist that teams include the language of learning in their goals. This is contrary to the traditional approach of writing goals that focus on evidence of what teachers will do rather than on evidence of what students will learn. Statements such as, "We will integrate technology into our course," "We will align our curriculum with the newly adopted textbook," or "We will increase the use of cooperative learning activities," may describe worthwhile initiatives, but they do not represent goals. If the purpose of these initiatives is to increase student learning, that purpose should be explicitly stated in a goal that

One of the most effective strategies for bringing district goals to life is to insist that all schools create goals that are specifically linked to district goals.

SMART Goal Worksheet: Third-Grade Team

School: George Washington Elementary   **Team Name:** Third-Grade Team   **Team Leader:** Theresa Smith

Team Members: Ken Thomas, Joe Ramirez, Cathy Armstrong, Amy Wu

District Goal(s): We will increase student achievement and close the achievement gap in all areas of our middle and secondary schools, using a variety of local, state, and national indicators to document improved learning on the part of our students.

School Goal(s): We will:

1. Increase the percentage of students demonstrating proficiency on both a national reading proficiency assessment and on the state test.

2. Eliminate the achievement gap for minority students.

Team SMART Goal	Strategies and Action Steps	Responsibility	Timeline	Evidence of Effectiveness
Our Reality: Last year, 18% of our third graders were unable to meet grade-level proficiency standards in reading fluency and comprehension as measured by a standardized, individualized assessment program for early literacy development. Six percent of Caucasian and 33% of minority students were unable to demonstrate proficiency.	We will create a common team schedule that reserves 8:30 to 10:30 for language arts each day. We will designate 45 minutes (9:45 to 10:30) each day for regrouping students into three groups (intensive support, strategic support, and achieving benchmark) based on demonstration of reading fluency and comprehension.	Third-grade team will adhere to the agreed-upon schedule and identify the appropriate reading group for each student by the end of September.	End of September	Students will be assigned to one of three groups on the basis of individual reading assessment results.

SMART Goal Worksheet: Third-Grade Team (continued)

Team SMART Goal	Strategies and Action Steps	Responsibility	Timeline	Evidence of Effectiveness
Our Goal: This year, 100% of third graders will demonstrate proficiency in reading fluency and comprehension as measured by the standardized, individualized program for early literacy.	The team will expand to include the special education teacher, Title I teacher, speech therapist, and literacy coach during the designated 45 minutes each day. Students in need of intensive support will be assigned to a member of the team in groups of no more than four students. Students in need of more strategic support will be assigned to groups of no more than eight students. Students at benchmark proficiency will be assigned to the remaining team members for reading enrichment and extension activities created by the team. Student proficiency will be monitored on an ongoing basis and membership in the groups will be fluid.	The team will: 1. Work with the principal and staff members listed above to create the schedule that allows for this intervention. 2. Create a series of ongoing assessments of reading fluency and comprehension and analyze the results. 3. Align assessments with the content and format of the state test for language arts. 4. Identify specific and precise instructional strategies to address the needs of students assigned to each group. 5. Create a variety of enrichment activities for proficient readers, including Junior Great Books reading circles, independent and group research projects, computer-based explorations, silent sustained reading, and teacher read-alouds.	The team will administer the standardized assessment three times this year: in mid-September, January, and late April. The team will develop and administer its own assessments every 6 weeks.	Evidence will include: 1. Student movement to higher groups 2. All students demonstrating fluency and comprehension on the standardized assessment 3. All students meeting the proficiency standard on the state test in language arts

SMART Goal Worksheet: Eighth-Grade Math

School: Thomas Jefferson Middle School **Team Name:** Eighth-Grade Math **Team Leader:** Chris Rauch

Team Members: Chris Carter, Dolores Layco, Mary Fischer

District Goal(s): We will increase student achievement and close the achievement gap in all areas of our middle and secondary schools, using a variety of local, state, and national indicators to document improved learning on the part of our students.

School Goal(s): We will:

1. Reduce the failure rate in our school.

2. Increase the percentage of students scoring at or above the established proficiency standard on the state assessment in all areas.

Team SMART Goal	Strategies and Action Steps	Responsibility	Timeline	Evidence of Effectiveness
Our Reality: Last year, 24% of our students failed one or more semesters of math. And 31% percent of our students were unable to meet the state proficiency standard in math.	We will align each unit of our math program with state standards, study the results of the last state assessment, identify problem areas, and develop specific strategies to address those areas in our course.	Entire team	We will complete the analysis on the teacher workday prior to the start of the year. We will review our findings prior to the start of each new unit.	Written analysis of state assessment and strategies to address weaknesses
Our Goal: This year, we will reduce the percentage of failing grades to 10% or less and the percentage of students unable to meet state standards to no more than 15%.	Develop common formative assessments and administer them every 3 weeks. These assessments will provide repeated opportunities for students to become familiar with the format used on the state assessment.	Entire team	Formative assessments will be created prior to the start of each unit of instruction throughout the year. They will be administered on a day designated by the team.	Student performance on team-endorsed common assessments

SMART Goal Worksheet Eighth-Grade Math (continued)

Team SMART Goal	Strategies and Action Steps	Responsibility	Timeline	Evidence of Effectiveness
	After each common assessment, we will identify any student who does not meet the established proficiency standard and will work with the counselor to have those students re-assigned from study hall to the math tutoring center.	Members of entire team will request tutoring as their supervisory responsibility; team leader will work with the counselor after each assessment.	Assessments administered every 3 weeks. Students will be assigned to the tutoring center within 1 week of assessment.	Daily list of students receiving tutoring in math
	Replace failing grades from our common assessments with the higher grade earned by students who are able to demonstrate proficiency in key skills on subsequent forms of the assessment after completing tutoring.	Entire team will create multiple forms of each assessment. Tutors will administer the assessment after a student has completed the required tutoring.	Multiple forms of an assessment will be created prior to the start of each unit of instruction. Tutors will administer the second assessment within 2 weeks of a student's assignment to the tutoring center.	Compilation of results from subsequent assessments
	Examine the results of each common assessment in an effort to determine which member of the team is getting the best results on each skill, and then share ideas, methods, and materials for teaching those skills more effectively.	Each member of the team	Ongoing throughout the year each time a common assessment is administered.	■ Analysis of findings after each common assessment is administered ■ Decrease in the failure rate ■ Increase in percentage of students proficient on state assessment

Learning by Doing © 2006 Solution Tree ■ www.solution-tree.com

SMART Goal Worksheet: American Government

School: John Adams High School   **Team Name:** American Government Team   **Team Leader:** Tom Botimer

Team Members: Dan Hahn, Andy Bradford, Nick Larsen, Helen Harvey

District Goal(s): We will provide more students with access to our most rigorous curriculum in each subject area and grade level.

School Goal(s): We will increase by at least 10% the number of students enrolling in:

1. Advanced placement courses

2. Capstone courses in a departmental sequence

Team SMART Goal	Strategies and Action Steps	Responsibility	Timeline	Evidence of Effectiveness
Our Reality: All students must complete a semester of American Government as a graduation requirement. Last year only 10% of the graduating class fulfilled that requirement by enrolling in advanced placement (AP) American Government.	We will make a presentation in each section of United States History, encouraging students to enroll in AP American Government and listing the advantages for doing so.	Team leader will coordinate the schedule for these presentations with the team leader for United States History. Each member of the team will assist in making these presentations and will distribute a written list of advantages created by the team.	Complete presentations by the end of January prior to students registering for their courses for next year.	The presentation has been made in every United States History class
Our Goal: At least 20% of the current junior class will enroll in and complete the advanced placement American Government class next year.	We will coordinate with the guidance department to ensure that when counselors register students for classes, they encourage any student who receives an A at the end of the first semester of United States History to enroll in AP American Government.	Team leader will attend the counselors' team meeting to enlist their support, explain advantages of the AP program, and share the team's strategies for supporting students in AP Government.	End of first semester	Minutes of meeting

SMART Goal Worksheet: American Government (continued)

Team SMART Goal	Strategies and Action Steps	Responsibility	Timeline	Evidence of Effectiveness
	We will advise parents of the benefits of AP American Government.	The team will draft a letter to parents of students who earn an A in United States History at the end of the semester. The letter will list the advantages of completing this course while in high school for any student planning on attending college. It will also include the team's strategy to provide students with additional support. The team will also create a flyer on the benefits of the AP program to be distributed during parent open house.	The flyer will be created for distribution at the open house in early October. The letter will be sent at the end of the first semester.	Completed documents
	We will create study groups to review material prior to the comprehensive assessments we administer every 6 weeks.	The team will create the common comprehensive assessments. Each member will be responsible for conducting one study group to help students review for these tests. Study groups will be held on three evenings in the week prior to the test.	Ongoing throughout the semester	Completion of common assessments and student performance on common assessments. The number of students earning honor grades on the AP exam in American Government will double over last year's total.

Learning by Doing © 2006 Solution Tree ■ www.solution-tree.com

SMART Goal Worksheet

School: _____

Team Members: _____

District Goal(s): _____

School Goal(s): _____

Team Name: _____

Team Leader: _____

Team SMART Goal	Strategies and Action Steps	Responsibility	Timeline	Evidence of Effectiveness

Effective team goals will focus on the intended outcome rather than on the strategies to achieve the outcome.

will help answer the question, "How will we know if our strategies are resulting in gains in student learning?" Effective team goals will focus on the intended outcome rather than on the strategies to achieve the outcome.

Create Short-Term Goals

Although a district should sustain the pursuit of a few key goals for an extended period of time, teams should be encouraged to create short-term goals that serve as benchmarks of progress. Frequent feedback and intermittent reinforcement are two factors that help sustain the effort essential to achieving challenging goals (Kouzes & Posner, 1999). A team that establishes a goal of improving student performance on a state test receives neither feedback nor reinforcement for almost a year unless it establishes some short-term goals.

For example, one team discovers that 23% of students demonstrate proficiency on a pre-assessment instrument it has administered at the beginning of the unit. The team then establishes a short-term goal that 90% of the students will demonstrate proficiency by the end of the unit. Another team reviews the results from the common assessments its members administered the previous year to determine that 64% of students were able to meet the established standard for writing proficiency by the end of October. The team sets a goal that 75% of students will meet that standard by the same date this year. In both instances, short-term goals can inform the team of progress and create a basis for celebration.

Part Three
Here's Why

Why should educators abandon traditional strategic planning and focus instead on ensuring that each collaborative team in every school is working toward SMART goals that are specifically linked to a few school and district goals? Most simply, because there is no evidence that strategic planning leads to improved results. In his study of "great" organizations, Collins (2001) was unable to discover any link between formal planning and organizational effectiveness. Pfeffer and Sutton (2000) were even more emphatic when they concluded, "Existing research on the effectiveness of formal planning efforts is clear: Planning is essentially unrelated to organizational performance" (p. 42). In his study of strategic planning in education, Reeves (2006) actually found a negative correlation between district-led formal strategic planning and improved student achievement.

Whereas effective leaders are skillful in making the complex simple, strategic planning almost inevitably makes the simple complex. The one thing most strategic plans for school districts have in common is their girth. Voluminous tomes place far too many initiatives upon schools and obscure rather than clarify priorities. The ambiguity and interchangeable use of terms adds to the confusion. How many people can assert with confidence that they can specify the differences between a strategic goal, a key objective, and a performance outcome? Furthermore, strategic plans often serve as a barrier to the relentless action orientation of effective organizations (Pfeffer & Sutton, 2000). Far too many school districts confuse developing or possessing a plan with taking meaningful action to ensure that something actually happens.

The biggest factor in the ineffectiveness of formal strategic planning rests on its faulty underlying assumption: some people in organizations (the leaders) are responsible for thinking and planning while others (the workers) are responsible for carrying out those plans. This separation of thought and action is the antithesis of a learning community, which requires widely dispersed leadership and strategic thinkers *throughout* the organization (Fullan, 2005a). Asking employees to follow a 5-year strategic plan chartered by others does little to generate a focus on or commitment to improved results. Engaging those employees in a process of *ongoing* continuous improvement in which they establish their own short-term goals, develop their own plans to achieve them, act on those plans, and make frequent adjustments based on their analysis of evidence is much more likely to instill a results orientation throughout the organization.

Mike Schmoker (1999, 2003) has made the most compelling case for replacing strategic planning with short-term goals created and pursued by collaborative teams of teachers. He writes, "Without explicit learning goals, we are simply not set up and organized for improvement, for results. Only such goals will allow us to analyze, monitor and adjust practice toward improvement" (1999, p. 18).

Not only do collaborative teams represent the optimum setting for the pursuit of meaningful SMART goals, but SMART goals represent an essential tool in developing powerful collaborative teams. Teams benefit when they have a few key goals that clarify the results they seek and how each member can contribute to achieving those results (Lencioni, 2005; Schaffer & Thomson, 1998). They are more effective when they see how their goals and their efforts are linked to the larger organization (Druskat & Wolf, 2001). They are strengthened from the accomplishment and celebration of short-term wins (Collins, 2001; Katzenbach & Smith, 1993; Kotter, 1996; Kouzes & Posner, 1987). They are more committed, empowered, and motivated when they set their own targets and create their own plans to achieve them (Axelrod, 2002; Csikszentmihalyi, 1997).

There is no evidence that strategic planning leads to improved results. Effective leaders are skillful in making the complex simple; strategic planning almost inevitably makes the simple complex.

In short, there is nothing more important in determining the effectiveness of a team than each member's understanding of and commitment to the achievement of results-oriented goals to which the group holds itself mutually accountable. Helping teams translate long-term purpose into specific, measurable short-term goals, and then helping members develop the skills to achieve those goals, is one of the most important steps leaders can take in building the capacity of a group to function as a high-performing collaborative team (Katzenbach & Smith, 1993).

Attainable Goals Versus Stretch Goals

When building a results-oriented culture, leaders must find a balance between the *attainable* goals teams feel they can achieve in the short term and *stretch* goals—goals so ambitious they could not possibly be achieved unless practices within the organization change significantly (Tichy, 1997). Stretch goals have also been referred to as BHAGs: Big Hairy Audacious Goals (Collins & Porras, 1997). Attainable goals are intended to document incremental progress and build momentum and self-efficacy through short-term wins. Stretch goals are intended to inspire, to capture the imagination of people within the organization, to stimulate creativity and innovation, and to serve as a unifying focal point of effort.

President John F. Kennedy announced one of the most famous stretch goals in American history when, in 1961, he declared the United States would "land a man on the moon and return him safely to earth" by the end of the decade, despite the fact that the necessary technology to achieve that goal did not exist. His pronouncement galvanized and energized the scientific community and the nation and led to the largest non-military technological endeavor ever undertaken by the United States.

But merely proclaiming stretch goals does not improve an organization. In 1989 President George Bush announced Education Goals 2000, boldly proclaiming the nation would achieve such stretch goals as, "All children in America will start school ready to learn" and, "United States students will be first in the world in mathematics and science achievement" by the new millennium. Neither goal was achieved because neither resulted in meaningful action.

Stretch goals are effective only if they stimulate action, if people begin to behave in new ways. Pronouncements without action are hopes, not goals. Furthermore, stretch goals must be *goals*, not mission statements. They must set specific targets rather than offer vague expressions or beliefs. Kennedy did not say, "We need to do something to strengthen the space program," or, "We believe in the potential of space." He said, "We will land a man on the moon." "We believe in high levels of learning for all students" is not a stretch goal. "We will

Attainable goals document incremental progress and build momentum and self-efficacy through short-term wins.

Stretch goals inspire, capture imagination, stimulate creativity and innovation, and unify.

ensure all students demonstrate proficiency on the state assessment," "We will eliminate achievement gaps based on socioeconomic status," and "We will ensure the academic success of every student in every grade level" are examples of stretch goals because they are stated as targets.

If schools and districts limit themselves to the pursuit of *attainable* goals they run the risk of never moving outside their comfort zones. Organizations are unlikely to experience dramatic improvement if they are content with creeping incrementalism—slowly inching forward over time. If the only goals educators pursue are easily attainable, the focus shifts to how good do we *have* to be rather than how good *can* we be.

On the other hand, if the only goals educators pursue are stretch goals, teachers and principals are prone to give up in hopelessness. If educators perceive goals as so unrealistic that they are unattainable and there are no successes to celebrate, they will be discouraged from taking action to achieve them.

Once again, we believe the solution to this dilemma of attainable goals versus stretch goals is found not in the "Tyranny of Or," but in the "Genius of And." In the early stages of building a PLC, celebrating small wins is key to sustaining the effort, and attainable goals are an essential element of results-oriented small wins. Therefore, we strongly recommend that goals established by collaborative teams should be *attainable*. Teams should feel reasonably confident they have the capacity to achieve their goals. They should be able to say, "If we seek and implement best practices, we have reason to believe we will achieve our team goal."

District goals, however, should be clearly linked to the purpose of learning for all students, should establish challenging targets, and should require innovation and long-term commitment if they are to be achieved. District goals should be so bold that they require the development of new capacities. The best district goals will present "adaptive challenges": challenges for which the solution is not apparent, challenges that cause us to experiment, discover, adjust, and adapt (Heifetz & Linsky, 2002).

Part Four
Assessing Your Place on the PLC Journey

The PLC Continuum

Working individually and quietly, review the continuum of a school's progress on the PLC journey (page 139). Which point on the continuum gives the most accurate description of the current reality of your school or district? Be prepared to support your assessment with evidence and anecdotes.

After working individually, share your assessment with colleagues. Where do you have agreement? Where do you find discrepancies in the assessments? Listen to the rationales of others in support of their varying assessments. Are you able to reach agreement?

Where Do We Go From Here?

The challenge confronting a school that has engaged in the collective consideration of a topic is answering the questions, "So what?" and, "What, if anything, are we prepared to do differently?" Now consider each indicator of a professional learning community described in the left column of the Where Do We Go From Here? Worksheet on page 140, and then answer the questions listed at the top of the remaining four columns.

The Professional Learning Community Continuum

Element of a PLC	Pre-Initiation Stage	Initiation Stage	Developing Stage	Sustaining Stage
Creating a Focus on Results That Impacts Schools, Teams, and Teachers	There is no effort to establish specific district goals intended to impact the direction of each school. The district reacts to problems as they arise and does little to either focus on the future or promote continuous improvement.	The district establishes multiple long-range goals as part of a comprehensive strategic planning process. Schools may create annual school improvement plans in response to district requirements, but those plans have little impact upon classroom practices.	The district has identified a few key goals. Every school then adopts goals designed to help the district achieve its targets. Every collaborative team in every school adopts SMART goals specifically aligned with its school goals. A process is in place to monitor each team's progress throughout the year.	Educators throughout the district have a results orientation. Collaborative teams of teachers establish both annual goals and a series of short-term goals to monitor their progress. They create specific action plans to achieve goals and clarify the evidence they will gather to assess the impact of their plans. This tangible evidence of results guides the work of teams as part of a continuous improvement process. Each member understands the goals of the team, how those goals relate to school and district goals, and how he or she can contribute to achieving the goals.

Where Do We We Go From Here? Worksheet
School Improvement Goals Drive Team Goals

Describe one or more aspects of a professional learning community that you would like to see in place in your school.	What steps or activities must be initiated to create this condition in your school?	Who will be responsible for initiating or sustaining these steps or activities?	What is a realistic timeline for each step or phase of the activity?	What will you use to assess the effectiveness of your initiative?
Each team translates school goals into a team goal. Goals are SMART: Strategic, Specific, Measurable, Attainable, Result-Oriented, and Timebound. Team members assist one another as they work together interdependently to achieve their collective goal.				

Part Five
Tips for Moving Forward:
Using Goals to Focus on Results

 Limit the number of district initiatives and make certain the initiatives reflect the priority of high levels of learning for all students.

 Require each school and each collaborative team within the school to establish a *limited* number of SMART goals that are specifically aligned with district goals.

 Provide templates for goal setting for every team. The templates should reinforce the premise that the team must focus on results rather than activities and must clarify how the achievement of the goal will be monitored and measured.

 Make certain goals are team goals rather than individual goals. Remember that an effective goal will require team members to work together *interdependently* in order to achieve it. Members should be able to clarify both individual responsibilities and collective responsibilities.

 Team goals should be established *by* teams rather than *for* teams. Teams should be expected to create goals that align with school and district goals and to write goals that are consistent with specified parameters. Each team should, however, enjoy considerable autonomy in articulating its goals.

 Monitor work toward a goal by requiring teams to create specific products (norms, common assessments, collective analysis of results, improvement plans, and so on) that are directly related to the goal.

 Celebrate progress. Plan for, seek out, and celebrate small wins.

The high levels of learning a school or team seeks for its students need not be limited to academic areas. Affective areas (for example, responsibility, empathy, self-efficacy, independence, and so on) are perfectly legitimate areas for establishing goals. There is a tendency when establishing such goals, however, to be content with the implementation of new programs or the nobleness of the cause. Neither the completion of projects nor the unassailability of good intentions should substitute for goals. Teams must discipline themselves to address the question, "How will we know our students are achieving this goal?" for every goal they establish.

District goals should include stretch goals. These goals will be so challenging that people throughout the organization will be called upon to build new capacities in order to achieve them.

Be wary of the complacency that can set in when a stretch goal has been achieved. It is easy for an organization to drift into the "we have arrived" mode when it has been successful in the pursuit of a challenging goal (Collins & Porras, 1997). Combat that tendency and promote continuous improvement by celebrating the accomplishment and then creating a new stretch goal.

Part Six
Questions to Guide the Work of Your Professional Learning Community

To Assess the Commitment to a Results Orientation in Your School or District, Ask:

1. What evidence do we have that district goals are directly impacting the work of schools and collaborative teams within the school?

_____

_____

2. Does every collaborative team have a goal that aligns with district and school goals?

_____

_____

3. Are team goals SMART: strategic, specific, measurable, attainable, results-oriented, and time-bound?

_____

_____

4. Is there a plan in place to monitor the progress of each team? Does the plan include monitoring products created by the team as it works towards its goals?

_____

_____

5. Are teams provided with relevant and timely feedback regarding their progress? Remember that goals are effective motivators, but only if teams receive feedback (Kouzes & Posner, 1999).

_____

_____

6. Is a plan in place to identify, acknowledge, and celebrate small wins as teams make progress toward their goals?

_____

_____

7. Do district goals include stretch goals?

_____

_____

Final Thoughts

The way in which a school or district structures its planning and goal-setting process can help or hinder the adoption of PLC concepts. The most effective structures will directly impact the work and decisions of schools, the collaborative teams within the schools, and the teachers in their classrooms. Those teams and teachers must have timely access to relevant information in order to make the adjustments essential to achieving their goals. Chapter 7 describes how to provide the critical resource of timely and relevant information.

Chapter 7

Using Relevant Information to Improve Results

In a professional learning community, educators are hungry for evidence of student learning. Relevant, timely information is the essential fuel of their continuous improvement process.

Part One
The Case Study:
The Reluctance to Use Information

After attending a Professional Learning Communities Institute, the school improvement committee of Gladys Knight Charter School (nickname: The Pips) unanimously resolved to use the model as the framework for improving their school. Their principal pledged her full support for the initiative. Over the summer, committee members sent supporting materials and articles on PLCs to the entire staff. When the teachers returned in August, the committee convened small-group faculty meetings to respond to any questions and concerns regarding their proposal to implement PLC concepts.

The staff's response was generally very positive. Teachers agreed it made sense to work together in collaborative teams once they were assured that work would occur during their contractual day. They acknowledged the benefits of working together to clarify what students were to learn. They agreed the school should build systematic interventions to ensure students who struggled received additional time and support for learning, and they supported the premise that common curriculum pacing was an important element in an effective intervention system.

The one aspect of the committee's proposal that met with resistance was requiring teams to develop and administer common formative assessments multiple times throughout the year in language arts and math. The committee reasoned that the results of the assessments could be used to identify students in need of additional assistance, to discover problem areas in the curriculum, and, very importantly, to help individual staff members discover strengths and weaknesses in their teaching.

Teachers raised a number of concerns regarding the use of common assessments. They expressed confidence in the competence of every teacher and argued that differences in student achievement on common assessments could be attributed to a number of factors—including the effort and ability of students—rather than to the effectiveness of the instruction. They felt any attempt to use data from common assessments to make inferences regarding the proficiency of teachers was invalid. They saw the potential for great harm: Results could be used to evaluate teachers or to create winners and losers among the staff. Teachers' self-esteem could suffer. Common assessments could be a first step in a scheme to establish merit pay.

Teachers also argued that common team-developed assessments would not contribute to school improvement. They maintained that if teachers agreed to work together collaboratively to clarify essential learning and to plan effective lessons, student achievement would be certain to improve. If, as the research suggested, collaborative processes among teachers were truly linked to higher levels of student learning, teachers need only focus on the process, confident that improved results would be the inevitable consequence of their efforts. If results became the focus, they argued, teachers would pay less attention to meaningful collaboration and would merely teach to the test.

Finally, they argued that the only results that mattered in the state accountability system were the results from the state test. If teachers were to spend time on data analysis, they should focus on student performance on the state test rather than on creating another entire level of assessment.

Reflection

Consider the case study and the arguments presented by those who oppose the use of common assessments to monitor results. Should the committee abandon the proposal to ask each grade-level team to develop common formative assessments?

Part Two
Here's How

The very reason to engage in the PLC process is to improve results; therefore, it is incongruous to argue that the process should be inattentive to results. For too long schools have focused on process and inputs, operating under the faulty assumption that improved learning is guaranteed if we select the right curriculum, create the right schedule, buy the right textbook, increase graduation requirements, extend the school year, and so on. That assumption has repeatedly, consistently, and invariably proven to be incorrect. Schools only become PLCs if they switch their focus from inputs to outcomes and from activities to results.

> Schools only become PLCs if they switch their focus from inputs to outcomes and from activities to results.

Those who think teachers can substitute discussion about how to teach a concept at the outset of a unit for systems that ensure each teacher gets useful information on results ignore an important point: All opinions are not of equal value. Two teachers can be passionately convinced of the superiority of their respective strategies for teaching a concept. How is it possible to determine if one of those teachers has, in fact, discovered a powerful way to teach that concept? It is through the collective examination of results—tangible evidence of student learning—that teachers' dialogue moves from sharing opinions to building shared knowledge, which is an essential step on the journey to developing the capacity to function as a PLC.

In the previous chapter, we argued that one powerful strategy to help create a results orientation in a school is to ask the collaborative teams within it to establish SMART goals that are specifically aligned with the goals of the school and district. Results-oriented goals are *essential* to effective teams. And the capacity of teams to achieve their goals improves dramatically when members have access to feedback that informs their individual practice—feedback that helps them discover what is working and what is not working in their instructional strategies.

The challenge for schools then is to provide each teacher with the most powerful and authentic information in a timely manner so that it can impact his or her professional practice in ways that enhance student learning. As we mentioned in chapter 3, state and provincial assessments fail to provide such feedback. Classroom assessments, on the other hand, can offer the timely feedback teachers need, and when those assessments are developed by a collaborative team of teachers, they also offer a basis of comparison that is essential for informing professional practice.

Schools have been called upon to become more "data driven"; however, this focus is misplaced because schools have never suffered from a lack of data.

> *The challenge for schools is to provide each teacher with powerful and authentic information in a timely manner in order to impact his or her professional practice in ways that enhance student learning.*

"An astonishing number of educational leaders make critical decisions . . . on the basis of information that is inadequate, misunderstood, misrepresented, or simply absent." (Reeves, 2002, p. 95)

Every teacher who works in isolation can generate a mountain of data with every test he or she administers: mean, mode, median, percentage passing, percentage failing, and so on. Teachers can give their same individual assessments over a period of years, get similar results year after year, and thus have access to longitudinal data. But unless they have a basis of comparison, they cannot identify strengths and weaknesses in their teaching, and they are unable to determine if an area in which students are struggling is a function of the curriculum, their strategies, or their students.

Lack of data is not the problem. Schools typically suffer from what Robert Waterman (1987) has called the DRIP syndrome: They are Data Rich but Information Poor. Data alone will not inform a teacher's professional practice and thus cannot become a catalyst for improvement unless those data are put in context to provide a basis for comparison. Even then, the basis of comparison must be valid. For generations, teachers with high rates of failing students have not been persuaded by comparative data. They have quickly dismissed the results as an indication of their colleagues' lower standards. But when a teacher has access to data that compares the performance of his or her students to similar students taught by colleagues, on an assessment that he or she helped to write, it becomes much more difficult to dismiss unfavorable results.

The old adage, "practice makes perfect," is patently false. Those who continue to engage in ineffective practices are unable to improve, much less reach perfection. A student who completes 50 math problems with the same multiplication error repeated over and over has not improved his ability to solve math problems. The golfer who hits bucket after bucket of golf balls with a major flaw in her swing does not improve her ability to make par. And a teacher who uses the same ineffective practices over and over again can work harder and harder at those practices, and still not improve learning for students. What each person in these examples requires is feedback—the more timely, frequent, and precise, the better. Then, of course, each will need support as they attempt to implement the strategies recommended for improvement.

The old adage, "practice makes perfect," is patently false. Those who continue to engage in ineffective practices are unable to improve, much less reach perfection.

It could be argued that teacher supervision and evaluation programs have been established to provide feedback to teachers, but any candid educator would be forced to acknowledge the limits of these programs in impacting teacher practice. Even if the feedback is precise, it is neither timely nor frequent. Furthermore, rarely have we seen veteran teachers respond with enthusiasm to a supervisor's suggestion that practices they have embraced for years are ineffective.

The best way to provide powerful feedback to teachers and to turn data into information *that can improve teaching and learning* is through team-developed and team-analyzed common formative assessments. If the school in this case study, or any school, is to develop the capacity of the faculty to function as a PLC, it must create systems to ensure that each teacher:

1. Receives *frequent and timely feedback* on the performance of his or her students,

2. in meeting an *agreed-upon proficiency standard* established by the collaborative team,

3. on a *valid assessment* created by the team,

4. *in comparison to other students* in the school attempting to meet that same standard.

Finally, the school must also ensure that each teacher has the benefit of a collaborative team to turn to and learn from as he or she explores ways to improve learning for students.

Chapter 3 describes the process teams should use in developing common formative assessments and explains in detail the reasons why such assessments are vital to progressing as a PLC. The power of common formative assessments is diminished, however, if individual teachers are not provided with a basis of comparison as they examine the results for their students.

The leading authorities on school improvement are remarkably consistent in their position on this strategy. Their "Here's How" response to the question of how to improve student achievement invariably calls upon teams to develop common formative assessments, to work together as they analyze results, and to help each other become more effective as individual teachers and as a team. Doug Reeves (2002) calls for "common collaboratively scored assessments" at least every quarter (p. 37). Michael Fullan (2004) contends the process is "one of the most powerful, high leverage strategies for improving student achievement that we know of" (p. 71). Rick Stiggins (2005) concludes the extent to which teams engage in the process will allow them to benefit from their collective wisdom "about how to help our students grow as learners" (p. 82). Mike Schmoker (2005) calls this process a "well-established way to appreciably improve both teaching quality and levels of learning" (p. xi).

It has been said that collecting data is only the first step toward wisdom: sharing data is the first step toward community. If the school in this case study is to become a professional learning *community*, it must create the structures and the culture to ensure data from common formative assessments become easily accessible and openly shared among teachers who are working together interdependently toward the same SMART goal that represents higher levels of learning for their students. Every teacher should be able to ascertain how the performance of his or her students compares to all similar students taking the

> The best way to provide powerful feedback to teachers and to turn data into information *that can improve teaching and learning* is through team-developed and team-analyzed common formative assessments.

same assessment. Only then will individuals and teams receive the information vital to continuous improvement and a focus on results.

Part Three
Here's Why

No school that purports a commitment to help all students learn can be inattentive to results. Learning organizations are, by definition, "organizations where people continually expand their capacities to create the *results* [italics added] they truly desire" (Senge, 1990, p. 3). A focus on results:

- Is essential to organizational effectiveness
- Is essential to the effectiveness of teams
- Serves as a powerful motivator
- Is essential to continuous improvement

A Focus on Results Is Essential to Organizational Effectiveness

Whereas ineffective organizations are "activity centered, a fundamentally flawed logic that confuses ends with means, processes with outcomes" (Schaffer & Thomson, 1998, p. 191), effective organizations "create results driven improvement processes" that focus on achieving specific, measurable improvement goals (p. 193). They continuously improve and renew by gathering and disseminating comparative data to inform the practice of people throughout the organization (Kotter, 1996; Waterman, 1987). Leaders of these organizations are "fanatically driven, infected with an incurable desire to produce *results* (Collins, 2001, p. 30) because results are what leadership is all about (Drucker, 1996). "The outcome of effective leadership is simple: it must turn aspirations into actions. . . . It will not be enough to declare an intent; leaders will have to deliver results" (Ulrich, 1996, p. 211).

Schools and districts that focus on results by creating specific learning goals for students and monitoring learning on a timely, systematic basis are more effective in raising student achievement (Cawelti & Protheroe, 2001; Council of Chief School Officers, 2002; Lezotte, 1997; Marzano, 2003). The major distinction between schools that are able to close the achievement gap among groups of students and those unable to do so is how schools use data (Symonds, 2004). Teachers in gap-closing schools use assessments more often, use data more frequently, and work collaboratively to analyze and act upon the data.

Teachers in gap-closing schools use assessments more often, use data more frequently, and work collaboratively to analyze and act upon the data.

Without attention to results, it is impossible for any group or organization to assess the effectiveness of improvement processes (Schmoker, 1996). As James Champy (1995) advised, "Unless you can subject your decision-making to a ruthless and continuous *judgment by results,* all your zigs and zags will only be random lunges in the dark" (p. 120). No wonder school leaders have been advised to "manage by results rather than by programs and inspire others to manage by results as well" (Schlecty, 1997, p. 71).

A Focus on Results Is Essential to Team Effectiveness

Teams that focus on results are more effective than those that center their work on activities and tasks (Katzenbach & Smith, 1993). Whereas inattention to results is characteristic of dysfunctional teams, the "ultimate measure of a great team" is the results it achieves (Lencioni, 2005, p. 69). Teams accomplish the most when they are clear and unambiguous about what they want to achieve, when they clarify how they will measure their progress, and when they create a scoreboard that helps keep them focused on results (Lencioni, 2005). When teams work together to establish measurable goals, collect and analyze data regarding their progress, and monitor and adjust their actions, they produce results that "guide, goad, and motivate groups and individuals" (Schmoker, 1996, p. 38).

A Focus on Results Can Serve as a Powerful Motivator

In chapter 2, we described the need for incremental gains or "small wins" to sustain an improvement initiative. Those gains are discernible only if close attention is paid to results. Furthermore, providing evidence of results is one of the most effective ways to win the support of resisters. Some people need to see tangible evidence of results before they will commit. But when skeptics "feel the magic of momentum, when they can begin to see tangible results—that is when they will get on board" (Collins, 2001, p. 178).

A Focus on Results Is Essential to Continuous Improvement

Frederick Winslow Taylor, the father of scientific management, called upon leaders to identify the "one right way" to perform a task and then create systems to ensure that employees adhered to that specific practice. His philosophy, which provided the conceptual framework for the factory assembly line, required management to get it right and then keep it going. Public schools borrowed heavily from scientific management, calling for leaders to select the appropriate inputs and systems (curriculum, schedules, materials) and for workers (that is, teachers) to adhere to the decisions made by others. This legacy has created a tradition in which "schools are structured to reinforce continuity, not continuous improvement" (Consortium on Productivity in Schools, 1995, p. 51).

No organization can continue to improve unless the people within it engage in ongoing learning.

> Timely feedback is a critical element in any process to promote continuous learning. Individuals and teams must have access to the data and information that enable them to make adjustments as they are engaged in their work, rather than when it is completed.

In contrast, PLCs are committed to continuous improvement, an essential element of any learning organization. Members of PLCs recognize their challenge is not to get it right and keep it going, but to "get it right and make it better and better and better" (Champy, 1995, p. 27). No organization can continue to improve unless the people within it engage in ongoing learning. Therefore, leaders of PLCs build continuous learning into the work processes of every individual and every team by working with staff to create clearly defined goals, to align activities around those goals, to clarify measurements of progress, and to focus on results (Deming, 2000; Drucker, 1992). Without this commitment to continuous improvement, schools and districts will be unable to meet the challenges that confront them (American Association of School Administrators, 1999).

Timely feedback is a critical element in any process to promote continuous learning. Individuals and teams must have access to the data and information that enable them to make adjustments as they are engaged in their work, rather than when it is completed (Covey, 1996; Pfeffer & Sutton, 2000). The information gleaned from an "instructionally useful test will enable teachers to do a better job of instructing their students. And that, after all, should be the reason we test students in the first place" (Popham, 2003, p. 49).

Once again, summative state and provincial assessments fail to provide such feedback. As Rick Stiggins (2004, p. 23) observed, these assessments are "grossly insufficient" as a tool for school improvement and offer "little value at the instructional level" (2001, p. 385). A comprehensive review of research found that formative assessments are far more powerful in promoting improvement than summative assessments. As a summary of that research concluded, "few initiatives in education have had such a strong body of evidence to support a claim to raise standards" as formative assessment (Black, Harrison, Lee, Marsh, & William, 2004, p. 9).

The Central Importance of a Results Orientation

The process of becoming a PLC is designed to achieve a very specific purpose: to continuously improve the collective capacity of a group to achieve intended results. Therefore, it is incongruous to engage in elements of the process and ignore results. When Edward Deming introduced continuous improvement into industry, he presented a four-step feedback loop (see the figure on the left) to allow workers to identify and improve upon problem areas:

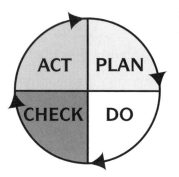

1. **Plan:** Design processes to improve results.

2. **Do:** Implement the plan and measure its performance.

3. **Check:** Analyze, assess, and report on the results.

4. **Act:** Decide what changes must be made to improve the process, and adjust accordingly.

Schools and districts that ignore results, or allow only a few members of the organization to concern themselves with results while others ignore them, do not engage in continuous improvement. Their cycle is not Plan, Do, Check, Act (and Adjust), but rather Plan, Do, Do, Do. Soon they are spinning their wheels, stuck in a rut. Improving schools avoid this trap by engaging the people who do the work, teachers and principals, in ongoing processes to identify and monitor results they recognize as valid and relevant (Dolan, 1994). These processes are essential to continual improvement, and a culture of continuous improvement is the "most important change to bring to the school" (Barth, 1991, p. 127).

Throughout this book we have referred to collaborative teams as the engine that drives the PLC process, so consider a sports analogy and assess the likelihood of success of the following football teams:

Tom Petty High School. The Heartbreakers. Team Motto: "Why Bother?" Students sign up for the team, but never take steps to create a team. They never select a captain, assign positions, or schedule a practice. In fact, they never even get in the game.

Harry Houdini High School. The Magicians. Team Motto: "Committed to the Art of Illusion." Students sign up for the team and are given a playbook. No time is spent studying the playbook or practicing the plays. At game time, each player freelances.

Alfred E. Neuman High School. The Lethargics. Team Motto: "What, Me Worry?" Students sign up for the team, receive a playbook, and attend practices to work on their plays, but absenteeism at practice is a chronic problem. Those who do attend frequently engage in horseplay and spend time talking about their social problems rather than focusing on the task.

George Santayana High School. The Historians. Team Motto: "Those Who Do Not Learn From the Past Are Condemned to Repeat It." Students sign up for the team, receive a playbook, attend practices faithfully, and devote practice time to becoming proficient at running a few plays on offense and operating a basic defense. At game time they run those same plays and present the same defensive alignment, regardless of the score, the situation, or the team they are playing. Opponents know exactly what to expect from this team.

W. C. Fields High School. The Competitors. Team Motto: "If at First You Don't Succeed, Try Again. Then Quit. No Sense in Being a Darn Fool About It." Students sign up for the team, receive a playbook, attend practices faithfully, and use practice time to develop their proficiency on offense, defense, and specialty teams. They use basic statistics to determine the strengths and weaknesses of the teams they are to play: Are they a passing team or a running team? Are they vulnerable to the pass or the run? They prepare their game plan accordingly and execute it without deviation. If, however, the opponent deviates from the expected, the team is unable to adjust.

Lake Wobegon High School. The Prairie Companions. Team Motto: "Good Is the Enemy of Great." Students sign up for the team, receive a playbook, and use practice time purposefully. The team uses statistics (that is, data) as part of their routine practice. They carefully review game films of their opponents to discover their strengths, weaknesses, and tendencies. The team builds common knowledge: Our opponent runs off left tackle on short yardage plays over 70% of the time, if the quarterback rolls left he will throw an out pattern, their blitz comes from the linebackers rather than the cornerback almost 100% of the time, and so on. They also examine the statistics and films of their own games to discover areas needing attention. In order to achieve the overarching goal—victory—each group in the team establishes specific goals: The defense will yield no more than 250 total yards and will create at least one turnover. The offense will gain at least 150 yards on the ground and control the ball for 60% of the game. Each member of the team knows the goals and how he or she can contribute to achieving them.

Vince Lombardi High School. The Champions. Team Motto: "The Quality of a Person's Life Is in Direct Proportion to His or Her Commitment to Excellence." This team replicates everything done by team Wobegon, but in addition, they are hungry for data and use both data and individual and collective experience to make adjustments throughout the game. Players examine pictures on the sidelines to come to a better understanding of what their opponents are doing and collaborate regarding how they might respond. They openly share concerns and ideas. With the help of their coaches, they reflect on their experience at half time and create new strategies to achieve their goals. They are committed to working interdependently to achieve goals for which they are mutually accountable, and they use data to establish interim goals, to monitor their progress, and to make adjustments in order to increase the likelihood of achieving their shared purpose.

We have seen examples of each of these teams in schools and districts that characterize themselves as professional learning communities. In some, a pronouncement is made, "We are a professional learning community," but nothing changes: No steps are taken to begin the process. They never get in the game. In others, teachers are given state standards and district curriculum guides to direct their work, but they never come together to clarify the curriculum or how it could best be taught and assessed. In some, teachers are provided with time to collaborate, but the time is wasted as they focus on matters unrelated to teaching and learning. In others, they collaborate on essential learning and create common assessments, but they do nothing with the results other than to assign grades. No effort is made to identify individual students who need help on specific skills, nor do members of the team use data to inform and improve their practice.

In schools and districts that are progressing as PLCs, teams gather and collaborate about data and use data to monitor student learning and to set SMART goals. Members of the team understand their individual roles and responsibilities and work together to achieve their targets. Finally, in PLCs, teams view data as an essential component of their process of continuous improvement. They use the results of every common assessment to identify individual students who need additional time and support for learning, to discover strengths and weaknesses in their teaching, and to inform and adjust their practice to increase the likelihood they will achieve their shared purpose: higher levels of learning for all students. They are not satisfied with taking a few half-steps on the road to becoming a PLC. They commit fully to stay the course.

Once again, there is no recipe or step-by-step manual for becoming a PLC, but there are some things that must be done as part of the process. Using results to inform and improve practice is one of those things, and schools that are sincere in their desire to create a PLC will act accordingly. Inattention to results is antithetical to becoming a PLC.

Inattention to results is antithetical to becoming a PLC.

Part Four
Assessing Your Place on the PLC Journey

The PLC Continuum

Working individually and quietly, review the continuum of a school's progress on the PLC journey (page 156). Which point on the continuum gives the most accurate description of the current reality of your school or district? Be prepared to support your assessment with evidence and anecdotes.

After working individually, share your assessment with colleagues. Where do you have agreement? Where do you find discrepancies in the assessments? Listen to the rationales of others in support of their varying assessments. Are you able to reach agreement?

Where Do We Go From Here?

The challenge confronting a school that has engaged in the collective consideration of a topic is answering the questions, "So what?" and, "What, if anything, are we prepared to do differently?" Now consider each indicator of a professional learning community described in the left column of the Where Do We Go From Here? Worksheet on page 157, and then answer the questions listed at the top of the remaining four columns.

The Professional Learning Community Continuum

Element of a PLC	Pre-Initiation Stage	Initiation Stage	Developing Stage	Sustaining Stage
A Focus on Results	There are no processes to use results as a tool for improvement. Teachers fall into a predictable pattern: They teach, they test, they hope for the best, and then they move on to the next unit.	District leaders analyze results from high-stakes summative tests such as state and provincial examinations. Data are shared with each school, and principals and teachers are encouraged to review the results and address weaknesses as part of their school improvement plan.	The school has created a specific process to bring together collaborative teams of teachers several times throughout the year to analyze results from common formative assessments. Teams identify areas of concern and discuss strategies for improving the collective results. Assessments are also used to identify students who are experiencing difficulty, and the school creates systems to provide those students with additional time and support for learning.	Collaborative teams of teachers regard ongoing analysis of results as a critical element in the teaching and learning process. They are hungry for information on student learning and gather and analyze evidence from a variety of sources. Results from their common formative assessments are compared to results from state and provincial assessments to validate the effectiveness of their local assessments. Teachers use results to identify strengths and weaknesses in their individual practice, to help each other address areas of concern, and to improve their effectiveness in helping all students learn. Strategically linked SMART goals drive the work of each collaborative team. Analysis of the performance of individual students enables the team and school to create efficient and timely interventions. Improved results and achievement of goals are the basis for a culture of celebration within classrooms, the school, and the district.

Learning by Doing © 2006 Solution Tree ■ www.solution-tree.com

Where Do We Go From Here? Worksheet
Collaborative Teams Turn Data Into Information for Continuous Improvement

Describe one or more aspects of a professional learning community that you would like to see in place in your school.	What steps or activities must be initiated to create this condition in your school?	Who will be responsible for initiating or sustaining these steps or activities?	What is a realistic timeline for each step or phase of the activity?	What will you use to assess the effectiveness of your initiative?
Collaborative teams of teachers regard ongoing analysis of results as a critical element in the teaching and learning process.				
Data are transformed into information that impacts practice because evidence of results is easily accessible and openly shared among teammates.				
Teachers use results to identify strengths and weaknesses in their individual practice, to help each other address areas of concern, and to improve their effectiveness in helping all students learn.				
The focus on results is critical to both the school's system of interventions and their culture of celebration.				

Part Five
Tips for Moving Forward:
Creating a Results Orientation

1 **Use feedback on results to inform, not punish.** In order to promote continuous improvement, feedback must not only be timely, it must also be effective. Feedback can encourage effort and improvement, but it can and often is used in ways that create a sense of hopelessness. The lessons learned from research on feedback for students can be applied to adults as well. Whenever an activity is viewed as a competition, there will be winners and losers. When feedback to students takes the form of grades, they are likely to see assessment as a competition or a way to compare their achievement with others. Students with a track record as losers see little point in trying; however, when they are clear on intended learning outcomes and are provided with feedback as part of a formative process for improving their work, and are then given support in clarifying how they can close the gap, they are more likely to continue working until they achieve the targets (Black, Harrison, Lee, Marsh, & William, 2004; Chappuis, 2005; Stiggins, 2001).

Schools that hope to create a culture of continuous improvement should provide every teacher with results from frequent, common formative assessments on a timely basis, *but they should not use those results to compare and assess teachers.* For more than 20 years, Stevenson High School in Lincolnshire, Illinois, has used frequent, common formative assessments developed by collaborative teams of teachers to drive its continuous improvement process—a process that has made Stevenson one of the most celebrated schools in America. Over the course of those two decades, common assessments have been administered thousands of times, *and on every one of those assessments, one teacher found that his or her students had the lowest scores on the team.* Stevenson administrators and teachers recognize there will always be a teacher with the lowest results on any given common assessment, just as there will always be 50% of the students in the bottom half of the graduating class. Therefore, when teams work collaboratively to analyze the results from common assessments, their focus is not on who had the best or the worst results, but rather on what they can do collectively to improve student learning.

Conversely, if a collaborative team develops and administers common assessments in the worst, most ineffective schools in the nation, one of those ineffective teachers will have the best results. It makes little sense to focus on comparison of teachers; there will always be a best and a worst. The goal is to provide each team and each teacher with the information and support necessary to fuel continuous improvement. The underlying assumption of the continuous improvement philosophy demands that we *use ourselves as benchmarks* and then work to improve upon our previous performance (Gerstner, Semerad, Doyle, & Johnston, 1995). The most effective organizations focus less on using data "to try to assess individual performance and more [on using data] to focus attention on factors critical to organizational success" (Pfeffer & Sutton, 2000, p. 173).

Attention to results can serve many purposes: identifying students who need additional time and support in order to become proficient in an essential skill, helping teams mark progress toward their goals, providing individual teachers with timely feedback on the effectiveness of their strategies, and providing a basis of celebration for small wins. But we strongly advise against using results to assess individual teachers. There is no benefit—but rather there is considerable detriment—to the school when they are used for that purpose.

 Provide the basis of comparison that translates data into information. Remember that data alone will not help individuals or teams improve. They need the context of valid comparison to identify strengths and weaknesses.

 Use apples-to-apples comparisons. Comparisons are most informative when conditions are similar. Schools with students from high-performing communities often take great satisfaction in "comparing" the performance of their students to state averages, but such comparisons do little to promote improvement. If a school places students into classrooms on the basis of multiple ability groups, it accomplishes little to compare the performance of students in the highest group to those in the lowest. Equivalent situations yield the most meaningful comparisons. Remember Gerstner's admonition that the comparisons most effective in promoting continuous improvement are comparisons to ourselves: What evidence do we have that we are becoming more effective?

Use balanced assessments. No single assessment source yields the comprehensive results necessary to inform and improve practice. The best strategy to gather results is to seek *balanced assessment* (National Education Association, 2003). Part of that balance is between summative assessments *of* learning and formative assessments *for* learning. Summative state and provincial assessments provide an important accountability tool for schools and districts. They demonstrate how local students perform compared to others in the state seeking the same outcomes, and they provide a means to certify the validity of local formative assessments. Common formative assessments created within a school or district can direct teacher practice and identify students needing assistance on a timely basis. Both are important and should be utilized in a school or district assessment program.

Balanced assessment can also refer to using different types of formative assessments based upon the knowledge or skills students are called upon to demonstrate. Rather than relying exclusively on one kind of assessment—multiple choice tests, performance-based assessments, constructed response tests, and so on—teachers should attempt to determine the best evidence of student learning and the most effective ways to gather that evidence. Schools and teams must develop multiple ways for students to demonstrate proficiency.

5 **Teachers and principals must engage in data analysis rather than outsourcing the task to others.** It is not realistic to expect teachers and principals to become statisticians. The central office can and should take steps to ensure information is provided to schools and teams in an easily interpreted, user-friendly format. It should not, however, exempt the educators in the building from doing their own analysis of the information. "There is no substitute for classroom-by-classroom, school-by-school analysis" by the people who are called upon to develop the improvement strategies: teachers and principals (Reeves, 2002, p. 107).

6 **A fixation with results does not mean inattention to people.** There are those who suggest an organization committed to results will be inattentive to the needs of the people within it, willing to sacrifice individuals on the altar of the bottom line. These people fall victim to the "Tyranny of Or." Professional learning communities are committed to both results *and* relationships. They recognize that the best way to achieve the collective purpose of the group is through collaborative relationships that foster the ongoing growth and development of the people who produce the results. They recognize that the very key to school improvement is people improvement, and they commit to creating cultures that help individuals become more proficient, effective, and fulfilled by virtue of the fact that they work in that school or district.

Part Six
Questions to Guide the Work of Your Professional Learning Community

To Assess the Results Orientation of Your School or District, Ask:

1. What evidence do we have that district goals are directly impacting the work of schools and collaborative teams within the school?

_____

_____

2. Have we identified the evidence we must gather to determine if all students are acquiring the knowledge, skills, and dispositions we have determined are most essential? What does that evidence include?

_____

_____

3. Do we provide students with a variety of ways to demonstrate they are proficient? Can we identify a variety of ways in which students in our school are able to demonstrate they are proficient? What does our list include?

_____

_____

4. Who analyzes evidence of student learning in our school and district? What happens as a result of that analysis? What evidence can we cite that it impacts classroom practice?

_____

_____

5. Does our assessment program enable us to identify, on a timely basis, students who need extra time and support for learning? At what point does our systematic process enable us to identify students who require intervention?

_____

_____

6. Does our assessment program provide every teacher with timely and valid feedback on the extent to which his or her students are becoming proficient in comparison to other similar students in our school or district who are attempting to meet the same standard? If not, what steps must we take to provide every teacher with this timely information?

_____

_____

7. Do we have a balanced assessment program that includes formative and summative assessments, local and state or provincial assessments, and a variety of performance-based and written assessments?

_____

_____

8. Do we use evidence of student learning as part of a continuous improvement process? Is our assessment program helping us to become better as a school?

_____

_____

9. Does our assessment program encourage or discourage student learning?

_____

_____

Final Thoughts

If working together effectively and making data easily accessible and openly shared among team members are critical elements of a PLC, then unproductive conflict and individuals resistant to collaboration and attention to results represent significant obstacles to progress on the PLC journey. Chapter 8 considers those obstacles and offers strategies for addressing them.

Chapter 8

Consensus and Conflict in a Professional Learning Community

| Part One |
| The Case Study: Building Consensus and Responding to Resistance |

Members of a professional learning community view conflict as a source of creative energy and an opportunity for building shared knowledge. They create specific strategies for exploring one another's thinking, and they make a conscious effort to understand as well as to be understood.

David C. Roth, the principal of Van Halen High School, was annoyed. He knew how hard he had worked to build consensus for moving forward with professional learning community concepts. He provided the entire staff with research and readings on the benefits of PLCs. He sent key teacher leaders to conferences on PLCs and used those staff members as a guiding coalition to promote the concept. He encouraged interested staff to visit schools that were working as PLCs. He met with the entire faculty in small groups to listen to their concerns and answer their questions. Finally, at the end of this painstaking process, he was convinced the faculty was ready to move forward. He assigned teachers into subject area teams and asked each team to work collaboratively to clarify the essential outcomes of their courses and to develop common assessments to monitor student proficiency.

Within a month, the Sophomore English Team met with Principal Roth to ask if the team could exempt one of its members from meetings. They explained that Fred made it evident he was opposed to the entire idea of collaborative teams and common assessments. Fred made no effort to contribute and his ridicule and sarcasm were undermining the team. Principal Roth assured them he would look into the situation and attempt to remedy it.

The next day Principal Roth called Fred to his office to discuss Fred's attitude toward his colleagues and the collaborative team process. After listening to the principal's concerns, Fred expressed his unhappiness with the heavy-handed, top-down dictate of working in teams. He rejected the idea that the staff had arrived at consensus. Not only was he opposed to the initiative, he knew many other teachers who were as well. It was fine with him if the team did not want him to participate, because he had no interest in participating. He had always been an effective teacher, and he did not need some artificial process of working with colleagues to become effective.

Principal Roth resented Fred's characterization of the decision-making process and his assertion that the staff had never arrived at consensus. As he expressed that resentment, it was evident that the emotions of both men were becoming more heated. Principal Roth decided the prudent course would be to adjourn the meeting.

Throughout the day the principal struggled with his dilemma. On the one hand, he was not amenable to exempting Fred from the PLC process. He was wary of establishing a precedent that released overt resisters from the obligation to contribute to their collaborative teams. He was concerned that others on the staff would resent devoting time and energy to collaboration if their colleagues were able to opt out of the process. On the other hand, he knew Fred could be difficult and he considered it unlikely that Fred could be persuaded to change his attitude.

After much deliberation, Principal Roth decided to ask the English team to continue working with Fred in the hope that his attitude would improve over time. The team was unhappy with his response.

Reflection

Consider Principal Roth's efforts to build consensus for an improvement process and his approach to dealing with a staff member who was unwilling to support the process. What is your reaction? Can you identify alternative strategies the principal might have used that would have been more effective?

Part Two
Here's How

In chapter 2, we offered suggestions for developing consensus: Create a guiding coalition, build shared knowledge, and engage in dialogue with staff members in small groups to listen to and address concerns. Principal Roth was attentive to each of these suggestions, yet he still encountered difficulties. The problem arose, in part, because no clear, operational definition of consensus guided the decision-making process in the school. Principal Roth was certain the staff supported moving forward with the PLC concept, while Fred was equally convinced that staff members opposed the concept. Without a shared understanding, people were left to determine their own standard for consensus.

Without a shared understanding, people are left to determine their own standard for consensus.

Have We Arrived at Consensus on Consensus?

In our work with schools, we frequently ask a straightforward question: "How do you define 'consensus' when your staff considers a proposal?" The responses we hear vary greatly. We have established a continuum of consensus based on the typical responses. Consider the following continuum and select the point at which you feel you have reached agreement on a proposal in your own school.

We have arrived at consensus in our school when:

1. All of us can embrace the proposal.

2. All of us can endorse the proposal.

3. All of us can live with the proposal.

4. All of us can agree not to sabotage the proposal.

5. We have a majority—at least 51%—in support of the proposal.

The most common outcome of this survey is a staff distributed all along the continuum because members *do not have consensus on the definition of consensus.* Disagreements and allegations are inevitable when a faculty does not understand the standard that must be met in order to make a collective decision.

Actually, we advise staffs to reject all points on the 5-point continuum. In our view (a view not universally shared by others), it is difficult to maintain that you have the consent of the group to move forward with a simple majority—a standard that can disregard the perspective of 49% of the group. On the other hand, every other point on the continuum goes beyond consensus when it calls for "all of us" to reach a level of agreement. While it is wonderful to strive for unanimity, there is a difference between unanimity and consensus. In the real world of schools, if *all of us* must agree before we can act, if every member of the staff can veto taking action, we will be subjected to constant inaction, a state of perpetual status quo.

The definition of consensus we prefer establishes two simple standards that must be met in order to move forward when a decision is made by consensus. A group has arrived at consensus when:

1. All points of view have been heard.

2. The will of the group is evident even to those who most oppose it.

A group has arrived at consensus when:

1. All points of view have been heard.

2. The will of the group is evident even to those who most oppose it.

This definition can, and typically does, result in moving forward with a proposal despite the fact that some members of the organization are against it.

If this standard had been applied in the case study, Principal Roth and his guiding coalition would have certainly built shared knowledge and engaged in small group dialogues to address concerns. At some point, however, they would have also presented a specific proposal such as this:

> In order to create a guaranteed and viable curriculum, establish consistency in assessing student proficiency, and promote a collaborative culture, we will work together in collaborative teams that clarify essential learning by course, create common formative assessments, and analyze the results from those assessments to improve student achievement.

The staff would then be *randomly* divided into two groups. The first group would be asked to work together to create a comprehensive list of all the reasons the faculty should oppose the proposal. The second group would be called upon to create a comprehensive list of all the reasons the staff should support the proposal. At this point, personal feelings about the proposal do not to come into play. Each member of the staff is to engage in an intellectual exercise to list all the possible pros and cons regarding the specific idea under consideration.

In the next step of the process, the first group presents all the reasons they listed to oppose the suggestion. Members of the second group are asked to listen attentively until the opposed group has completed their list, and then they are invited to add to that list with other objections that might not have been identified. The process is then repeated with the proponent group announcing their comprehensive list in support of the decision, with the objectors then being invited to add to it. Participants are then encouraged to ask for clarification on any point they do not understand. If done correctly, no one will know where any member of the staff stands on the issue personally, although all points of view have been heard.

The next step is to determine the will of the group. A quick and simple way to do so is to use the "fist to five" strategy. Once everyone is clear on the proposal and all pros and cons have been offered, each person is asked to indicate a level of support as shown in the feature box on page 167.

The facilitator for the process ensures that everyone understands the issue under consideration and how to express themselves through fist to five. All members of the staff are then asked to express their position simultaneously by raising their hands with the appropriate indication of support (that is, the number of fingers best expressing their level of support). Each participant is then able to look around the room to ascertain the support for the proposal. If participants

Fist to Five Strategy

5 Fingers:	I love this proposal. I will champion it.
4 Fingers:	I strongly agree with the proposal.
3 Fingers:	The proposal is okay with me. I am willing to go along.
2 Fingers:	I have reservations and am not yet ready to support this proposal.
1 Finger:	I am opposed to this proposal.
Fist:	If I were king or queen, I would veto this proposal, regardless of the will of the group.

do not support the proposal, or the vote is too close to determine the will of the group at a glance, the proposal does not go forward. Pilot projects may be run, more time can be taken to build shared knowledge, and in time the proposal may be presented again; however, if support is not readily apparent, the standard of consensus has not been met. If, however, it is evident by looking around the room that it is the will of the group to move forward (the number of hands with 3, 4, and 5 fingers clearly outnumber those with 2, 1, and fists), consensus has been reached and all staff members will be expected to honor the decision.

There are certainly variations on this format. For example, if the technology is available, staff could vote anonymously and have the tally reported instantly. If there are concerns about intimidation, an anonymous paper vote may be necessary as long as the process for counting the votes is accepted as fair by all concerned. In very large schools, the vote may take place in a series of small-group staff meetings rather than one large-group meeting. In that case, it is prudent to have the teachers' association appoint a representative to attend all of the meetings in case concerns emerge about the accuracy of the reporting. But while the format may vary, one thing does not: Decision-making is easier, more effective, and less likely to end in disputes about process when a staff has a clear operational definition of consensus.

The Need to Confront

A faculty that has built a solid foundation for a PLC by carefully crafting consensus regarding their purpose, the school they seek to create, their collective commitments, the specific goals they will use to monitor their progress, and the strategies for achieving those goals, has not eliminated the possibility of conflict. The real strength of a PLC is determined by the response to the disagreements and violations of commitments that inevitably occur.

The real strength of a PLC is determined by the response to the disagreements and violations of commitments that inevitably occur.

Every organization will experience conflict, particularly when the organization is engaged in significant change. Every collective endeavor will include instances when people fail to honor agreed-upon priorities and collective commitments. The ultimate goal, of course, is to create a culture that is so strong and so open that members throughout the organization will use the violation as an opportunity to reinforce what is valued by bringing peer pressure to bear on the offender, saying, in effect, "That is not how we do it here." In the interim, however, it typically will be the responsibility of the leader (that is, principal or administrator) to communicate what is important and valued by demonstrating a willingness to confront when appropriate. Nothing will destroy the credibility of a leader faster than an unwillingness to address an obvious violation of what the organization contends is vital. A leader must not remain silent; he or she must not be unwilling to act when people disregard the purpose and priorities of the organization.

Confrontation does not, however, involve screaming, demeaning, or vilifying. It is possible to be tough-minded and adamant about protecting purpose and priorities while also being tender with people. One of the most helpful resources we have found for engaging in frank dialogue when "the stakes are high, opinions vary, and emotions run strong" is *Crucial Conversations* by Patterson, Grenny, McMillan, and Switzler (2002, p. 3). They contend that skillful communicators reject the false dichotomy of the "Suckers Choice": I can either be honest and hurtful *or* be kind and withhold the truth. Instead, they search for the "Genius of And"—a way to be both honest *and* respectful, to say what needs to be said to the people who need to hear it without brutalizing them or causing undue offense.

Some of the strategies offered in *Crucial Conversations* for engaging in honest and respectful dialogue include:

1. Clarify what you want and what you do not want to result from the conversation.

2. Attempt to find mutual purpose.

3. Create a safe environment for honest dialogue.

4. Use facts because "gathering facts is the homework required for crucial conversations" (p. 127).

5. Share your thought process that has led to the conversation.

6. Encourage recipients to share their facts and thought process.

Let us apply these strategies to the situation Principal Roth is facing. Prior to initiating the conversation with Fred, Principal Roth might clarify his position in his own mind: "I want all students to have the benefit of a teacher who is a member of a high-performing collaborative team. Therefore, I want Fred to honor the commitments we made as a staff to the collaborative process by making a positive contribution to his team. I do not want Fred to think we are questioning his expertise or diminishing his contribution to the school." Principal Roth would then think of how he might achieve what he wants and avoid what he does not want through a meaningful, respectful dialogue with Fred.

During the conversation with Fred, the principal could attempt to find mutual purpose: "I believe we both want a school that is committed to helping all students achieve at high levels and to providing teachers with a satisfying and fulfilling professional experience." He could ask Fred if he agrees with that assessment of their mutual purpose.

Roth could attempt to create a safe environment for dialogue by sharing facts, speaking tentatively, inviting Fred to clarify any mistakes in his thinking, and encouraging the teacher to elaborate on his own thought process: "I feel very strongly that developing our capacity to work together collaboratively on significant issues centered in teaching and learning is vital to both raising student achievement and creating a rewarding workplace. Our staff has made commitments to work together with the colleagues on their teams, and I was wondering if that commitment is problematic for you. Here are some of the events that caused me to raise this question. I understand you frequently do not attend the meetings of your collaborative team, and that you have not made any contribution to creating common assessments. I received several complaints from students and parents that you had not taught the skills assessed on the last common test. I recognize the contribution you have made to this school over the years, and I don't want to diminish that contribution in any way. In fact, I think your teammates could benefit from your experience. So help me understand. Are my facts incorrect? Are there issues of which I am unaware? I'm very interested in hearing your perspective and your assessment of any factors that may be impacting your contribution to your collaborative team."

At this point it is important for Principal Roth to listen carefully to Fred, to make a good faith effort to understand Fred's perspective. In *Difficult Conversations,* another helpful study of how to address differences through dialogue, the authors advise, "Listening is not only the skill that lets you into the other person's world; it is the single most powerful move you can make to keep the conversation constructive" (Patterson, Grenny, McMillan, and Switzler, 2000, p. 202).

If Fred agrees with the mutual purpose but cites conditions that are impeding his ability to contribute to the team, the principal and Fred can brainstorm solutions and commit to carry out their agreed-upon plan. If Fred can express his reasons for resisting the proposal, the principal may be able to modify the context of the proposal in a way that resonates with Fred. For example, we know

"Listening is not only the skill that lets you into the other person's world; it is the single most powerful move you can make to keep the conversation constructive." (Stone, Patton, & Heen, 2000, p. 202)

of a teacher who argued he should not be required to work with his team because he was only 2 years from retirement and was already getting the best results in his department. The principal acknowledged those points and complimented the teacher on the craft knowledge he had developed over the years. The principal then pointed out that all that accumulated knowledge would walk out the door with him on his retirement day unless he shared it with his colleagues. By shifting the focus from "participate to improve" to "participate to ensure your ongoing legacy," the principal convinced the teacher to commit to contribute to his team.

It is possible, however, that Fred rejects the mutual purpose. He might say: "My primary job is to give students the opportunity to demonstrate that they have learned what I taught, and I don't need to collaborate with peers to do my job. I see your insistence on collaboration as an attempt to deprive me of my autonomy. As a professional I have a right to determine what I will teach, the instructional strategies I deem appropriate, and how I will assess my students. If others elect to collaborate, it is their choice, but I choose not to participate."

In this situation, Principal Roth should:

1. Continue to work with Fred in a respectful and professional manner. Losing his composure or arguing with Fred serves no one's interest.

2. Acknowledge that there are fundamental differences in their perspectives; however, those differences do not exempt Fred from participating in the collaborative process in a productive way. Principal Roth must send a clear message to Fred that the need for change is immediate and imperative.

3. Clarify the specific behaviors he requires of Fred. Admonitions such as, "You need to do a better job with your team," or, "You need to improve your attitude toward collaboration" do not provide Fred with the precise direction that is needed. A far more effective strategy might sound like this: "Fred, there are three things I need you to begin doing immediately. First, you *must* attend all of your team meetings. Second, you *must* honor each of the norms your team has established regarding how members will fulfill their responsibilities and relate to one another. Third, you *must* provide me with specific evidence each week that you are (1) teaching your students the essential learning outcomes established by your team and (2) preparing your students to demonstrate their attainment of those outcomes on the common assessments created by the team. We can discuss different ways you might provide me with such evidence. To ensure that there are no misunderstandings, I will provide you with a written directive detailing these expectations."

"Successful groups know how to fight gracefully—they embrace the positive aspects of conflict and actively minimize the negative aspects. . . . Conflict is an important resource for forging better practices."
(Garmston & Wellman, 1999, p. 183)

4. Invite Fred to offer any suggestions, support, training, or resources he might need to comply with the directive.

5. Clarify the specific consequences that will occur if Fred ignores the directive he has been given: "Fred, if you disregard what I have directed you to do, I will have no choice but to consider your actions as insubordination. At that point I will suspend you without pay and take the matter to the Board of Education."

6. Establish strategies to monitor Fred's behavior rather than his attitude. When good-faith efforts to engage in meaningful dialogue reveal fundamental differences rather than common ground, and when attempts to participate in crucial conversations lead to impasse rather than agreement, attempts to "talk" a person into a new attitude are almost always unproductive.

7. Acknowledge and celebrate any efforts Fred may make to change his behavior.

8. Apply the specified consequences if necessary.

Leaders are always in a better position to confront when they act as the promoters and protectors of decisions, agreements, and commitments of the group.

Leaders are always in a better position to confront when they act as the promoters and protectors of decisions, agreements, and commitments of the group. Appeals to hierarchy—"Do it because I am the boss and I said so"—may eventually become necessary on occasion, but in raising an issue initially, leaders are more effective utilizing the moral authority that comes with defending the articulated collective aspirations of the people within the organization.

Part Three
Here's Why

As we emphasized in chapter 2, research has consistently concluded that effective leaders build shared vision and a shared sense of purpose that binds people together. But unless vision and purpose result in action, nothing is accomplished (Decrane, 1996; Klein, Medrich, & Perez-Ferreiro, 1996; Pfeffer & Sutton, 2000; Ulrich, 1996). So what are leaders to do when some members of the organization are opposed to taking action that is critical to moving forward? The best leaders will create a "critical mass" of those willing to act (Klein, Medrich, & Perez-Ferreiro, 1996) and will then move to action without expecting universal support (Evans, 1996; Burns, 1978).

Conflict is an inevitable by-product of the substantive change processes in schools (Evans, 1996; Lieberman, 1995; Louis, Kruse, & Marks, 1996). As James Champy (1995) wrote: "A culture that squashes disagreement is a culture doomed to stagnate, because change always begins with disagreement. Besides, disagreement can never be squashed entirely. It gets repressed, only to emerge later as a sense of injustice, followed by apathy, resentment, and even sabotage" (p. 89).

In fact, the absence of conflict suggests the changes are only superficial because "*conflict* is *essential* to any successful change effort" (Fullan, 1993, p. 27). Therefore, those who hope to lead the effort effectively must learn how to manage conflict productively rather than focusing on how to kill it or avoid it (Newmann & Wehlage, 1996). Effective leaders will surface the conflict, draw out and acknowledge the varying perspectives, and search for a common ground that everyone can endorse (Goleman, 2002). When managed well, conflict can serve as an engine of creativity and energy (Saphier, 2005), build shared knowledge (Maxwell, 1995), clarify priorities (Bossidy & Charan, 2002), and develop stronger teams (Lencioni, 2005).

Repeated conflict over the same issues can certainly represent a drain on an organization's time and energy, and at some point there is a need for closure. But when educational leaders at the district or school level avoid confrontation because they favor keeping the peace over productive conflict, they can do tremendous damage to any improvement process. As we wrote in *Professional Learning Communities at Work*™ (1998):

> The school suffers when individuals are free to act in a manner the staff as a whole has agreed is contrary to the school's best interest. The principal suffers because his or her credibility as a leader is diminished by an unwillingness to confront an obvious problem. The individual acting inappropriately suffers because he or she has been deprived of an opportunity for learning and growth. Most important, the improvement initiative suffers because the staff will soon come to recognize that the principal assigns a higher priority to avoiding conflict than to advancing the vision and values of the school. (p. 113)

How Are Attitudes Changed?

The most frequent issue raised by participants in our workshops is help in dealing with "resisters." Teachers and administrators alike want to know how to change the minds of those who persist in their opposition to an agreed-upon initiative. Gladwell (2002) contends there is a tendency to overestimate the importance of character (for example, "June is just a negative person") and underestimate the power of context: the cultural norms and peer pressure that influence behavior. We concur and join the legion of educational writers (Barth, 2001; Elmore, 2002; Fullan, 1993; Louis, Kruse, & Raywid, 1996; Marzano, Waters, & McNulty, 2005; Newmann & Associates, 1996; Sarason, 1996; Schlechty, 1997) who have urged leaders to move beyond structural changes and

When educational leaders at the district or school level avoid confrontation because they favor keeping the peace over productive conflict, they can do tremendous damage to any improvement process.

to address culture as a critical part of the improvement process. Focusing on changing the culture is one of the most powerful strategies for converting people to the cause of improvement, because most people are powerfully influenced by the culture in which they work.

But changing culture is a long-term process. What short-term strategies are available to persuade reluctant staff members to join the improvement initiative? Howard Gardner (2004) has identified seven factors that can be used to bring about changes in people's thinking. The first six of those strategies include:

1. **Reason:** Appealing to rational thinking and decision-making.

2. **Research:** Building shared knowledge of the research base supporting a position.

3. **Resonance:** Connecting to the person's intuition so that the proposal "feels right."

4. **Representational Re-descriptions:** Changing the way the information is presented (for example, using stories or analogies instead of data).

5. **Resources and Reward:** Providing people with incentives to embrace an idea.

6. **Real-World Events:** Presenting real-world examples where the idea has been applied successfully.

Gardner believes that the greatest likelihood of changing the thinking of others occurs when these six factors work in consort, but he acknowledges that even if each has been addressed, resistance is still likely to occur. He advises that *resistance must be identified and dealt with rather than ignored, and that direct confrontation of resistance is an important seventh factor in changing someone's mind.*

Howard Gardner's Factors to Change People's Thinking (2004)

1. Reason

2. Research

3. Resonance

4. Representational Re-descriptions

5. Resources and Reward

6. Real-World Events

7. Confrontation

Don't focus on the attitude; focus on the behavior.

But what is an effective way to confront resistance? We are often asked for advice on what to say to convert those with "bad attitudes"—those who remain opposed to moving forward despite every effort to convince them to support an initiative. Our advice is simple: Don't focus on the attitude—focus on the behavior. Research in the fields of psychology, organizational development, and education concur that changes in attitudes follow, rather than precede, changes in behavior. When work is designed to require people to *act* in new ways, the possibility of new experiences are created for them. These new experiences, in turn, can lead to new attitudes over time (Champy, 1995; Kotter, 1996; Pfeffer & Sutton, 2000; Reeves, 2002; Wheelis, 1973).

In the final analysis, however, it is important to recognize that it is quite probable some people will *never* embrace PLC concepts despite overwhelming evidence of the benefits and the best efforts of leaders to bring them on board. Teachers who believe it is their job to teach and the students' job to learn, who are convinced that learning is a function of the aptitude of the student rather than the expertise of the teacher, who define professionalism as the autonomy to do as they please, or who take pleasure in wallowing in negativity will always find a way to dismiss PLC concepts.

So what is a leader to do when she continues to meet with defiance even though she has listened respectfully, made a good faith effort to find common ground, exhausted every art of persuasion, and prescribed the specific behaviors she expects an individual staff member to demonstrate despite his or her reservations or concerns? The traditional school response is to avoid the problem (Evans, 1996; Sarason, 1996). Leaders must overcome this tradition if they want to avoid stalling their improvement efforts.

Many leaders conclude, perhaps rightly, that there is very little hope of changing the hard-core resisters, and so they begin to ignore their repeated disregard for and violations of the agreed-upon commitments to implement the improvement agenda. Leaders must persist, nevertheless, and follow through on the specific consequences they have outlined to those who violate the collective commitments. *They must keep in mind that the goal in addressing these violations is not only to bring about change in the resister, but also to communicate priorities throughout the organization.* Unwillingness to follow through sends mixed messages about what is important and valued. As Evans (2001) concluded, the need to confront resistance is "one of the toughest truths of change in school" (p. 276) because "confrontation forms a matching bookend with clarity and focus" (p. 288). In every school that we have seen succeed as a PLC, a defining moment has occurred when a leader chose to confront rather than avoid saboteurs. We are convinced their schools' improvement efforts could not have gone forward had they ignored violations of collective commitments.

We know that many veteran administrators will dismiss this advice to confront resisters as out of touch with the realities of schooling. They could point to the difficulties they face when it comes to dismissing a tenured teacher, and in that respect, they would be right. For example, in 1985, Illinois passed reform legislation intended to make it easier to dismiss teachers for incompetence. A recent study of the impact of the legislation found, on average, only 2 of the 95,000 teachers in the state are dismissed for incompetence each year. The study also found that the cost of bringing a tenured teacher through the laborious and time-consuming process for dismissal averaged $100,000 ("Protecting Mediocre Teachers," 2005).

Unwillingness to follow through sends mixed messages about what is important and valued.

In his study of effective organizations, Collins (2001) found they not only were committed to getting "the right people on the bus," but they were equally attentive to getting "the wrong people off the bus" (p. 41). Educators often reply that this advice does not apply in their settings because of the difficulty of removing staff. We are convinced, however, that Collins' finding has merit, even when confronting veteran staff members who enjoy the protection of tenure. Although it may be difficult to remove saboteurs from the bus in education, we can take steps to ensure that they are not in the driver's seat. We can change their seats and reduce their relevance in the decisions regarding the route we will take.

We know of a high school principal who inherited a leadership structure that included a chairperson of each department. Seniority was king in the school. New teachers were assigned to classes perceived as least desirable and chairmanships were awarded as a matter of right to the most veteran staff member in the department. The principal soon discovered that the department chairs considered themselves the champions of the status quo (primarily because the quo gave them a certain degree of status). They were adamantly opposed to any proposal for even the smallest of changes in the practices of the school. Their negativity routinely tainted any attempts to engage the staff in dialogue through department meetings. When the principal met with each chair to express his concerns about the role they were playing in thwarting any consideration of steps that could be taken to improve the school, he found that behind the scenes they had cemented their alliance and were uniformly opposed to exploring improvement strategies.

Rather than waiting to improve the school "one retirement at a time," the principal set out to reduce the relevance of the department chairs. He created a school improvement task force and recruited some of the most highly respected members of the faculty to serve on it. He created schedules to ensure members of the task force were available to meet with him on a regular basis, and he began communicating with department chairs through memos rather than meetings. As the task force went through the process of building shared knowledge and soliciting the concerns of the staff, the principal conducted small-group inter-disciplinary dialogues rather than meeting with the entire faculty or single departments. As the task force built support for some changes, new project teams were created to address specific elements of the improvement plan, and interested staff members were recruited to serve on each project team. As more staff members became involved in the process, more people became invested in the improvement effort. Leadership was widely dispersed. In short, the princi-pal broke free from the traditional bureaucracy and utilized a new structure of ad hoc task forces and project teams, a structure described as "*the* most power-ful tool we have for effecting change" (Waterman, 1993, p. 16). Department chairs remained on the bus, but they were no longer driving.

Another concern that can arise when confronting resisters is the human tendency to want positive relationships, particularly with our working col-leagues. The good news is that "the single factor common to every successful change initiative is that relationships improve" (Fullan, 2001, p. 5). The bad news is that conflict is an inevitable by-product of those initiatives, and there will be strains on relationships during the process. It is not uncommon for lead-ers to be vilified at the outset, despite every effort they may have taken to build consensus and to listen to and honor those who opposed the change. Even if the will of the group to go forward is evident, adamant resisters may disparage the leader and the strategies used to arrive at consensus. They may say, "She manip-ulated the process. People are really opposed but were intimidated because they knew she wanted to do it. The dialogue was a farce. She dismissed counter argu-ments without considering them. She is just attempting to use us to make a name for herself so she can climb the administrative ladder."

In his Pulitzer Prize–winning book on leadership, James McGregor Burns (1978) offered advice to those faced with this dilemma: "No matter how strong the yearning for unanimity . . . [leaders] must settle for far less than universal affection. . . . They must accept conflict. They must be willing and able to be unloved" (p. 34). The recognition that they will not be universally loved despite their best efforts may trouble leaders initially; however, once they come to accept that truth, it can be quite liberating.

We have seen schools and districts held hostage by a few recalcitrant staff members who veto any attempt to move forward, but that situation can only occur when leaders allow it. As Jonathon Saphier (2005) wrote, "Day after day in schools across America, change initiatives, instructional improvement, and bet-ter results for children are blocked, sabotaged, or killed through silence and inac-tion . . . this lack of follow-through results from the avoidance or inability to face conflict openly and make it a creative source of energy among educators" (p. 37).

English philosopher Edmund Burke once observed, "The only thing necessary for the triumph of evil is for good men to do nothing." In no way do we mean to suggest that those unwilling to consider more effective ways to meet the needs of students are evil. Often they are good people who have been burned too many times by initiatives launched with enthusiasm only to be quickly abandoned. We do, however, think a paraphrase of Burke is appropriate: All that is necessary for the triumph of those who resist school improvement is for educational leaders to do nothing.

All that is necessary for the triumph of those who resist school improvement is for educational leaders to do nothing.

Leaders who face a scenario similar to the one described in this chapter must be unequivocal in confronting the problem and demanding change. Daniel Goleman is an ardent advocate of the importance of emotional intelligence, a concept anchored, in part, in the critical significance of skillful relationship building characterized by high levels of empathy for others. Yet even Goleman (1998) advises:

> Persuasion, consensus building, and all the other arts of influence don't always do the job. Sometimes it simply comes down to using the power of one's position to get people to act. A common failing of leaders from supervisors to top executives is the failure to be *emphatically assertive* [italics added] when necessary. (p. 190)

Part Four
Assessing Your Place on the PLC Journey

The PLC Continuum

Working individually and quietly, review the following continuum of a school's progress on the PLC journey (page 178). Which point on the continuum gives the most accurate description of the current reality of your school or district? Be prepared to support your assessment with evidence and anecdotes.

After working individually, share your assessment with colleagues. Where do you have agreement? Where do you find discrepancies in the assessments? Listen to the rationales of others in support of their varying assessments. Are you able to reach agreement?

Where Do We Go From Here?

The challenge confronting a school that has engaged in the collective consideration of a topic is answering the questions, "So what?" and, "What, if anything, are we prepared to do differently?" Now consider each indicator of a professional learning community described in the left column of the Where Do We Go From Here? Worksheet on page 179, and then answer the questions listed at the top of the remaining four columns.

The Professional Learning Community Continuum

Element of a PLC	Pre-Initiation Stage	Initiation Stage	Developing Stage	Sustaining Stage
Responding to Conflict in a PLC	People react to conflict with classic flight or fight responses. Most staff members withdraw from interactions in order to avoid those they find disagreeable. Others are perpetually at war in acrimonious, unproductive arguments that never seem to get resolved. People seem more interested in winning arguments than in resolving differences. Groups tend to regard each other as adversaries.	School and district leaders take steps to resolve conflict as quickly as possible. Addressing conflict is viewed as an administrative responsibility. The primary objective of administrators in addressing disputes is to restore the peace.	Staff members have created norms or protocols to help them identify and address the underlying issues causing conflict. Members are encouraged to explore their positions and the fundamental assumptions that have led them to their positions. They attempt to use a few key, guiding principles to assist them in coming to closure.	Staff members view conflict as a source of creative energy and an opportunity for building shared knowledge. They create specific strategies for exploring one another's thinking, and they make a conscious effort to understand as well as to be understood. They seek ways to test competing assumptions through action research and are willing to re-think their position when research, data, and information contradict their suppositions. Because they have found common ground on their purpose and priorities, they are able to approach disagreements with high levels of trust and an assumption of good intentions on the part of all members.

Where Do We Go From Here? Worksheet
Building Consensus and Responding to Resistance

Describe one or more aspects of a professional learning community that you would like to see in place in your school.	What steps or activities must be initiated to create this condition in your school?	Who will be responsible for initiating or sustaining these steps or activities?	What is a realistic timeline for each step or phase of the activity?	What will you use to assess the effectiveness of your initiative?
Members of our staff have identified specific strategies for resolving conflict and practice those strategies to become more proficient. Members of our staff seek ways to test competing assumptions through action research and are willing to re-think their position when research, data, and information contradict their suppositions. Members of our staff are able to approach disagreements with high levels of trust and an assumption of good intentions on the part of all members because they have found common ground in their purpose and priorities.				

Part Five
Tips for Moving Forward: Building Consensus and Responding to Resistance

 Teach and practice skills for dealing with conflict.

 Ask teams to apply Senge's strategies for inquiry and advocacy (presented in chapter 5) to a current issue that is not laden with emotion. For example, a team could consider, "Should we keep minutes of our team meetings?" Debrief at the end of the exercise. What did we observe? What did we learn? How did we feel? Did we stay with the strategy? When would it be appropriate to use? How could we use it more effectively?

 Ask teams to role-play a situation regarding a more volatile issue using the crucial conversation strategies we presented in this chapter. Once again, debrief at the end of the exercise.

 Visit the Crucial Skills web site (www.vitalsmarts.com) and click on "Free Stuff" to get free video clips and role-play exercises for crucial conversations.

 Create cues you can use to refocus when participants seem to be resorting to fight or flight. Signal timeout or simply ask, "Are we moving away from dialogue?"

 Remember that facts are the required homework for any crucial conversation. What are the facts you can bring to the dialogue?

 Build shared knowledge when faced with contrasting positions. Seek agreement on what research or evidence could help lead you to a more informed conclusion.

 Use action research to explore differences. Create strategies that allow participants to put their theories to the test.

 Recognize that conflicts are more productive when members have found common ground on major issues and approach one another with an assumption of good intentions.

Remember that you are attempting to develop new skills that will require practice. As Patterson, Grenny, McMillan, and Switzler advise, "Don't expect perfection; aim for progress" (p. 228).

Be tender with one another.

(continued)

Part Six
Questions to Guide the Work of Your Professional Learning Community

To Assess the Climate for Creating Consensus and Responding to Resistance in Your School or District, Ask:

1. What evidence do we have that district goals are directly impacting the work of schools and collaborative teams within the school?

   _____

   _____

2. Do we have an operational definition of consensus in our school? Do we know at what point in the decision-making process we will move forward with an initiative?

   _____

   _____

3. Do we have a sense of what decisions require consensus? When do we want to involve all staff in the decision-making process? Who decides who decides?

   _____

   _____

4. Should individual members of our staff be permitted to disregard agreements we have made as a staff? What is the appropriate response if they do?

   _____

   _____

5. Identify a conflict that has emerged in our school in the past. How was that conflict addressed?

   _____

   _____

6. Are we building shared knowledge and conducting action research in an effort to address conflict productively? Can we cite an example in which we resolved a difference of opinion through examining the research or conducting our own action research?

   _____

   _____

7. Describe the process we currently use to resolve conflict. What skills could we identify and practice to become more effective in this important area?

_____

_____

8. Do we view conflict as something to be avoided?

_____

_____

9. Do we expect administrators to resolve conflict or do we work together to address it in ways that improve our effectiveness?

_____

_____

10. Are we developing our skills to hold crucial conversations? (For a free team assessment tool, go to www.vitalsmarts.com/CrucialSkills/FreeStuff and click on "Where Do You Stand.")

_____

_____

11. Do we have a common understanding of our purpose—learning for all—and of our priorities, our goals, and our expectations of one another that are aligned with that purpose? Does this shared understanding allow us to be open with each other? Do we operate with an assumption of the good intentions of our members?

_____

_____

Final Thoughts

Educational leaders who make a good faith effort to implement every suggestion presented in the preceding chapters will nevertheless confront a brutal fact: Leading a substantive change process, one that impacts the very culture of the organization, is a complex and often bewildering endeavor. Chapter 9 examines what we have come to understand about the change process in schools and school districts.

Chapter 9

The Complex Challenge of Creating Professional Learning Communities

John Gardner (1988) once observed that "the impulse of most leaders is much the same today as it was a thousand years ago: accept the system as it is and lead it" (p. 24). Those who hope to serve in any leadership capacity in building PLCs must overcome that impulse. They must help people break free of the thicket of precedent, the tangle of unquestioned assumptions, and the trap of comfortable complacency. Their task is not only to help people throughout the organization acquire the knowledge and skills to solve the intractable challenges of today, but also to develop their capacity and confidence to tackle the unforeseen challenges that will emerge in the future. No program, no textbook, no curriculum, no technology will be sufficient to meet this challenge. Educators will remain the most important resource in the battle to provide every child with a quality education, and thus leaders must commit to creating the conditions in which those educators can continue to grow and learn as professionals.

We use the term *leaders* here in an inclusive sense that goes far beyond administrators. Throughout this book we have referenced many leadership roles for teachers: as member of a guiding coalition, participants on task forces, team leaders, and informal leaders who exert their authority through their expertise and character rather than their position. We also include, of course, those who are formally placed into positions of leadership: superintendents, principals, department chairpeople, district coordinators, and so on. Widely dispersed leadership is essential in building and sustaining PLCs, and it is important that individuals at all levels lead effectively.

We acknowledge that the challenge of leading effectively is formidable. Most efforts to improve schools tinker at the edge of existing practice. A new program may be added, but everything else in the structure and culture of the school remains much the same. But as Andy Hargreaves (2004) observed, "A

The choice facing educators is not, "Shall we do the easy work of maintaining traditional schools or the difficult work of creating a PLC?" The real issue is to assess honestly which kind of hard work offers the greatest hope for success for students and professional satisfaction for educators. We have always worked hard. Will we now choose to work smart?

professional learning community is an ethos that infuses every single aspect of a school's operation. When a school becomes a professional learning community, everything in the school looks different than before" (p. 48).

When a school moves from traditional practice to create a PLC, it undergoes a seismic cultural shift. On pages 187–189 we offer a brief review of the shifts we have referenced in this book.

There is a corollary to Hargreaves' observation that becoming a PLC "changes everything": It also changes everyone. Every educator—every teacher, counselor, principal, central office staff member, and superintendent—will be called upon to re-define his or her role and responsibilities. People comfortable working in isolation will be asked to work collaboratively. People accustomed to hording authority will be asked to share it. People who have operated under certain assumptions their entire careers will be asked to change them.

In their comprehensive study of school leadership, Marzano, Waters, and McNulty (2005) distinguish between first-order and second-order change. The former is incremental, representing the next step on an established path and operating within existing paradigms. The change can be implemented by utilizing the existing knowledge and skills of the staff. The goal of first-order change is to help us get better at what we are already doing. Second-order change, however, is a dramatic departure from the expected and familiar. It is perceived as a break from the past, is inconsistent with existing paradigms, may seem to be at conflict with prevailing practices and norms, and will require the acquisition of new knowledge and new skills (p. 113). The goal of second-order change is to modify the very culture of the organization and the assumptions, expectations, habits, roles, relationships, and norms that make up that culture. Transforming schools into PLCs demands second-order change, and engaging in second-order change is particularly problematic.

Finally, what we advocate in this book is not a program, but an *ongoing, never-ending* process specifically designed to change the very culture of schools and districts. Educators are accustomed to a predictable cycle of initiatives with short life spans, launched with fanfare and promises, only to be buffeted by confusion, concerns, criticisms, and complaints, until ultimately drowning in despair. Educators are very familiar with *initiating* change, but the idea of a process that continues forever is foreign to them.

There is only one conclusion that can be drawn about a transformation that changes everything, changes everyone, represents a departure from the familiar, demands the acquisition of new skills, and continues forever: This transformation requires substantive change—real change—and *real change is real hard!*

What we advocate in this book is not a program, but an *ongoing, never-ending* process specifically designed to change the very culture of schools and districts.

(continued on page 190)

Cultural Shifts in a Professional Learning Community

A Shift in Fundamental Purpose

From a focus on teaching . . .	to a focus on learning
From emphasis on what was taught . . .	to a fixation on what students learned
From coverage of content . . .	to demonstration of proficiency
From providing individual teachers with curriculum documents such as state standards and curriculum guides . . .	to engaging collaborative teams in building shared knowledge regarding essential curriculum

A Shift in Use of Assessments

From infrequent summative assessments . . .	to frequent common formative assessments
From assessments to determine which students failed to learn by the deadline . . .	to assessments to identify students who need additional time and support
From assessments used to reward and punish students . . .	to assessments used to inform and motivate students
From assessing many things infrequently . . .	to assessing a few things frequently
From individual teacher assessments . . .	to assessments developed jointly by collaborative teams
From each teacher determining the criteria to be used in assessing student work . . .	to collaborative teams clarifying the criteria and ensuring consistency among team members when assessing student work
From an over-reliance on one kind of assessment . . .	to balanced assessments
From focusing on average scores . . .	to monitoring each student's proficiency in every essential skill

A Shift in the Response When Students Don't Learn

From individual teachers determining the appropriate response . . .	to a systematic response that ensures support for every student
From fixed time and support for learning . . .	to time and support for learning as variables
From remediation . . .	to intervention
From invitational support outside of the school day . . .	to directed (that is, required) support occurring during the school day
From one opportunity to demonstrate learning . . .	to multiple opportunities to demonstrate learning

(continued)

Cultural Shifts in a PLC (continued)

A Shift in the Work of Teachers

From isolation . . .	to collaboration
From each teacher clarifying what students must learn . . .	to collaborative teams building shared knowledge and understanding about essential learning
From each teacher assigning priority to different learning standards . . .	to collaborative teams establishing the priority of respective learning standards
From each teacher determining the pacing of the curriculum . . .	to collaborative teams of teachers agreeing on common pacing
From individual teachers attempting to discover ways to improve results . . .	to collaborative teams of teachers helping each other improve
From privatization of practice . . .	to open sharing of practice
From decisions made on the basis of individual preferences . . .	to decisions made collectively by building shared knowledge of best practice
From "collaboration lite" on matters unrelated to student achievement . . .	to collaboration explicitly focused on issues and questions that most impact student achievement
From an assumption that these are "my kids, those are your kids" . . .	to an assumption that these are "our kids"

A Shift in Focus

From an external focus on issues outside of the school . . .	to an internal focus on steps the staff can take to improve the school
From a focus on inputs . . .	to a focus on results
From goals related to completion of project and activities . . .	to SMART goals demanding evidence of student learning
From teachers gathering data from their individually constructed tests in order to assign grades . . .	to collaborative teams acquiring information from common assessments in order to (1) inform their individual and collective practice, and (2) respond to students who need additional time and support

Cultural Shifts in a PLC (continued)

A Shift in School Culture

From independence . . .	to interdependence
From a language of complaint . . .	to a language of commitment
From long-term strategic planning . . .	to planning for short-term wins
From infrequent generic recognition . . .	to frequent specific recognition and a culture of celebration that creates many winners

A Shift in Professional Development

From external training (workshops and courses) . . .	to job-embedded learning
From the expectation that learning occurs infrequently (on the few days devoted to professional development) . . .	to an expectation that learning is ongoing and occurs as part of routine work practice
From presentations to entire faculties . . .	to team-based action research
From learning by listening . . .	to learning by doing
From learning individually through courses and workshops . . .	to learning collectively by working together
From assessing impact on the basis of teacher satisfaction ("Did you like it?") . . .	to assessing impact on the basis of evidence of improved student learning
From short-term exposure to multiple concepts and practices . . .	to sustained commitment to limited, focused initiatives

Confronting the Brutal Facts of Substantive Change

Those who hope to transform their schools and districts into PLCs should heed the advice of Jim Collins (2001): "You absolutely cannot make a series of good decisions without first confronting the brutal facts" (p. 70). The first and most brutal fact that must be confronted in creating PLCs is that the task is not merely challenging; it is daunting. It is disingenuous to suggest that the transformation will be easy or to present it with a rosy optimism that obscures the inevitable turmoil ahead.

The recommendations we present throughout this book are grounded in solid research from a number of different fields. We can point to schools throughout North America who have successfully implemented the recommendations. And as we stated at the outset, the most frequent reaction of those who attend our workshops is, "This just makes sense." But the fact that a concept is backed by research, evidence, and logic does not mean it will be embraced by those who are called upon to abandon the comfort and security of their known practices in order to implement that concept.

The response to any significant change is typically not logical; it is emotional. In examining the psychology of change, Robert Evans (1996) found that even when change is recognized as positive, it is accompanied by a sense of loss and causes a kind of bereavement. We are more prone to protect the assumptions that have guided us than to re-examine them because those assumptions have provided us with a sense of identity; they have helped us make sense of our world. Therefore, we are likely to react defensively if our assumptions are called into question. Change also challenges our competence. When we are called upon to develop new proficiencies (for example, to become a contributing member of a collaborative team), we are likely to feel the anxiety that accompanies moving outside our comfort zone. Change creates confusion. The clarity and predictability of the status quo are replaced by uncertainty. Change can open old wounds and rekindle lingering resentment from those who committed to previous innovations only to see them abandoned or from those whose own calls for change about which they cared deeply were ignored by others (Evans, 1996).

Finally and inescapably, substantive change creates conflict. When schools are engaged in second-order change, staff members may perceive that the culture of their school has been weakened, their opinions are not valued, and that the stability and order of the school have been undermined (Marzano, Waters, & McNulty, 2005). When people are called upon to do differently, it is inevitable that they question why and challenge both the need for and the specifics of the change. It serves no purpose to ignore, obscure, or brush aside these brutal facts. Those who hope to help their schools and districts become PLCs will embrace them, respect them, and most importantly, address them. Recognition of the harsh realities must be a part of any implementation plan.

The Need for Leadership

The current emphasis on shared decision-making, dispersed leadership, staff empowerment, collaboration, and collegiality has tended to obscure another harsh reality about substantive change: It demands the sustained attention, energy, and effort of school and district leaders. The idea of bottom-up reform is great, but it is unrealistic to assume that one day a group of educators gathered together in the faculty lounge will suddenly begin to re-examine the basic assumptions, beliefs, and practices that constitute the culture of their school. Major change almost never begins from the bottom (Evans, 1996). There are examples of departments or grade-level teams who operate according to PLC concepts in a school that does not, but we know of no instances in which a *school-wide* PLC was created and sustained without effective leadership from the principal. Some responsibilities simply cannot be delegated, and at the school level, it is the principal who creates the conditions that allow PLC concepts to flourish (McLaughlin & Talbert, 2001). Conversely, a change as significant as creating a PLC cannot survive a principal's indifference or opposition.

School leaders cannot passively wait for substantive change to "bubble up." They must understand that deep reform will require support *and* pressure. There is a tendency in education to regard support as inherently positive and pressure as intrinsically negative. We have seen educators ask, "Will you support me?" as a litmus test for their leaders, assuming a "good" leader will assure them of unwavering support. Effective leaders, however, will not support ineffective practice, cruel comments, or deliberate violations of collective commitments. In those instances, support would be no virtue. We have also heard from educators who oppose an improvement initiative, regardless of its merits, for one reason: It came from the administration. They expect us to be appalled at the disclosure of a top-down initiative. But top-down leadership has its place. It is far more productive to recognize that effective change processes demand both pressure and support. Effective leaders at both the district and building level must be willing to exert top-down pressure when needed. They will embrace the advice of Robert Evans (1996): "Bottom-up as possible, top-down as necessary" (p. 245).

If leaders allow participation in PLC processes to be optional, they doom the initiative to failure. Piloting a program with interested staff can be a valuable way to build shared knowledge regarding its effectiveness, but substantive change that transforms a culture will ultimately require more than an invitation. The challenging of deep assumptions inherent in changing the culture of a school or district requires leaders to assert their influence, to get and hold people's attention. In short, leaders must be willing to lead.

*Deep reform will require support **and** pressure.*

One of the great ironies in education is that it takes strong and effective educational leaders to create truly empowered people who are capable of sustaining improvement after the leader has gone.

When Jim Collins (2001) set out to determine what distinguished "great" companies from those that were less effective, he made a conscious decision to exclude leadership as a factor because he felt it was simplistic to attribute the success or failure of an organization to its leaders. The empirical evidence, however, brought him to an inescapable conclusion: Every great company was characterized by effective leadership. Furthermore, Collins found that those leaders were not charismatic, flamboyant personalities, but rather self-effacing individuals with a ferocious resolve to make their organizations great and a fanatical fixation on results. Their goal was to build the capacity of their organizations to be successful long after they had retired.

Collins argues that his findings apply not only to the private sector but to other organizations as well—including schools and school districts. We believe he is right, particularly on the significance of leadership. Leaders do not empower teachers by disempowering themselves. Self-directed teams and highly autonomous schools characterized by shared decision-making are important targets toward which to strive. In fact, one of the reasons for becoming a PLC is to lessen the dependency on individual leaders and to build the capacity of staff to sustain a strong culture despite changes in leadership. But these laudable conditions simply cannot occur without key leaders assuming personal responsibility for initiating the process. One of the great ironies in education is that it takes strong and effective educational leaders to create truly empowered people who are capable of sustaining improvement after the leader has gone.

Advice for Leading a PLC Initiative

If, as we have argued thus far, (1) implementing PLC concepts is complex and challenging and (2) it is impossible to meet that challenge without the advocacy and attention of effective leaders, then it is important to explore the most promising leadership strategies. We offer the following insights.

Link the Change Initiative to Current Practices and Assumptions When Possible

Educators are more inclined to support what is presented as evolution rather than revolution. Therefore, leaders should, if possible, attempt to connect an innovation to existing practices and principles. In effect, they should show that the proposal represents a natural next step in the school's ongoing effort to improve results for students. They should be certain to honor rather than demean past efforts and paradigms. The message should be, "We did then what we knew how to do. Now that we know better, we can do better."

Focus First on the "Why" of Change, Then Focus on the "How"

One of the most effective strategies for linking substantive change to the past is demonstrating how the change will advance the articulated purpose of the school. As mentioned previously, virtually all schools and districts have written "mission" statements that solemnly assert the intention to have a profound and positive impact on the lives of the students they serve. In effect, those statements declare that the school is committed to serving a moral purpose. Leaders should return to that purpose, provide evidence that current practices, although well-intentioned, are failing to achieve it, and clarify how the proposed change will enhance the school's ability to achieve the purpose. Fullan (2001) lists "moral purpose" as a critical element in his framework for effective leadership. He argues that leadership, if it is to be effective, has to:

1. Have an explicit "making-a-difference" sense of purpose.

2. Use strategies that mobilize many people to tackle tough problems.

3. Be held accountable by measured and detectable indicators of success.

4. Be ultimately assessed by the extent to which it awakens people's intrinsic commitment, which is none other than the mobilizing of everyone's sense of moral purpose. (pp. 19–20)

"Good leaders lead from something deep in the heart" (Bolman & Deal, 1996, p. 5), and we have found the most effective leaders of PLCs publicly and repeatedly cite their commitment to an overarching purpose. It might be eliminating the achievement gap, breaking the cycle of poverty, responding to the individual needs of each student, expanding access to opportunities, or promoting excellence and equity. This direct appeal to collective purpose calls upon a staff to unite in order to achieve a higher end. Staff may be anxious to hear a detailed explanation of "How?" (knowing the devil is in the details), but leaders should start with and repeatedly return to "Why?" They should create a story with a teachable point of view—a succinct explanation of the school or district's purpose and how the initiative is advancing that purpose—and they should repeat that story with boorish redundancy. They should repeatedly address the idea of "who we are and who we are becoming" because one of the most important tasks of leadership is "to make sure that the organization knows itself" (Wheatley, 1999, p. 156).

Align Actions With Words

Articulating a mission or purpose does nothing to close the knowing-doing gap unless people act upon that mission. Leaders establish personal credibility far more readily by what they do than by what they say. Expressions of commitment to strong moral purpose only generate cynicism if the commitment is not manifested through behavior. If leaders are to be believed they must establish their personal integrity, and "integrity requires action. . . . Authentic leaders embody character in action: they don't just say, they do" (Evans, 1996, p. 90).

Unfocused and undirected action, however, detracts from rather than enhances the clarity and coherence of a leader's communication. Clarity demands focused, sustained attention and consistent direction over time. Building the capacity of staff to work as a PLC represents a *major* initiative, and effective leaders will do everything in their power to protect the staff from other intrusions on their time and energy (Marzano, Waters, & McNulty, 2005). They will demonstrate a fundamental premise of effective leadership: "The main thing is to keep the main thing the main thing" (Covey, 1994).

Be Flexible on Implementation but Firm on the Essence of the Initiative

This is merely another way to call upon leaders to demonstrate loose *and* tight leadership (see chapter 3). There are typically multiple ways to solve a given problem, and leaders should be open to exploring alternative strategies for implementation (Klein, Medrich, & Perez-Ferreiro, 1996). An unwillingness to consider alternative strategies or to amend timelines for implementation will impede rather than enhance the PLC journey. Leaders must be willing to listen and to adapt. There will be battles to fight, but drawing a line in the sand regarding the specifics of implementation is typically the wrong battle.

On the other hand, leaders must hold firm to the core principles that underlie PLC concepts if those concepts are to take root. Imagine a principal who presents her staff with all the evidence in support of PLCs and how the concept is aligned with the school's commitment to high levels of learning for all students. She paints a portrait of a school in which the entire staff works collaboratively to clarify the knowledge, skills, and dispositions each student must acquire in each grade level and unit; to monitor the learning of each student on a timely basis; and to create systematic interventions to ensure students receive additional time and support for learning. She describes teachers working together to examine multiple sources of evidence of student learning and using that evidence as part of a process of continuous improvement. After much dialogue, the faculty achieves consensus to work to create such a school.

As the initiative moves forward, however, staff members begin to propose compromises to expedite the process: "Couldn't we simply use the questions from the textbook to monitor student learning instead of working together to create common assessments?" "Can't an individual teacher opt out of the collaborative team meetings as long as he is getting good results?" "Shouldn't students who fail to demonstrate proficiency suffer the consequences rather than being provided additional opportunities to learn?" "Aren't systematic interventions 'enabling' students?" "Do we really need to examine student achievement data?" Questions like these do not represent issues of implementation or timelines. They get to the very heart of PLC concepts. We are convinced that the most common cause of the demise of PLC initiatives is not the result of a single cataclysmic event, but rather repeated compromises regarding the fundamental premises of PLCs. There is no one fatal blow: PLCs die from a thousand small wounds.

One of the most common small wounds inflicted on a PLC initiative occurs with protestation of the lack of time to implement PLC concepts. We have made the point repeatedly that the process does take time, and we have emphasized that staff members should be provided with time to work at the process during their contractual day and within their contractual year. We recognize the significance of time, but leaders cannot accept scarcity of time as justification for not moving forward. The best thinking in time management boils down to a single principle: "Organize and execute around priorities" (Covey, 1989, p. 149). A principal who alleges she is too busy doing her job to work on building a PLC must be reminded that the very essence of her job is to create the conditions in which a PLC will flourish. A teacher who contends he is too busy teaching to work with colleagues to clarify what students must learn, the methods to be used in monitoring student learning, and the strategies to be implemented when students struggle with their learning must be told such work is critical to the effective teaching process. A counselor who professes she is too busy writing college recommendations to monitor the academic and emotional well-being of her students must be told to redefine her role and her priorities. In each case a sincere attempt can be made to explore options for removing less essential tasks from the staff member's duties in order to address the issue of time, but the work of building a PLC should never be considered an "add on." No one who has worked in schools for any length of time would question whether educators work hard. They do. The challenge for leaders and the key to the success of a school is to ensure they are doing the *right* work (Elmore, 2003). The priority work of effective schools, and the educators within them, is building the collective capacity to function as a PLC.

Build a Guiding Coalition and Move Forward Without Unanimity

We have stressed that leadership is essential to successful implementation of PLCs; however, leadership is not a solo act. In studying thousands of cases of effective leadership, Kouzes and Posner (2003) could not find a single example

We are convinced that the most common cause of the demise of PLC initiatives is not the result of a single cataclysmic event, but rather repeated compromises regarding the fundamental premises of PLCs. There is no one fatal blow: PLCs die from a thousand small wounds.

Leadership is not a solo act.

of extraordinary achievement that occurred without the active involvement and support of many people:

> We've yet to find a single instance in which one talented person—leader or individual contributor—accounted for most, let alone 100 percent, of the success. Throughout the years, leaders from all professions, from all economic sectors, and from around the globe continue to tell us, "You can't do it alone." Leadership . . . is a team performance. . . . The winning strategies will be based on the "we not I" philosophy. Collaboration is a social imperative. Without it people can't get extraordinary things done in organizations. (p. 20)

In his study, Collins (2001) found ineffective organizations tended to operate under the model of one genius leader with lots of helpers. The leaders of effective companies, on the other hand, created a powerful leadership team that energized the improvement effort. Furthermore, the creation of that team came early in the process—often preceding the specific improvement initiative—as leaders focused on getting the "right people on the bus" (p. 41).

Another comprehensive study discovered building a guiding coalition was "an essential part of the early stages" of leading a change process (Kotter, 1998). In creating that coalition, leaders:

1. Recruited partners with broad experience, high credibility, and real leadership skills

2. Expanded the coalition at every opportunity

3. Structured the coalition as a real team rather than as a collection of individuals

Members of the coalition committed to working together interdependently in order to achieve a collective purpose and common goal for which they were mutually accountable.

As we stressed in chapter 8, however, leaders cannot wait for unanimity before moving forward with an improvement process. Because proposals for significant change are certain to generate concerns, leaders must encourage the articulation of those concerns, seek to understand them, and address them honestly. Again, they can acquire important insights from those who challenge their assumptions, reasoning, and proposals. Throughout this book we have offered advice in building consensus, conducting crucial conversations, using the art of persuasion, and implementing strategies to enlist resisters in the initiative. A leader can execute flawlessly every step we have proposed and still experience both overt and covert resistance. This situation does not represent failure on the part of the leader; it represents the reality of substantive change.

We have seen principals who respond to this reality by ignoring the willingness and readiness of a staff to implement PLC concepts in order to devote their effort and energy to convincing a few holdouts of the worthiness of the initiative. In these instances, instead of using shared decision-making and participatory processes as a springboard to action, they allow participation to become a quagmire that prevents action.

A far more effective strategy is for leaders to work with the leadership team to ensure there is a critical mass of people willing to move forward and then to push forward despite the objections of those who are not in favor of doing so. Margaret Mead once observed, "Never doubt that a small group of thoughtful, committed people can change the world. Indeed, it is the only thing that ever has." This power of small groups to have an enormous impact is cited repeatedly in contemporary research. Malcolm Gladwell (2002) refers to the "Law of the Few": the ability of a small close-knit group of people to champion an idea or proposal until it reaches the "tipping point" and spreads like an epidemic throughout the organization. The Law of the Few, critical mass, and tipping points are useful concepts for those who lead PLC initiatives; the quest for unanimity as a prerequisite for action is not.

Expect to Make Mistakes and Learn From Them

Murphy's Law promises, "If anything can go wrong, it will." In reflecting on the problem of school change, psychologist Seymour Sarason (1996) concluded Murphy was an optimist and Murphy's Law was a "gross underestimation. Changing the school culture is conceptually and practically a bewildering, complex affair" (p. 339). Leaders should approach the change process honestly and advise staff that it is unrealistic to expect flawless execution in initial efforts to implement complex concepts. The best-laid plans and noblest of efforts will typically fall short of the desired results, at least initially. Staff must be assured that these setbacks are simply a natural part of the learning process rather than a failure of will or skill. Rather than being branded as failures, setbacks should be viewed as opportunities to begin again, this time with the benefit of greater insight and experience.

If our earliest efforts in technology were regarded as final products rather than first drafts, we would all still be driving model Ts and computers would be stored in warehouses rather than sitting on our laps. Similarly, there is no reason to believe first efforts to transform a school will lead to spectacular results. Resilient leaders will celebrate effort, learning, and progress even when things do not go well, but they will also immediately start to think about how they can make the situation better (Goleman, 1998). Their resilience allows them to accept criticism, acknowledge setbacks, and welcome recommendations for

Setbacks should be viewed as opportunities to begin again, this time with the benefit of greater insight and experience.

"The answer to the knowing-doing problem is deceptively simple: *embed more of the process of acquiring new knowledge in the actual doing of the task* and less in the formal training programs that are frequently ineffective. If you do it, then you will know it."
(Pfeffer & Sutton, 2000, p. 27)

alternative strategies for achieving shared purpose at the same time they remain optimistic about the final outcome. They keep the faith.

Learn by Doing

One of the most common traps that prevent organizations from closing the knowing-doing gap is reliance upon learning by training rather than learning by doing. As Pfeffer and Sutton (2000) concluded, "The answer to the knowing-doing problem is deceptively simple: *embed more of the process of acquiring new knowledge in the actual doing of the task* [italics added] and less in the formal training programs that are frequently ineffective. If you do it, then you will know it" (p. 27).

The learning by doing characterized by an action orientation is a critical factor in both organizations in general and schools in particular (Bennis, 1997; Block, 2003; Collins & Porras, 1997; Elmore, 2003). Yet we have seen schools devote years of training to becoming a PLC according to elaborate improvement plans. The first year may be devoted to helping staff learn to work in teams through training in consensus building, conflict resolution, and norm writing. The second year may be devoted to examining and rewriting curriculum. In the third year, staff are trained in writing good assessments, in the fourth staff learn how to analyze data from assessments, and so on. Meanwhile, as they are *preparing* to become a PLC, other schools roll up their sleeves and dig into the work of PLCs. They learn by doing and they build community by doing the work together (Fullan, 2001; McLaughlin & Talbert, 2001). As questions arise, appropriate training is provided to help staff resolve the questions as part of their ongoing process. Schools make the most progress on the PLC journey when they demonstrate an action orientation.

When we wrote *Professional Learning Communities at Work™*, we made a conscious decision to emphasize *work* in order to stress the importance of an action orientation in PLCs. We didn't refer to "PLCs at training," "PLCs at study," "PLCs at reading," or "PLCs at staff development." Now that we have had the opportunity to work with school systems throughout North America, we are more convinced than ever that schools develop as PLCs when their staffs actually *work* at the process rather than train for the process.

Pfeffer and Sutton (2000) contend that most organizations already have all the knowledge they need to improve—they simply do not implement what they already know. What those organizations typically require to move forward is more will than skill. As Peter Block wrote, "We deny ourselves action when we keep looking for more and more information to ensure greater certainty as a condition for moving on" (p. 42). Those who hope to lead PLCs should stop waiting for more training, more knowledge, and more skills, and instead create the conditions that enable staff members to learn by doing.

Keep Hope Alive

Even the most powerful vision of a better future will inspire people to act only if they have a strong sense of self-efficacy, the belief that they can create their future through their own purposeful actions. Fostering this self-efficacy by helping people to believe in themselves is one of a leader's highest duties (Gardner, 1988). This responsibility is particularly important in building a PLC because the concept rests upon the premise that the best way to improve the school or district is by developing the people within it. Leaders of PLCs must consistently communicate, through their words and actions, their conviction that the people in their school or district are capable of accomplishing great things through their collective efforts. Conventional wisdom asks if people in an organization believe in their leaders. While that question is significant, the question, "Do the leaders believe in their people?" may be even more relevant to the successful implementation of PLC concepts.

Leaders of PLCs must consistently communicate, through their words and actions, their conviction that the people in their school or district are capable of accomplishing great things through their collective efforts.

We are arguing here that leaders must not only personally keep the faith; they must also foster hope throughout the organization. In fact, Evans (1996) argues, "Of all the factors vital to improving schools, none is more essential— or vulnerable—than hope" (p. 290). Alexander Pope was wrong. Hope does not "spring eternal in the human breast"; it is a fragile emotion that can be easily eroded and destroyed.

Hope is more than sunny optimism. It is the conviction that you have both the will and the way to accomplish your goals, whatever they might be (Snyder, Harris, Anderson, & Holleran, 1991). People with hope do not succumb to a defeatist attitude in the face of challenges or setbacks. They are able to motivate themselves, to reassure themselves when confronted with obstacles, to break down formidable tasks into smaller steps, and to find different ways of achieving their objectives when initial strategies do not generate the desired results.

Most importantly, hope and self-efficacy are not simply innate; they can be learned, and the leader is in the key position to teach those emotions. Psychologist Daniel Goleman (2002) concluded that the passion, energy, enthusiasm, and self-efficacy of the leader are contagious, invigorating people throughout the organization. Fullan (2001) also found that the most effective leaders conveyed an optimism, confidence, and determination to persevere that were infectious. A comprehensive review of the research on the principalship found that principals, for better or worse, set the emotional tone of their building, and that one of the most significant responsibilities of the principal was "portraying a positive attitude about the ability of the staff to accomplish substantive things" (Marzano, Waters, & McNulty, 2005, p. 56).

Hope burns brightest in those who believe in their ability to impact the future. Leaders of learning communities will keep hope alive in their schools and districts by modeling that belief and calling upon all staff to do the same.

Cynics, pessimists, and those who do not believe in the ability of their colleagues make poor leaders. Communicating confidence and hopefulness in good times is important in any organization, but demonstrating confidence and hopefulness in trying times is imperative. This imperative is only heightened in schools where the collective efficacy of a staff is a better predictor of student success than the socioeconomic status of the students (Goddard, Hoy, & Hoy, 1994). For the sake of their students, teachers *need* to believe that their collective efforts can make a difference.

During our workshops we sometimes ask participants which students they would prefer in their classrooms next fall: those who believe their achievement is strictly a function of their ability or those who believe that their achievement will be determined largely by their effort. Invariably the entire group opts for students who believe in effort-based ability, students who are convinced that "smart is not something you just are; smart is something you can get" (Efficacy Institute, 2005). Educators have good reason to make that choice, given the well-established link between a student's sense of self-efficacy and his or her academic achievement. The next question we pose is, "If we want students to believe in effort-based ability, aren't we obligated to model the principle of effort-based ability ourselves? Shouldn't we demonstrate a core belief that our collective efforts as a staff can have a tremendous impact on the learning of our students?" Hope burns brightest in those who believe in their ability to impact the future. Leaders of learning communities will keep hope alive in their schools and districts by modeling that belief and calling upon all staff to do the same.

Passion and Persistence

But is there any reason to be hopeful given the state of education in North America today when schools are bashed by critics from all sides and publicly branded as failures as part of a punitive accountability system? Do PLC concepts have the potential to generate hope in the face of such challenges? We are convinced the answer to both questions is, "Yes!" We addressed those issues in the concluding chapter of *Professional Learning Communities at Work™*. We are more certain than ever that what we presented in that chapter remains valid, and we will conclude this book by reiterating and building upon what we wrote then.

Creating a PLC is not advancing through a checklist of tasks to be accomplished: It is a passionate, nonlinear, and persistent endeavor. The process is most successful when it taps into the wellsprings of emotion within the professionals of the school or district. Therefore, leaders of the process must make a conscious effort to bring those emotions to the surface and express explicitly what often is left unsaid. As John Gardner (1988) wrote:

> One of the deepest truths about the cry of the human heart is that it
> is so often muted, so often a cry that is never uttered. To be sure

> there are needs and feelings that we express quite openly; lying deeper are emotions we share only with loved ones, and deeper still the things we tell no one. . . . It is strange that members of a species renowned for communicative gifts should leave unexpressed some of their deepest yearnings. (p. 6)

Creating a PLC is not advancing through a checklist of tasks to be accomplished: It is a passionate, nonlinear, and persistent endeavor.

Psychologists have sought to discover those unspoken yearnings people hope will be addressed in their lives and in their work. They found a basic human desire to feel successful in one's work, to believe we are good at what we do. It is difficult to address this need in the world of traditional schools with the steady drumbeat of accusations that schools are failing our students and our society. Furthermore, teachers have little opportunity to discover their strengths. While interviewing a high school physics teacher who had been teaching for 20 years, Rick asked a straightforward question: "What evidence do you have that you have been a successful teacher?" After a long pause, the teacher replied:

> I have no evidence, nothing I can point to. To be honest, I don't know if my students learned more about physics than students taught by other teachers in our school or other teachers in our state. Occasionally a former student will tell me my course helped him or her in college, but I really cannot provide any substantive evidence of my effectiveness.

The fact that a veteran teacher, someone who had worked at his craft for 20 years, had no basis for identifying his strengths and weaknesses is profoundly sad, but it is commonplace in our profession. Most teachers have no basis of comparison that allows them to celebrate strengths or make progress on weaknesses. Furthermore, the lack of agreement about what students must learn; the disparities in the way students are assessed; the different criteria used to judge the quality of their work; the focus on summative assessments that rob teachers of timely feedback; and the lack of specific, measurable, results-oriented goals that impact classroom practice all make it difficult for educators to address, much less satisfy, the need to feel successful at their work. Traditional schools have simply not been organized to address that need.

So PLCs make a conscious and sustained effort to create the conditions that allow educators to become more skillful in their profession. They engage the staff in ensuring clarity regarding exactly what students must learn and be able to do. They make certain staff members understand how students will be assessed and the criteria that will be used in judging the quality of student work. They provide teachers with timely, ongoing feedback regarding the progress of each student so teachers can discover who is learning and who is having difficulty. They create support systems to ensure students receive additional time and support outside of the regular classroom but during the school day.

Professional learning communities ensure that each teacher gets timely feedback regarding the learning of his or her students *in comparison to other students* who are striving to meet the same outcomes so that every teacher can identify strengths and weaknesses in their instruction. They provide all staff members with systematic access to colleagues and well-defined processes so that they can learn from each other. They set specific, measurable, attainable, results-oriented, and timebound goals for every team so that every professional is monitoring and measuring improvement. And they *celebrate*: They plan for short-term wins and honor individuals and teams for effort, progress, and achievement. They ensure that everyone on the staff hears the repeated message, "We are getting better, individually and collectively, at the important job of ensuring learning for every student." Members of effective PLCs are reminded—in a conscious, deliberate, ongoing way—that they are becoming more and more successful at their work.

There is also an innate human desire to belong, to connect, to be a part of a collective endeavor that is larger than oneself. As Mahatma Gandhi observed, "Interdependence is and ought to be as much the ideal of man as self-sufficiency. Man is a social being." The need for connection with others demands more than proximity. Connection means mutual caring and mutual support. Once again, this desire is typically not addressed in the "lonely profession" because schools have been structured to promote isolation rather than collaboration. Teachers can work in close proximity to one another yet remain professionally and emotionally isolated, year after year. Professional learning communities tear down those walls of isolation and purposefully create interdependent relationships. They ensure that everyone on the staff has a well-defined support system, and colleagues to lean on and learn from.

Above all else, there is a basic human desire to live a life of meaning, to serve a higher purpose, to make a difference in this world. It has been argued that this search for meaning, for significance, is the primary force in human life (Frankl, 1959). It is the desire to make a difference in the lives of students that continues to be the single most powerful factor cited by those entering the teaching profession. The most striking finding in a nonpartisan national survey of new teachers was their passion for teaching—a passion fueled by their fervent desire to make a difference for their students. Teaching was a conscious choice for them, a response to a calling. Only 12% indicated that they fell into the profession by chance, and the zeal of the new teachers for their work far exceeded their contemporaries who entered the private sector (Farkas, Johnson, Foleno, Duffett, & Foley, 2000).

Most of those same enthusiastic teachers soon discovered, however, that they were ill equipped to deal with issues such as classroom management, inspiring unmotivated students, and meeting the needs of struggling students. Within a short period of time, almost 75% doubted whether the efforts of a staff could transform a low-performing school. They attributed problems they were encountering to circumstances beyond their control and doubted their ability to make things better. When pressed for what they might do to improve their situation, they proposed finding a school with more motivated students and more supportive parents as their best alternative. In a very short time, the passion and fervor of these new teachers and their desire to make a difference began to be eroded by a collective sense of resignation and helplessness (Farkas, Johnson, Foleno, Duffett, & Foley, 2000).

Professional learning communities set out to restore and increase the passion of teachers by not only reminding them of the moral purpose of their work, but also by creating the conditions that allow them to do that work successfully. The focus is on making a positive difference in the lives of kids rather than on raising test scores. There is constant emphasis that the staff must work collectively, as a community, if they are to meet the needs of students because they cannot adequately respond to students if they work in isolation. Leaders provide constant reminders of the impact teachers and teams are having on the lives of students. They make heroes of staff members by weaving a never-ending story of committed people who touch both the minds and hearts of their students.

Those who regard these direct appeals to emotions as too "touchy-feely" for the "bottom-line" mentality that should drive results-oriented schools are mistaken. Daniel Goleman (2002) presents a compelling argument that "great leadership works through the emotions" (p. 3). Educators hunger for evidence that they are successful in their work, that they are part of a significant collective endeavor, and that their efforts are making a positive difference in the lives of the students they serve. By addressing these emotional needs, the PLC concept offers the most promising hope for sustained and substantive school improvement.

There is another reason for hope when approaching the challenge of building a PLC. George Bernard Shaw wrote, "The true joy of life is being used for a purpose recognized by yourself as a mighty one." When that purpose is shared and pursued jointly with others, the joy is only magnified.

Those who have succeeded in developing PLCs attest to the energy and enthusiasm—the joy—generated by committed people working together, sharing ideas, and accomplishing goals they value. Fullan (2001) found that once teachers begin to experience the benefits of a PLC, "they literally can't get enough of it" (p. 99). In her study of schools characterized by shared purpose, collaborative teams, data-driven decisions, and job-embedded learning, Joan Richardson (2004) found faculties infused with passion and benefiting from powerful, positive relationships. Some of the ways they described their working environment appear on page 204.

Professional learning communities set out to restore and increase the passion of teachers by not only reminding them of the moral purpose of their work, but also by creating the conditions that allow them to do that work successfully.

What Faculties Are Saying . . .

"There is something about this place that is just kind of magical." (p. 20)

"I feel supported here. My colleagues are loyal to me and I feel loyal to them. . . . What we do works, and it works better every year." (p. 57)

"We are set up to be successful. . . . I think if we couldn't work together like this, we would just wither up and die." (p. 106)

"The best graduate course you could ever take is working at this school." (p. 113)

"In this school you are able to draw on an awful lot of expertise." (p. 124)

"Teaching at this school is a better experience than I could have ever hoped for. . . . It is amazing." (p. 125)

"People share what they have because they want to be better. It's a culture in which everyone really wants to succeed because they want the school to succeed." (p. 126)

High school faculties are notorious for their recalcitrance, but in their study of high schools, McLaughlin and Talbert (2001) found that even teachers at the high school level were energized and renewed by the power of working in PLCs: "In collaborative professional communities teachers experience careers marked by collective accomplishments and a sense of continuing professional growth" (p. 91). Teachers in those schools offered the observations on page 205.

Particularly striking in McLaughlin and Talbert's study were the sharply differing perspectives and attitudes of teachers in two different departments *in the same school*—departments that were close in physical proximity but miles apart in terms of their cultures. The English department was organized into collaborative teams while social studies teachers worked in isolation. English teachers raved about their relationship with their colleagues, while social studies teachers complained bitterly about others in their department. English teachers attacked problems collectively. Social studies teachers worried alone. English teachers were uniformly positive regarding their students, describing them as "excellent," "bright," and "cooperative." They responded to students who experienced academic difficulties by assigning them to an "intensive care" list to receive additional support. Social studies teachers considered the same students unmotivated and apathetic and offered no response to students who struggled.

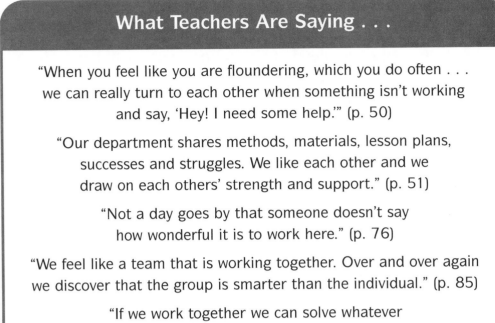

What Teachers Are Saying . . .

"When you feel like you are floundering, which you do often . . . we can really turn to each other when something isn't working and say, 'Hey! I need some help.'" (p. 50)

"Our department shares methods, materials, lesson plans, successes and struggles. We like each other and we draw on each others' strength and support." (p. 51)

"Not a day goes by that someone doesn't say how wonderful it is to work here." (p. 76)

"We feel like a team that is working together. Over and over again we discover that the group is smarter than the individual." (p. 85)

"If we work together we can solve whatever problems we have." (p. 88)

English teachers expressed pride in their department and pleasure in their work. They felt they were becoming more competent, more professional, and more successful. Social studies teachers, unsupported in their fractured department, were bitter regarding the diminished rewards of the profession and sought opportunities to escape it.

Creating the culture of a PLC is indeed hard work; however, what is the alternative? Teaching in isolation in traditional schools is also very hard work, and the teachers in the social studies department in the McLaughlin and Talbert study were feeling worn down by the demands being placed upon them. The choice facing educators is not, "Shall we do the easy work of maintaining traditional schools or the difficult work of creating a PLC?" The real issue is to assess honestly which kind of hard work offers the greatest hope for success for students and for professional satisfaction for educators. We have always worked hard. Will we now choose to work smart? The path to school improvement has never been clearer. We know what to do, but will we demonstrate the discipline to do it? Will we close the knowing-doing gap by taking purposeful action because, at long last, we acknowledge that "to *know* and not to *do* is really not to know" (Covey, 2002, p. xiv)?

And will we act with the sense of urgency the situation demands when considering the impact on the lives of students if we continue with ineffective practices and school cultures that are inhospitable to the concept of learning for all despite the assertions of our mission statements? The words Martin Luther

*Will we close the knowing-doing gap by taking purposeful action because, at long last, we acknowledge that "to **know** and not to **do** is really not to know" (Covey, 2002, p. xiv)?*

King, Jr., used in 1967 to describe a different desperate situation ring true for educators today:

> We are confronted with the fierce urgency of now. In this unfolding conundrum of life and history there is such a thing as being too late. Procrastination is still the thief of time. We must move past indecision to action. Now let us begin. The choice is ours, and though we may prefer it otherwise, we must choose in this crucial moment of human history. (2001, p. 163)

Many who work through this handbook will endorse this call for action, will agree that something needs to be done, and then will wait for someone else to do it. There is a natural tendency to assign responsibility for improving schools to others. We have heard principals say, "I hope the central office heard your message and is prepared to do something about it," ignoring the fact that individual schools have become powerful PLCs without support from the central office. We have heard teachers say, "I sure hope the principal will take responsibility for implementing what you advocate," ignoring the fact that individual departments and grade-level teams have become islands representing powerful PLCs in schools that seem indifferent to the concept. Perhaps, as Michael Fullan (2005b) argues, the effort to create PLCs should be a tri-level effort involving the state or province, the district, and the individual school and community working in consort. But Fullan also warns it is a fundamental mistake to assume the system must change before we do. As he writes, "Each of us *is* the system" (p. 222), and therefore each of us must recognize his or her personal and individual responsibility to promote PLC concepts. Here is the brutal fact: The most common reason for failure to close the knowing-doing gap is not conflict with others, but conflict from within. We fail to do what we recognize we should do simply because it is easier to continue an unquestionably ineffective or bad practice than it is to adopt a new one. The ultimate challenge is not to manage others; the challenge is to manage ourselves and to demonstrate, day-by-day, the self-discipline to "put first things first" (Covey, 1989, p. 148).

Final Thoughts

This book has attempted to address some of the structural and cultural challenges of schooling that prevent schools and districts from making progress as professional learning communities. We have attempted to draw upon research from organizational development, education, leadership, psychology, and sociology to suggest alternative strategies for dealing with those challenges. Once again, however, it is not a "how to" book. The history, cultures, and contexts of each school and district are unique and must be considered in the improvement process. Furthermore, challenges to education will arise in the coming years that this book could not possibly anticipate. We remain convinced, however, that when educators learn to clarify their priorities, to assess the current reality of their situation, to work together, and to build continuous improvement into the very fabric of their collective work, they create conditions for the ongoing learning and self-efficacy essential to solving whatever problems they confront. We hope every school or district that begins the PLC journey will come to believe deeply in and, more importantly, act upon the advice attributed to Ralph Waldo Emerson: "What lies behind us and what lies ahead of us are insignificant compared to what lies within us."

Appendix

Developing Norms

Comments to the Facilitator: This activity will enable a group to develop a set of operating norms or ground rules. In existing groups, anonymity will help ensure that everyone is able to express their ideas freely. For this reason, it is essential to provide pens or pencils or to ask that everyone use the same type of writing implement.

Supplies: Index cards, pens or pencils, poster paper, display board, tape, tacks

Time: Two hours

Directions

1. Explain to the group that effective groups generally have a set of norms that govern individual behavior, facilitate the work of the group, and enable the group to accomplish its task.

2. Provide examples of norms by posting the list of norms that appears on page 212.

3. Recommend to the group that it establish a set of norms:

    - To ensure that all individuals have the opportunity to contribute in the meeting;

    - To increase productivity and effectiveness; and

    - To facilitate the achievement of its goals.

4. Give five index cards and the same kind of writing tool to each person in the group.

5. Ask each person to reflect on and record behaviors they consider ideal behaviors for a group. Ask them to write one idea on each of their cards. Time: 10 minutes.

6. Shuffle all the cards together. Every effort should be made to provide anonymity for individuals, especially if the group has worked together before.

7. Turn cards face up and read each card aloud. Allow time for the group members to discuss each idea. Tape or tack each card to a display board so that all group members can see it. As each card is read aloud, ask the group to determine if it is similar to another idea that already has been expressed. Cards with similar ideas should be grouped together.

8. When all of the cards have been sorted, ask the group to write the norm suggested by each group of cards. Have one group member record these new norms on a large sheet of paper.

9. Review the proposed norms with the group. Determine whether the group can support the norms before the group adopts them.

Developing Norms

WHEN ESTABLISHING NORMS, CONSIDER:	PROPOSED NORM
Time ■ When do we meet? ■ Will we set a beginning and ending time? ■ Will we start and end on time?	_____ _____ _____ _____ _____
Listening ■ How will we encourage listening? ■ How will we discourage interrupting?	_____ _____ _____ _____ _____ _____
Confidentiality ■ Will the meetings be open? ■ Will what we say in the meeting be held in confidence? ■ What can be said after the meeting?	_____ _____ _____ _____ _____
Decision Making ■ How will we make decisions? ■ Are we an advisory or a decision-making body? ■ Will we reach decisions by consensus? ■ How will we deal with conflicts?	_____ _____ _____ _____ _____
Participation ■ How will we encourage everyone's participation? ■ Will we have an attendance policy?	_____ _____ _____ _____ _____ _____
Expectations ■ What do we expect from members? ■ Are there requirements for participation?	_____ _____ _____ _____ _____

Used with permission of the National Staff Development Council, www.nsdc.org, 2006. All rights reserved. From *Keys to Successful Meetings* by Stephanie Hirsh, Ann Delehant, and Sherry Sparks. Oxford, OH: National Staff Development Council, 1994.

Norms of the National Staff Development Council
Board of Trustees and Staff

We will work together as a community that
values consensus rather than majority rule.

We will be fully "present" at the meeting by becoming
familiar with materials before we arrive and by being attentive
to behaviors which affect physical and mental engagement.

We will invite and welcome the contributions
of every member and listen to each other.

We will be involved to our individual level of comfort. Each of us
is responsible for airing disagreements during the meeting rather than
carrying those disagreements outside the board meeting.

We will operate in a collegial and friendly atmosphere.

We will use humor as appropriate to help us work better together.

We will keep confidential our discussions, comments, and deliberations.

We will be responsible for examining all
points of view before a consensus is accepted.

We will be guided by the NSDC mission statement,
which focuses on organization and professional development
to enhance success for all students.

Glossary of Key Terms
and Concepts

The following glossary provides a brief definition of key terms and concepts as they are used in the context of this book and in the context of professional learning communities in general.

action orientation: A predisposition to learn by doing; moving quickly to turn aspirations into actions and visions into realities. Members of PLCs understand that the most powerful learning always occurs in a context of taking action, and they value engagement and reflective experience as the most effective teachers.

adaptive challenges: Challenges for which the solution is not apparent; challenges that cause us to experiment, discover, adjust, and adapt (Heifetz & Linsky, 2002). Adaptive challenges may also be described as second-order change.

attainable goals: Goals perceived as achievable by those who set them. Attainable goals are intended to document incremental progress and build momentum and self-efficacy through short-term wins.

balanced assessment: An assessment strategy that recognizes no single assessment yields the comprehensive results necessary to inform and improve practice and foster school and system accountability; therefore, balanced assessments utilize multiple measures of student achievement including formative assessments *for* learning and summative assessments *of* learning. Balanced assessment also refers to using different types of formative assessments based upon the knowledge and/or skills students are called upon to demonstrate. Rather than relying exclusively on one kind of assessment, schools and teams develop multiple ways for students to demonstrate proficiency.

building shared knowledge: Learning together. When members of PLCs are called upon to resolve an issue or make a decision, they consistently attempt to learn together by clarifying questions and accessing the same information and knowledge base. Members of a PLC, by definition, will *learn* together.

capacity building: Developing the collective ability—the dispositions, knowledge, skills, motivation, and resources—to act together to bring about positive change (Fullan, 2005a, p. 4).

collaboration: A *systematic* process in which people work together, *interdependently*, to analyze and *impact* professional practice in order to improve individual and collective results. In a PLC, collaboration focuses on the critical questions of learning: What is it we want each student to learn? How will we know when each student has learned it? How will we respond when a student experiences difficulty in learning? How will we enrich and extend the learning for students who are proficient?

collective inquiry: The process of building shared knowledge by clarifying the questions that a group will explore together. In PLCs, collaborative teams engage in collective inquiry into both best practices regarding teaching and learning as well as the reality of the current practices and conditions in their schools or districts.

common formative assessment: An assessment typically created collaboratively by a team of teachers responsible for the same grade level or course. Common formative assessments are used frequently throughout the year to identify (1) individual students who need additional time and support for learning, (2) the teaching strategies most effective in helping students acquire the intended knowledge and skills, (3) program concerns—areas in which students generally are having difficulty achieving the intended standard—and (4) improvement goals for individual teachers and the team.

community: A group linked by common interests. Whereas the term "organization" tends to emphasize structure and efficiency, "community" suggests shared purpose, mutual cooperation, and supportive relationships.

consensus: Consensus is achieved when (1) all points of view have been heard and (2) the will of the group is evident even to those who most oppose it.

continuous improvement process: The ongoing cycle of planning, doing, checking, and acting designed to improve results—constantly. In a PLC, this ongoing cycle includes gathering evidence of current levels of student learning, developing strategies and ideas to build on strengths and address weaknesses in that learning, implementing those strategies and ideas, analyzing the impact of the changes to discover what was effective and what was not, and applying the new knowledge in the next cycle of continuous improvement.

criterion-referenced assessment: An assessment used to determine if a student or group of students have met a specific standard or intended learning outcome (Ainsworth & Viegut, 2006).

crucial conversation: Dialogue in which "the stakes are high, opinions vary, and emotions run strong" (Patterson, Grenny, McMillan, & Switzler, 2002, p. 3).

curriculum leverage: The skills, knowledge, and dispositions that will assist the student in becoming proficient in other areas of the curriculum and other academic disciplines (Reeves, 2002).

data versus information: Data represent facts or figures that, standing alone, will not inform practice or lead to informed decisions. To transform data into information requires putting data in context, and this typically requires a basis of comparison.

DRIP Syndrome (Data Rich/Information Poor): The problem of an abundance of data that does nothing to inform practice because it is not presented in context through the use of relevant comparisons.

endurance: The knowledge, skills, and dispositions students are expected to retain over time as opposed to merely learning something for a test (Reeves, 2002).

essential learning: The critical skills, knowledge, and dispositions each student must acquire as a result of each course, grade level, and unit of instruction. Essential learning may also be referred to as essential outcomes or power standards.

first-order change: Innovation that is incremental, representing the next step on an established path and operating within existing paradigms. The change can be implemented by using the existing knowledge and skills of the staff. The goal of first-order change is to help us get better at what we are already doing (Marzano, Waters, & McNulty, 2005).

formative assessment: An assessment *for* learning used to advance and not merely monitor each student's learning (Stiggins, 2002). Formative assessments are used to ensure any student who experiences difficulty reaching or exceeding proficiency is given additional time and support as well as additional opportunities to demonstrate his or her learning. Formative assessments are also used to help students monitor their own progress toward an intended standard of proficiency.

foundation of a professional learning community: PLCs rest upon a shared *mission* of high levels of learning for all students. In order to achieve that mission, educators create a common *vision* of the school they must create, develop *values* or *collective commitments* regarding what they will do to create such a school, and use *goals* as measurable milestones to monitor their progress.

"Genius of And": The ability to reject the "Tyranny of Or" and embrace paradox. Embracing the Genius of And allows an individual to avoid the choice between A *or* B and to choose both A *and* B at the same time (Collins & Porras, 1997). A commitment to simultaneous loose and tight leadership serves as an example of the Genius of And.

goals: Measurable milestones that can be used to assess progress in advancing toward a vision. Goals establish targets and timelines to answer the question, "What results do we seek and how will we know we are making progress?"

guaranteed and viable curriculum: A curriculum that (1) gives students access to the same essential learning regardless of who is teaching the class *and* (2) can be taught in the time allotted (Marzano, 2003).

guiding coalition: An alliance of key members of an organization who are specifically charged to lead a change process through the predictable turmoil. Members of the alliance should have shared objectives and high levels of trust.

high expectations: The confident belief that all students can attain mastery of the essential learning and that the staff has the capability to help all students achieve that mastery. "High expectations for success will be judged, not only by the initial staff beliefs and behaviors, but also by the organization's response when some students do not learn" (Lezotte, 1991, p. 4).

knowing-doing gap: The disconnect between knowledge and action, the mystery of why knowledge of what needs to be done so frequently fails to result in action or behavior consistent with that knowledge (Pfeffer & Sutton, 2000).

Law of the Few: The ability of a small close-knit group of people to champion an idea or proposal until it reaches a tipping point and spreads like an epidemic throughout an organization (Gladwell, 2002).

learning: The acquisition of new knowledge or skills through ongoing action and perpetual curiosity. Members of a PLC engage in the ongoing study and constant reflective practice that characterize an organization committed to continuous improvement.

learning organization: "Organizations where people continually expand their capacities to create the results they truly desire, where new and expansive patterns of thinking are nurtured, where collective aspiration is set free, and where people are continually learning how to learn together" (Senge, 1990, p. 3).

mission: The fundamental purpose of an organization. Mission answers the question, "Why do we exist?"

moral purpose: "Acting with the intention of making a positive difference in the lives of employees, customers, and society as a whole" (Fullan, 2001, p. 3). Fullan lists a commitment to moral purpose as a critical element of effective leadership and contends leadership must be ultimately assessed by the extent to which it awakens and mobilizes the moral purpose of those within the organization.

norm-referenced assessment: An assessment designed to compare the performance of an individual or group with a larger "norm" group typically representing a national sample with a wide and diverse cross-section of students (Ainsworth & Viegut, 2006).

power standard: The knowledge, skills, and dispositions that have *endurance, leverage,* and are essential in preparing students for *readiness* at the next level (Reeves, 2002); the most essential learning or outcomes.

professional: Someone with expertise in a specialized field, an individual who has not only pursued advanced training to enter the field, but who is also expected to remain current in its evolving knowledge base.

professional development: A lifelong, collaborative learning process that nourishes the growth of individuals, teams, and the school through a daily job-embedded, learner-centered, focused approach (National Staff Development Council, 2000).

professional learning community (PLC): Educators committed to working collaboratively in ongoing processes of collective inquiry and action research to achieve better results for the students they serve. Professional learning communities operate under the assumption that the key to improved learning for students is continuous job-embedded learning for educators.

readiness for the next level of learning/prerequisite knowledge: The skills, knowledge, and dispositions essential for success in the next unit, course, or grade level (Reeves, 2002).

results orientation: A focus on outcomes rather than inputs or intentions. In PLCs, members are committed to achieving desired results and are hungry for evidence that their efforts are producing the intended outcomes.

school culture: The assumptions, beliefs, values, and habits that constitute the norm for the school and guide the work of the educators within it.

school structure: The policies, procedures, rules and hierarchical relationships within the school.

second-order change: Innovation that represents a dramatic departure from the expected and familiar. It is perceived as a break from the past, is inconsistent with existing paradigms, may seem to be at conflict with prevailing practices and norms, and will require the acquisition of new knowledge and new skills (Marzano, Waters, & McNulty, 2005).

simultaneous loose and tight leadership: A leadership concept in which leaders encourage autonomy and creativity (loose) within well-defined parameters and priorities that must be honored (tight). The concept has also been referred to as "directed empowerment" (Waterman, 1987) and a "culture of discipline with an ethic of entrepreneurship" (Collins, 2001, p. 124).

SMART goals: Goals that are Strategic & Specific, Measurable, Attainable, Results-oriented, and Timebound (O'Neill & Conzemius, 2005).

stretch goals: Goals intended to inspire, to capture the imagination of people within the organization, to stimulate creativity and innovation, and to serve as a unifying focal point of effort. Stretch goals are so ambitious that they typically cannot be achieved without significant changes in practice. Stretch goals are also referred to as BHAGs: Big, Hairy, Audacious Goals (Collins & Porras, 1997).

summative assessment: An assessment *of* learning (Stiggins, 2002) designed to provide a final measure to determine if learning goals have been met (Ainsworth & Viegut, 2006). Summative assessments yield a dichotomy: pass or fail, proficient or not proficient. Additional support is typically not forthcoming.

systematic intervention: A school-wide plan that ensures every student in every course or grade level will receive additional time and support for learning as soon as they experience difficulty in acquiring essential knowledge and skills. The intervention occurs during the school day and students are required rather than invited to devote the extra time and secure the extra support for learning.

systematic process: A specific effort to organize the combination of related parts into a coherent whole in a methodical, deliberate, and orderly way toward a particular aim.

teachable point of view: A succinct explanation of an organization's purpose and direction that can be illustrated through stories that engage others emotionally and intellectually (Tichy, 1997).

team: A group of people working *interdependently* to achieve a *common goal* for which members are held *mutually accountable*. Collaborative teams are the fundamental building blocks of PLCs.

team norms: "Ground rules or habits that govern a group (Goleman, 2002, p. 173). In PLCs norms represent protocols or commitments developed by each team to guide members in working together. Norms help team members clarify expectations regarding how they will work together to achieve their shared goals.

Time management: The ability to organize and execute one's time around priorities (Covey, 1989).

"Tyranny of Or": "The rational view that cannot easily accept paradox, that cannot live with two seemingly contradictory forces at the same time. We must be A or B but not both" (Collins & Porras, 1997, p. 44).

values: The specific attitudes, behaviors, and commitments that must be demonstrated in order to advance the organization's vision. Articulated values answer the question, "How must we behave in order to make our shared vision a reality?"

vision: A realistic, credible, attractive future for an organization. Vision answers the question, "What do we hope to become at some point in the future?"

References and Resources

Ainsworth, L., & Viegut, D. (2006). *Common formative assessments: An essential part of the integrated whole.* Thousand Oaks, CA: Corwin.

American Association of School Administrators. (1999). *Preparing schools and school systems for the 21st century.* Lanham, MD: Rowman and Littlefield.

Assessment Training Institute: www.assessmentinst.com

Autry, J. (2001). *The servant leader: How to build a creative team, develop great morale, and improve bottom-line performance.* New York: Three Rivers.

Axelrod, R. (2002). *Terms of engagement: Changing the way we change organizations.* San Francisco: Berrett-Koehler.

Barth, R. (1991). Restructuring schools: Some questions for teachers and principals. *Phi Delta Kappan, 73*(2), 123–128.

Barth, R. (2001). *Learning by heart.* San Francisco: Jossey-Bass.

Bardwick, J. (1996). Peacetime management and wartime leadership. In F. Hesselbein, M. Goldsmith, & R. Beckhard (Eds.), *The leader of the future* (pp. 131–140). San Francisco: Jossey-Bass.

Bennis, W. (1997*). Organizing genius: The secrets of creative collaboration.* Cambridge, MA: Perseus.

Black, P., Harrison, C., Lee, C., Marsh, B., & William, D. (2004). Working inside the black box: Assessment for learning in the classroom. *Phi Delta Kappan, 86*(1), 9–19.

Blanchard, K. (1996). Turning the organization upside down. In F. Hesselbein, M. Goldsmith, & R. Beckhard (Eds.), *The leader of the future* (pp. 81–88). San Francisco: Jossey-Bass.

Block, P. (2003). *The answer to how is yes: Acting on what matters.* San Francisco: Berrett-Koehler.

Bolman, L., & Deal, T. (1996). *Leading with soul: An uncommon journey of spirit.* San Francisco: Jossey-Bass.

Bolman, L., & Deal, T. (2000). *Escape from cluelessness.* New York: AMACOM.

Bossidy, L., & Charan, R. (2002). *Execution: The discipline of getting things done.* New York: Crown Business.

Brophy, J., & Good, T. (2002). *Looking in classrooms* (9th ed.). Boston: Allyn and Bacon.

Buckingham, M. (2005). *The one thing you need to know . . . about great managing, great leading and sustained individual success.* New York: Free Press.

Burns, J. (1978). *Leadership.* New York: Harper and Row.

Cawelti, G. (2003). The new effective schools. In W. Owings & L. Kaplan (Eds.), *Best practices, best thinking and emerging issues in school leadership* (pp. 45–52). Thousand Oaks, CA: Corwin.

Cawelti, G., & Protheroe, N. (2001). *High student achievement: How six school districts changed into high-performing systems.* Arlington, VA: Educational Research Service.

Champy, J. (1995). *Reengineering management.* New York: Harper Collins.

Chappuis, J. (2005). Helping students understand assessment. *Educational Leadership, 63*(3), 39–43.

Cole, R., & Schlechty, P. (1993). Teachers as trailblazers in restructuring. *Education Digest, 58*(6), 8–12.

Collins, J. (2001). *Good to great: Why some companies make the leap . . . and others don't.* New York: Harper Business.

Collins, J., & Porras, J. (1997). *Built to last: Successful habits of visionary companies.* New York: Harper Business.

Consortium on Productivity in Schools. (1995). *Using what we have to get the schools we need.* New York: Teachers College.

Cotton, K. (2000). *The schooling practices that matter most.* Alexandria, VA: Association for Supervision and Curriculum Development.

Council of Chief School Officers. (2002). *Expecting success: A study of five high-poverty schools.* Washington, DC: Council of Chief School Officers.

Covey, S. (1989). *The seven habits of highly effective people: Powerful lessons in personal change.* New York: Fireside.

Covey, S. (1994). *First things first: To live, to love, to learn, to leave a legacy.* New York: Fireside.

Covey, S. (1996). Three roles of the leader in the new paradigm. In F. Hesselbein, M. Goldsmith, & R. Beckhard (Eds.), *The leader of the future* (pp. 149–160). San Francisco: Jossey-Bass.

Covey, S. (2002). Introduction. In Patterson, K., Grenny, J., McMillan, R., & Switzler, A. (Eds.), *Crucial conversations: Tools for talking when stakes are high* (pp. xi–xiv). New York: McGraw-Hill.

Covey, S., Merrill, A., & Merrill, R. (1996). *First things first: To live, to love, to learn, to leave a legacy.* New York: Fireside.

Csikszentmihalyi, M. (1997). *Finding flow: The psychology of engagement with everyday life.* New York: Bantam.

Darling-Hammond, L. (1996). What matters most: A competent teacher for every child. *Phi Delta Kappan, 78*(3), 193–200.

Darling-Hammond, L. (2001). *The right to learn.* San Francisco: Jossey-Bass.

Deal, T., & Key, M. K. (1998). *Corporate celebration: Play, purpose and profit at work.* San Francisco: Berrett-Koehler.

Deal, T., & Peterson, K. (1999). *Shaping school culture: The heart of leadership.* San Francisco: Jossey-Bass.

Decrane, A. (1996). A constitutional model of leadership. In F. Hesselbein, M. Goldsmith, & R. Beckhard (Eds.), *The leader of the future* (pp. 249–256). San Francisco: Jossey-Bass.

Deming, W. E. (2000). *Out of the crisis.* Cambridge, MA: Massachusetts Institute of Technology.

Dilworth, R. (1995). The DNA of the learning organization. In C. Sarita & J. Renesch (Eds.), *Learning organizations: Developing cultures for tomorrow's workplace* (p. 243–254). Portland, OR: Productivity.

Dolan, P. (1994). *Restructuring our schools: A primer on systemic change.* Kansas City, MO: Systems and Organizations.

Drucker, P. (1992). *Managing for the future: The 1990s and beyond.* New York: Truman Talley.

Drucker, P. (1996). Not enough generals were killed. In F. Hesselbein, M. Goldsmith, & R. Beckhard (Eds.), *The leader of the future* (pp. xi–xvi). San Francisco: Jossey-Bass.

Druskat, V., & Wolf, S. (2001). Group emotional intelligence and its influence on group effectiveness. In C. Chernis & D. Goleman (Eds.), *The emotionally intelligent workplace* (pp. 132–155). San Francisco: Jossey-Bass.

DuFour, R. (2003a). Building a professional learning community. *The School Administrator, 60*(5), 13–18.

DuFour, R. (2003b). Central office support for learning communities. *The School Administrator, 60*(5), 15–16.

DuFour, R., & Eaker, R. (1998). *Professional learning communities at work™: Best practices for enhancing student achievement.* Bloomington, IN: Solution Tree (formerly National Educational Service).

DuFour, R., DuFour, R., Eaker, R., & Karhanek, G. (2004). *Whatever it takes: How a professional learning community responds when kids don't learn.* Bloomington, IN: Solution Tree (formerly National Educational Service).

Eaker, R., DuFour, R., & DuFour, R. (2002). *Getting started: Reculturing schools to become professional learning communities.* Bloomington, IN: Solution Tree (formerly National Educational Service).

Eastwood, K., & Louis, K. S. (1992). Restructuring that lasts: Managing the performance dip. *Journal of School Leadership, 2*(2), 213–224.

Eden, D. (1990). *Pygmalion in management: Productivity as a self-fulfilling prophecy.* Lanham, MD: Lexington Books.

Efficacy Institute: www.efficacy.org

Elmore, R. (2002, January/February). The limits of change. *Harvard Education Letter.* Retrieved January 6, 2006, from http://www.edletter.org/past/issues/2002-jf/limitsofchange.shtml

Elmore, R. (2003). *Knowing the right thing to do: School improvement and performance-based accountability.* Washington, DC: NGA Center for Best Practices.

Evans, R. (1996). *The human side of school change: Reform, resistance and the real-life problems of innovation.* San Francisco: Jossey-Bass.

Farkas, S., Johnson, J., Foleno, T., Duffett, A., & Foley, P. (2000). *A sense of calling: Who teaches and why—a report from Public Agenda.* New York: Public Agenda.

Fiske, E. (1992). *Smart schools, smart kids: Why do some schools work?* New York: Simon and Schuster.

Frankl, V. (1959). *Man's search for meaning.* New York: Pocket Books.

Fullan, M. (1993). *Change forces.* London: Falmer Press.

Fullan, M. (2001). *Leading in a culture of change.* San Francisco: Jossey-Bass.

Fullan, M. (2005a). *Leadership and sustainability: System thinkers in action.* San Francisco: Corwin.

Fullan, M. (2005b). Professional learning communities writ large. In R. DuFour, R. Eaker, & R. DuFour (Eds.), *On common ground: The power of professional learning communities* (pp. 209–223). Bloomington, IN: Solution Tree (formerly National Educational Service).

Gardner, H. (1990). *Leading minds.* New York: Basic Books.

Gardner, H. (2004). *Changing minds: The art and science of changing our own and other people's minds.* Boston: Harvard Business School.

Gardner, J. (1988). *Leadership: An overview.* Washington, DC: Independent Sector.

Garmston, R., & Wellman, B. (1999). *The adaptive school: A sourcebook for developing collaborative groups.* Norwood, MA: Christopher-Gorden.

Georgiades, W., Fuentes, E., & Snyder, K. (1983). *A meta-analysis of productive school cultures.* Houston: University of Texas.

Gerstner, L., Semerad, R., Doyle, D., & Johnston, W. (1995). *Reinventing education: Entrepreneurship in America's public schools.* New York: Penguin.

Gladwell, M. (2002). *The tipping point: How little things can make a big difference.* New York: Back Bay.

Goddard, R., Hoy, W., & Hoy, A. (1994). Collective efficacy beliefs: Theoretical developments, empirical evidence, and future directions. *Educational Researcher, 33*(3), 3–13.

Goldberg, M., & Cross, C. (2005). Time out. *Edutopia Magazine.* Retrieved August 18, 2005, from http://email.e-mailnetworks.com/ct/ct.php?t= 1018842&c=561784071&m=m&type=3

Goldsmith, M. (1996). Ask, learn, follow up, and grow. In F. Hesselbein, M. Goldsmith, & R. Beckhard (Eds.), *The leader of the future* (pp. 227–240). San Francisco: Jossey-Bass.

Goleman, D. (1998). *Working with emotional intelligence.* New York: Bantam.

Goleman, D. (2002). *Primal leadership.* Boston: Harvard Business School.

Goleman, D., Boyatzis, R., & McKee, A. (2002). *Primal leadership: Learning to lead with emotional intelligence.* Boston: Harvard Business School.

Hall, G., & Hord, S. (1987). *Change in schools: Facilitating the process.* Albany, NY: State of New York.

Handy, C. (1995). Managing the dream. In S. Chawala & J. Renesch (Eds.), *Learning organizations: Developing cultures for tomorrow's workplace* (pp. 45–56). New York: Productivity.

Handy, C. (1996). The new language of organizing and its implications for leaders. In F. Hesselbein, M. Goldsmith, & R. Beckhard (Eds.), *The leader of the future* (pp. 3–10). San Francisco: Jossey-Bass.

Hargreaves, A. (2004). Broader purpose calls for higher understanding: An interview with Andy Hargreaves. *Journal of Staff Development, 25*(2), 46–50.

Hargreaves, A., & Fink, D. (2006). *Sustainable leadership.* San Francisco: John Wiley.

Haycock, K. (1998). Good teaching matters . . . a lot. *Thinking K–16, 3*(2), 1–14.

Heifetz, R., & Linsky, M. (2002). Leadership on the line: Staying alive through the dangers of leading. Boston: Harvard Business School.

Heskett, J., & Schlesinger, L. (1996). Leaders who shape and keep performance-oriented culture. In F. Hesselbein, M. Goldsmith, & R. Beckhard (Eds.), *The leader of the future* (pp. 111–120). San Francisco: Jossey-Bass.

Hirsch, E. D. (1996). *The schools we need and why we don't have them.* New York: Doubleday.

Hord, S., Rutherford, W., Huling-Austin, L., & Hall, G. (1987). *Taking charge of change.* Alexandria, VA: Association for Supervision and Curriculum Development.

Interstate School Leaders Licensure Consortium. (1996). *Standards for school leaders.* Washington, DC: Council of Chief State School Officers.

Jacobs, H. H. (1997). *Mapping the big picture: Integrating curriculum and assessment K–12.* Alexandria, VA: Association for Supervision and Curriculum Development.

Jacobs, H. H. (2001). New trends in curriculum: An interview with Heidi Hayes Jacobs. *Independent School, 61*(1), 18–24.

Kanold, T. (2006). The continuous improvement wheel of a professional learning community. *Journal of Staff Development, 27*(2), 16–21.

Kanter, R. (1995). Mastering change. In S. Chawala & J. Renesch (Eds.), *Learning organizations: Developing cultures for tomorrow's workplace* (pp. 71–84). New York: Productivity.

Kanter, R. (2005, Winter). How leaders gain (and lose) confidence. *Leader to Leader, 35*, 21–27.

Katzenbach, J., & Smith, D. (1993). *The wisdom of teams: Creating the high-performance organization.* Boston: Harvard Business School.

Kegan, R., & Lahey, L. (2001). *How the way we talk can change the way we work: Seven languages for transformation.* San Francisco: Jossey-Bass.

Kendall, J., & Marzano, R. (2000). *Content knowledge: A compendium of standards and benchmarks for K–12 education* (3rd ed.). Alexandria, VA: Association for Supervision and Curriculum Development.

King, Jr., M. L. (2001). Beyond Vietnam: Address delivered to the clergy and laymen concerned about Vietnam. April 4, 1967. In C. Carson & K. Shepherd (Eds.), *A call to conscience: Landmark speeches of Martin Luther King, Jr.* (pp. 133–164). New York: Warner Books.

Klein, S., Medrich, E., & Perez-Ferreiro, V. (1996). *Fitting the pieces: Education reform that works.* Washington, DC: United States Department of Education.

Kotter, J. (1996). *Leading change.* Boston: Harvard Business School.

Kotter, J. (1998, Fall). Winning at change. *Leader to Leader, 10,* 27–33.

Kouzes, J., & Posner, B. (1987). *The leadership challenge: How to get extraordinary things done in organizations.* San Francisco: Jossey-Bass.

Kouzes, J., & Posner, B. (1996). Seven lessons for leading the voyage to the future. In F. Hesselbein, M. Goldsmith, & R. Beckhard (Eds.), *The leader of the future* (pp. 99–110). San Francisco: Jossey-Bass.

Kouzes, J., & Posner, B. (1999). *Encouraging the heart: A leader's guide to rewarding and recognizing others.* San Francisco: Jossey-Bass.

Kouzes, J., & Posner, B. (2003, Spring). Challenge is the opportunity for greatness. *Leader to Leader, 28,* 16–23.

The Leadership and Learning Center: www.makingstandardswork.com

Lencioni, P. (2003, Summer). The trouble with teamwork. *Leader to Leader, 29,* 35–40.

Lencioni, P. (2005). *Overcoming the five dysfunctions of a team: A field guide.* San Francisco: Jossey-Bass.

Lezotte, L. (1991). *Correlates of effective schools: The first and second generation.* Okemos, MI: Effective Schools Products. Retrieved January 6, 2006, from http://www.effectiveschools.com/ freestuff.asp

Lezotte, L. (1997). *Learning for all.* Okemos, MI: Effective Schools Products.

Lezotte, L. (2005). More effective schools: Professional learning communities in action. In R. DuFour, R. Eaker, & R. DuFour (Eds.), *On common ground: The power of professional learning communities* (pp. 177–191). Bloomington, IN: Solution Tree (formerly National Educational Service).

Lickona, T., & Davidson, M. (2005). *Smart and good high schools: Integrating excellence and ethics for success in school, work, and beyond.* Cortland, NY: Center for the 4th and 5th R's (Respect and Responsibility), and Washington, DC: Character Education Partnership.

Lieberman, A. (1995). Restructuring schools: The dynamics of changing practice, structure, and culture. In A. Lieberman (Ed.), *The work of restructuring schools: Building from the ground up* (pp. 1–17). New York: Teachers College.

Little, J. W. (1990). The persistence of privacy: Autonomy and initiative in teachers' professional relations. *Teachers College Record, 91*(4), 509–536.

Lortie, D. (1975). *Schoolteacher: A sociological study.* Chicago: University of Chicago.

Louis, K. S., Kruse, S., & Marks, H. (1996). Schoolwide professional community. In F. Newmann (Ed.), *Authentic achievement: Restructuring schools for intellectual quality* (pp. 179–204). San Francisco: Jossey-Bass.

Louis, K. S., Kruse, S., & Raywid, M. (1996). Putting teachers at the center of reform. *NASSP Bulletin, 80*(580), 9–21.

Mandl, A., & Sethi, D. (1996). Either/or yields to the theory of both. In F. Hesselbein, M. Goldsmith, & R. Beckhard (Eds.), *The leader of the future* (pp. 257–264). San Francisco: Jossey-Bass.

Marks, H., Doanne, K., & Secada, W. (1996). Support for student achievement. In F. Newmann (Ed.), *Authentic achievement: Restructuring schools for intellectual quality* (pp. 209–227). San Francisco: Jossey-Bass.

Marzano, R. (2003). *What works in schools: Translating research into action.* Alexandria, VA: Association for Supervision and Curriculum Development.

Marzano, R., Waters, T., & McNulty, B. (2005). *School leadership that works.* Alexandria, VA: Association for Supervision and Curriculum Development.

Maxwell, J. (1995). *Developing the leaders around you: How to help others reach their full potential.* Nashville, TN: Thomas Nelson.

McLaughlin, M., & Talbert, J. (2001). *Professional communities and the work of high school teaching.* Chicago: University of Chicago.

McTighe, J., & Wiggins, G. (2004). *Understanding by design: Professional development workbook.* Alexandria, VA: Association for Supervision and Curriculum Development.

Mintzberg, H. (1994). *The rise and fall of strategic planning.* New York: Free Press.

Naisbitt, J., & Aburdene, P. (1985). *Reinventing the corporation.* New York: Warner.

Nanus, B. (1992). *Visionary leadership.* San Francisco: Jossey-Bass.

National Center for Research on Evaluation, Standards and Student Testing (CRESST): www.cse.ucla.edu

National Commission on Teaching and America's Future. (2003). *No dream denied: A pledge to America's children.* Washington, DC: National Commission on Teaching and America's Future.

National Education Association. (2003). NEA's Keys Initiative. Retrieved January 6, 2006, from http://www.nea.org/schoolquality/index.html

National Staff Development Council. (1999, August/September). Developing norms. *Tools for Schools,* pp. 3–5.

National Staff Development Council. (2000). A staff development code of ethics. *Journal of Staff Development, 21*(2). Retrieved April 30, 2006, from http://www.nsdc.org/library/publications/jsd/ethics212.cfm

National Staff Development Council: www.nsdc.org

Newmann, F., & Associates. (Eds.). (1996). *Authentic achievement: Restructuring schools for intellectual quality.* San Francisco: Jossey-Bass.

Newmann, F., King, B., & Youngs, P. (2000, April) *Professional development that addresses school capacity.* Paper presented at the annual meeting of the American Research Association. New Orleans, LA.

Newmann, F., & Wehlage, G. (1995). *Successful school restructuring: A report to the public and educators by the center for restructuring schools.* Madison, WI: University of Wisconsin.

Newmann, F., & Wehlage, G. (1996). Restructuring for authentic student achievement. In F. Newmann (Ed.), *Authentic achievement: Restructuring schools for intellectual quality* (pp. 286–301). San Francisco: Jossey-Bass.

O'Neill, J., & Conzemius, A. (2006). *The power of SMART goals: Using Goals to improve student learning.* Bloomington, IN: Solution Tree.

Patterson, K., Grenny, J., McMillan, R., & Switzler, A. (2002). *Crucial conversations: Tools for talking when stakes are high.* New York: McGraw-Hill.

Perkins, D. (1992). *Smart schools: From training memories to educating minds.* NY: Free Press.

Perkins, D. (2003). *King Arthur's roundtable.* New York: Wiley.

Peters, T. (1987). *Thriving on chaos: A handbook for a management revolution.* New York: Knopf.

Peters, T., & Austin, N. (1985). *A passion for excellence: The leadership difference.* New York: Random House.

Peters, T., & Waterman, R. (1982*). In search of excellence: Lessons from America's best-run companies.* New York: Harper and Row.

Pfeffer, J., & Sutton, R. (2000). *The knowing-doing gap: How smart companies turn knowledge into action.* Boston: Harvard Business School.

Pinchot, G., & Pinchot, E. (1993). *The end of bureaucracy and the rise of the intelligent organization.* San Francisco: Berrett-Koehler.

Popham, J. (2003). The seductive allure of data. *Educational Leadership, 60*(5), 48–51.

Protecting mediocre teachers. (2005, December 9). *Chicago Tribune,* p. 18.

Purkey, S., & Smith, M. (1983). Effective schools: A review. *Elementary School Journal, 83*(4), 427–452.

Reeves, D. (2000). *Accountability in action: A blueprint for learning organizations.* Denver: Advanced Learning.

Reeves, D. (2002). *The leader's guide to standards: A blueprint for educational equity and excellence.* San Francisco: John Wiley and Sons.

Reeves, D. (2004). *Accountability for learning: How teachers and school leaders can take charge.* Alexandria, VA: Association for Supervision and Curriculum Development.

Reeves, D. (2005). Putting it all together: Standards, assessment, and accountability in successful professional learning communities. In R. DuFour, R. Eaker, & R. DuFour (Eds.), *On common ground: The power of professional learning communities* (pp. 45–63). Bloomington, IN: Solution Tree (formerly National Educational Service).

Reeves, D. (2006). *The learning leader.* Alexandria, VA: Association for Supervision and Curriculum Development.

Richardson, J. (2004). *From the inside out: Learning from the positive deviance in your organization.* Oxford, OH: National Staff Development Council.

Rose, L. C., & Gallup, A. M. (2005). The 37th annual Phi Delta Kappa / Gallup poll of the public's attitudes toward the public schools. *Phi Delta Kappan, 87*(1), 41–57.

Sagor, R. (1997). Collaborative action research for educational change. In A. Hargreaves (Ed.), *Rethinking educational change with heart and mind* (pp. 169–191). Alexandria, VA: Association for Supervision and Curriculum Development.

Saphier, J. (2005). *John Adams' promise: How to have good schools for all our children, not just for some.* Acton, MA: Research for Better Teaching.

Sarason, S. (1996). *Revisiting the culture of the school and the problem of change.* New York: Teachers College.

Schaffer, R., & Thomson, H. (1998). Successful change programs begin with results. In *Harvard Business Review on change.* Boston: Harvard Business School.

Schein, E. (1996). Leadership and organizational culture. In F. Hesselbein, M. Goldsmith, & R. Beckhard (Eds.), *The leader of the future* (pp. 59–70). San Francisco: Jossey-Bass.

Schlecty, P. (1990). *Schools for the 21st century.* San Francisco: Jossey-Bass.

Schlecty, P. (1997). *Inventing better schools: An action plan for educational reform.* San Francisco: Jossey-Bass.

Schmoker, M. (1999). *Results: The key to continuous school improvement* (2nd ed.). Alexandria, VA: Association for Supervision and Curriculum Development.

Schmoker, M. (2003). First things first: Demystifying data analysis. *Educational Leadership, 60*(5), 22–24.

Schmoker, M. (2004). Learning communities at the crossroads: A response to Joyce and Cook. *Phi Delta Kappan, 86*(1), 84–89.

Schmoker, M. (2005). Here and now: Improving teaching and learning. In R. DuFour, R. Eaker, & R. DuFour (Eds.). *On common ground: The power of professional learning communities* (pp. 135–153). Bloomington, IN: Solution Tree (formerly National Educational Service).

Senge, P. (1990). *The fifth discipline: The art & practice of the learning organization.* New York: Currency Doubleday.

Senge, P., Kleiner, A., Roberts, C., Ross, R., & Smith, B. (1994). *The fifth discipline fieldbook: Strategies and tools for building a learning organization.* New York: Doubleday/Currency.

Sergiovanni, T. (2005). *Strengthening the heartbeat: Leading and learning together in schools.* San Francisco: Jossey-Bass.

Snyder, C., Harris, C., Anderson, J., & Holleran, S. (1991). The will and the ways: Development and validation of an individual-differences measure of hope. *Journal of Personality and Social Psychology, 60*(4), 570–585.

Southern Regional Education Board. (2000). *Things that matter most in improving student learning.* Atlanta, GA: Southwest Regional Education Board.

Sparks, D. (2005). Leading for transformation in teaching, learning, and relationships. In R. DuFour, R. Eaker, & R. DuFour (Eds.), *On common ground: The power of professional learning communities* (pp. 155–175). Bloomington, IN: Solution Tree (formerly National Educational Service).

Steele, W. (1996). Key leadership challenges for present and future executives. In F. Hesselbein, M. Goldsmith, & R. Beckhard (Eds.). *The leader of the future.* San Francisco: Jossey-Bass.

Stevenson, H., & Stigler, J. (1992). *The learning gap: Why our schools are failing and what we can learn from Japanese and Chinese education.* New York: Simon and Simon.

Stiggins, R. (2001). *Student involved classroom assessment* (3rd ed.). Upper Saddle River, NJ: Prentice-Hall.

Stiggins, R. (2002). Assessment crisis: The absence of assessment for learning. *Phi Delta Kappan, 83*(10), 758–765.

Stiggins, R. (2004). New assessment beliefs for a new school mission. *Phi Delta Kappan, 86*(1), 22–27.

Stiggins, R. (2005). Assessment FOR learning: Building a culture of confident learners. In R. DuFour, R. Eaker, & R. DuFour (Eds.), *On common ground: The power of professional learning communities.* Bloomington, IN: Solution Tree (formerly National Educational Service).

Stone, D., Patton, B., & Heen, S. (2000). *Difficult conversations: How to discuss what matters most.* New York: Penguin.

Straus, D. (2002). *How to make collaboration work: Powerful ways to build consensus, solve problems, and make decisions.* San Francisco: Berrett-Koehler.

Symonds, K. (2004). *Perspectives on the gaps: Fostering the academic success of minority and low-income students.* Naperville, IL: North Central Regional Educational Laboratory.

Thompson, J. (1995). The renaissance of learning in business. In S. Chawala & J. Renesch (Eds.), *Learning organizations: Developing cultures for tomorrow's workplace* (pp. 85–100). New York: Productivity.

Tichy, N. (1997). *The leadership engine: How winning companies build leaders at every level.* New York: Harper Business.

Ulrich, D. (1996). Credibility X capability. In F. Hesselbein, M. Goldsmith, & R. Beckhard (Eds.), *The leader of the future* (pp. 209–220). San Francisco: Jossey-Bass.

Waterman, R. (1987). *The renewal factor: How the best get and keep the competitive edge.* New York: Bantam.

Waterman, R. (1993). *Adhocracy: The power to change.* New York: Norton.

Wehlage, G., Newmann, F., & Secada, W. (1996). Support for student achievement. In F. Newmann (Ed.), *Authentic achievement: Restructuring schools for intellectual quality* (pp. 21–48). San Francisco: Jossey-Bass.

Wheatley, M. (1999). Goodbye command and control. In F. Hesselbein & P. Cohen (Eds.), Leader to leader. San Francisco: Jossey-Bass.

Wheelis, A. (1973). How people change. New York: Harper and Row.

Wright, S., Horn, S., & Sanders, W. (1997). Teacher and classroom context effects on student achievement: Implications for teacher evaluation. *Journal of Personnel Evaluation in Education, 11,* 57–67.

Index

Make the Most of Your
Professional Development Investment

Let Solution Tree (formerly National Educational Service) schedule time for you and your staff with leading practitioners in the areas of:

- **Professional Learning Communities** with Richard DuFour, Robert Eaker, Rebecca DuFour, and associates
- **Effective Schools** with associates of Larry Lezotte
- **Assessment *for* Learning** with Rick Stiggins and associates
- **Crisis Management and Response** with Cheri Lovre
- **Classroom Management** with Lee Canter and associates
- **Discipline With Dignity** with Richard Curwin and Allen Mendler
- **PASSport to Success** (parental involvement) with Vickie Burt
- **Peacemakers** (violence prevention) with Jeremy Shapiro

Additional presentations are available in the following areas:

- At-Risk Youth Issues
- Bullying Prevention/Teasing and Harassment
- Team Building and Collaborative Teams
- Data Collection and Analysis
- Embracing Diversity
- Literacy Development
- Motivating Techniques for Staff and Students

Solution Tree
304 West Kirkwood Avenue
Bloomington, IN 47404
(812) 336-7700
(800) 733-6786 (toll free)
FAX (812) 336-7790
email: info@solution-tree.com
www.solution-tree.com

The Power of Professional Learning Communities at Work™

Featuring Richard DuFour, Robert Eaker, and Rebecca DuFour

This four-program video series takes you inside eight diverse schools, where teachers and administrators engage in candid conversations and collaborative team meetings. See how successful schools radically improve student learning, and learn the fundamentals of PLC with this powerful, fun staff development tool.   **VIF094**

Professional Learning Communities at Work™ Plan Book

Rebecca DuFour, Richard DuFour, and Robert Eaker

With space for eight class periods, this process book helps collaborative teacher teams address crucial, teacher-specific professional learning community concepts.   **BKF217**

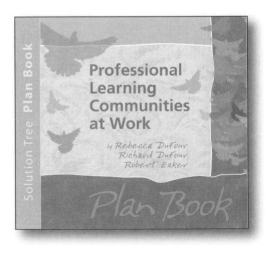

Whatever It Takes (Audio Book)

Richard DuFour, Rebecca DuFour, Robert Eaker, and Gayle Karhanek

Transform your daily commute into a learning opportunity with this convenient audio book to help you answer the question, "What do you do when, despite your best efforts, a student does not learn?"   **AUF003**

On Common Ground

Edited by Richard DuFour, Robert Eaker, and Rebecca DuFour

Examine a colorful cross-section of educators' experiences with PLC. This collection of insights and stories from practitioners throughout North America highlights the benefits of PLC and offers unique angles of approach to a variety of school improvement challenges.   **BKF180**